THE FOURTH EVANGELIST

BY THE SAME AUTHOR

THE PERSON OF OUR LORD AND
RECENT THOUGHT.

THE RISE OF THE CHRISTIAN
RELIGION.
A Study in Origins.

PUBLISHED BY MACMILLAN & CO., LTD.

EDITED BY REV. C. F. NOLLOTH.

THE CHRISTIAN FAITH.
Essays written at the instance of the Christian
Evidence Society. By various authors. Edited
with an Introduction by C. F. Nolloth.

PUBLISHED BY JOHN MURRAY.

THE
FOURTH EVANGELIST

HIS PLACE IN THE DEVELOPMENT OF RELIGIOUS THOUGHT

BY

CHARLES FREDERICK NOLLOTH,

M.A., D.Litt.

HON. FELLOW OF ORIEL COLLEGE, OXFORD
EXAMINING CHAPLAIN TO THE BISHOP OF ROCHESTER

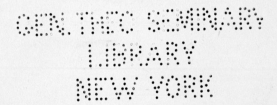
LONDON
JOHN MURRAY, ALBEMARLE STREET, W.
1925

PRINTED IN GREAT BRITAIN BY
WILLIAM CLOWES AND SONS, LIMITED, LONDON AND BECCLES

PREFACE

THE present book may be regarded as a continuation of two earlier works, *The Person of Our Lord and Recent Thought*, 1908, and *The Rise of the Christian Religion: a Study in Origins*, 1917, both published by Messrs. Macmillan.

In a kindly review of the latter book, the writer demurred to my attitude to the " Johannine " literature, with the result that I was led to continue my previous study of the Apostolic Age by a fresh investigation of the problems historical, literary, and theological, which confront the student of the Fourth Gospel.

It has lately been said that " the case against the old tradition of authorship is overwhelming." My own study of the subject has convinced me that this verdict is borne out neither by the witness of history nor by the literary and psychological considerations which emerge in the course of a critical investigation of the Gospel. At the same time, the hardihood of so dogmatic a statement is shown by the fact that it is opposed to the judgment of men like Professor Theodor Zahn, of Erlangen—the greatest of living New Testament scholars—the late Drs. Bernhard Weiss and C. R. Gregory, in Germany, and to much of the best scholarship in this country.

The chief difficulty of an undertaking like the present arises from the complexity of the issues involved. So few positions in this field of criticism can be said to be assured against all possible attack. On many points, if we look for certainty, we have to be content with a large measure of probability; while few literary problems have been made the subject of more wild and irresponsible theories.

Against the effect of this intellectual licence may be set the fact that the net result of the close scrutiny of the Gospel, which has been carried on from the publication of Bretschneider's famous work [1] until the present time, has been to place it securely upon the ground of historical trustworthiness and value.

For, apart from lack of agreement as to the hand that wrote it and as to the precise measure of its faithfulness as a record of fact and actuality, it is being increasingly admitted that, more than any other book of the New Testament, this Gospel brings us into the very presence of our Lord.

As in my other books, I have translated references to German writers for the convenience of my readers. The present work is intended for the educated layman as well as for the professed student of theology.

Professor C. H. Turner has read a considerable part of the book in manuscript. Professor C. C. J. Webb has read the proofs. I have to thank them both for very valuable suggestions and criticisms. The Rev. T. D. Raikes has given me much help in verifying references, in the preparation of the index and in other ways.

[1] *Probabilia de Evangelii et Epistolarum Joannis Apostoli Indole et Origine*, 1820.

C. F. NOLLOTH.

Oxford, *September*, 1925.

CONTENTS

vii

CHAPTER IV

The Authorship of the Fourth Gospel

Tradition

CHAPTER V

Papias

CHAPTER VI

The Alleged Martyrdom of St. John

CHAPTER VII

Mediating Theories of Authorship

CHAPTER VIII

The Relation of the Fourth Gospel to the other Johannine Books

CHAPTER IX

The Fourth Gospel and the Synoptic Gospels

Narrative

CHAPTER X

The Fourth Gospel and the Synoptic Gospels

The Discourses of Christ

CHAPTER XI

The Philosophy of St. John

CHAPTER XII

THE THEOLOGY OF ST. JOHN

The Humanity of Christ

CHAPTER XIII

THE THEOLOGY OF ST. JOHN

The Deity of Christ

CHAPTER XIV

THE TRANSITION TO CATHOLICITY

CHAPTER XV

THE CONTRIBUTION OF ST. JOHN TO RELIGIOUS THOUGHT

THE FOURTH EVANGELIST

CHAPTER I

INTRODUCTION

THE literary history of the five writings which, from the time of their inclusion in the New Testament Canon, have borne the name of St. John, presents a problem of great complexity.

Down to the close of the eighteenth century, it was the general belief [1] that they were all the work of the same man, John, the younger son of Zebedee and one of the primitive disciples of Christ. The writings themselves contain no precise statement upon the subject. It is true that the Gospel is very insistent in claiming for its author the certainty possessed by an eye-witness of what he records, while it identifies him with a disciple who became known among his friends as "the disciple whom Jesus loved." But it does not give his name.

The Apocalypse states that the recipient of its visions was a servant of Christ, whose name was John ; but it does not proceed to specify him.

Of the Epistles, the first has generally been assigned to the author of the Gospel. In phraseology and tone of thought, there is close resemblance between the two writings.[2] The two minor Epistles apparently disclose the same family connection.

---

[1] For exceptions to this rule, v. pp. 7, 31, 63.

[2] Speaking of the relation between the Fourth Gospel and the Epistles of St. John, J. H. Moulton remarks, " No one with the faintest instinct of style would detach (them) from it," in *Peake's Commentary on the Bible*, p. 592. *V.* Streeter, *The Four Gospels*, 1924, p. 460, " We are forced to conclude that all four documents are by the same hand."

I

In the Synoptic Gospels, the two sons of Zebedee were, with St. Peter, admitted to the closest intimacy with their Master. When we turn to the Fourth Gospel, the brothers are not even mentioned [1]; while throughout that Gospel, the name John is always applied to the Baptist, without explanation, as though no other person of the name would be thought of.

The younger son of Zebedee appears in the Book of Acts closely linked, as in the Synoptic Gospels, with his friend St. Peter. He takes part in the election of St. Matthias; he shares with the Twelve the experiences of Pentecost; he observes the stated hours of prayer in the Temple; he is with St. Peter at the healing of the lame man in the Temple gate, contributing his own spiritual influence to the act; he shares the consequences of the bold confession of the Sacred Name by which the miracle was wrought. Then, so far as the historian of Acts is concerned, he disappears from our sight.[2] We owe to St. Paul the knowledge that he was present and took part in the Council of Jerusalem in the spring of the year 49.[3]

From that time " John, son of Zebedee," vanishes from the pages of the New Testament. If referred to, it is either, as in the Fourth Gospel, under a different designation, or in a form so abbreviated (John) as to make his identity uncertain.[4] For his subsequent career we depend upon tradition. For determining his connection, if any, with the writings that bear his name, we must have recourse partly to tradition, partly to the indications afforded by the writings themselves.

We are sometimes assured that the question of authorship is after all quite a minor point.[5] But authorship and

[1] Except in the appendix, chap. xxi.

[2] Apart from the fact that he is mentioned in order to identify the James who was put to death by Herod in A.D. 44 (Acts xii. 2).

[3] Gal. ii. 9 ; v. Acts xv. 6 f. Here it is assumed that St. Paul's visit to Jerusalem (Gal. ii. 1 f.) corresponds with the third of those narrated in Acts, viz. the visit to the Council, xv. 4 f. Ramsay, *St. Paul the Traveller*, p. 153 f.; Emmet; Burkitt, *Christian Beginnings*, p. 130, identify it with that of Acts xi. 30, which was *c.* A.D. 47.

[4] Rev. i. 1, 4, 9.

[5] As, recently, by Heitmüller : " If the Gospel possessed great signifi-

genuineness are in most cases too closely connected to allow us to be indifferent as to whose hand we owe the writings in question. The matter ceases to be one of mere literary nicety. The considerations involved are too serious to warrant such an attitude.

At the same time, we are far from thinking that the question of authorship should be allowed so to dominate the situation as to disturb our estimate of their value. Works which have exercised so great an influence in the fashioning of saintly lives in every age of the Christian Church have an intrinsic value and significance, apart from their origin. No hesitation to accept the Fourth Gospel as the work of St. John the Apostle, should disturb our faith in the teaching which it was intended to impart. The power and inspiration of the book have been amply certified by what they have wrought. By whatever channel it has reached us, it brings its own guarantee that its writer was " borne along by the Holy Spirit." [1] The question is not one of belief or unbelief ; but very largely of literary criticism, in which every instrument that is ordinarily employed for the determination of a disputed authorship should be brought into play.

But if opponents of the traditional authorship of the Johannine writings are not to be charged, *ipso facto*, with disloyalty to the cause of Christ, neither are upholders of that authorship to be accused offhand of an obscurantist apologetic. The matter does not admit of such an alternative presentation. It lies within the province of historical criticism, and by the laws which govern all historical investigation its treatment must be directed and ultimately judged.

The danger-point emerges where full information is lacking ; and it is here that the investigator requires to be most anxiously on his guard. He will, of course, approach his task, if not with his mind made up, at least with certain

cance for its own time and has its value for ours, it is in the last resort quite indifferent whether it proceeds from the Apostle John or not." In J. Weiss, *D. Schriften des N.T.*, ii. p. 687.

[1] 2 Pet. i. 21.

prepossessions. We may almost say that to be destitute of any bias would argue a coldness and indifference to the issues of the inquiry that would unfit him for his work. No history that is worth the name was ever written in such a mood. A passionless calculation of probabilities, with no heart in the nature of the result, would fail to arrive even at the lifeless object at which the historian aimed. But the need to guard against mere predilection, against the tendency to subjectivity in weighing evidence, will be paramount throughout. The fact that a certain aspect of the matter in hand is edifying is no excuse for its retention in face of evidence to the contrary. We have to watch the effect upon our minds which a long tradition in art as well as in literature has insensibly woven about them. The devotional value of a view consecrated by ages of Christian thought and worship must not be placed in the scale against a valid result of historical inquiry.

On the other hand, we have to be equally on our guard against the fascination of methods which are purely scientific, and on that account are apt to lead the critic, through pride in their achievements, to disregard the claims of philosophy. A purely scientific handling of phenomena in which so complex a factor as the mind of man is involved, conducted without reference to the philosophic considerations which always dominate the whole inquiry, leads to results no less disastrous to the cause of truth than those brought about by the admission of religious sentiment into the determination of a matter of history. Moreover, by thus isolating itself, it ceases to be scientific. The laws which govern the pursuit of a pure science, such as mathematics, do not suffice to regulate an historical inquiry. The former deals with certainty. The latter has to be content with probability in by far the greater number of questions submitted to it ; and in working out its problems it has to bring into consideration the manifold possibilities of error to which the human mind is subject. In other words, a purely scientific treatment of history, isolated from the larger questions suggested by philosophy—as, for instance, the bearing of psychology on the production and interpretation of the evidence at disposal—is bound to fail. It will always be one-sided : its judgments are formed on a wholly insufficient induction.

The sweeping verdicts of a too hasty and narrow criticism are at once seen to miss the mark. Confronted by the results of a wider induction, which takes account of the human element involved, they appear inadequate and misleading.

The history of the Johannine problem affords many instances of this fact. Yet it does not mean that no such thing as certainty is attainable. A certainty there may be —if not the highest—yet sufficient for all practical purposes ; sufficient to form a foundation on which we may rear a true conception of the place and influence of the Johannine writings in the formation and development of Christian thought.

It will be generally admitted that a statement of historic fact, which has been handed down from a period hard by the time of its occurrence, presents a strong claim to be heard and, unless overborne by considerations which prove its falsity, to be accepted. For the very fact that the statement was made has been shown by long experience to be a point in its favour. Men do not recklessly assert what could at once be disproved by their contemporaries. *The mere existence of a tradition is something in its favour.* But when the tradition, after surviving the preliminary stage of its origin, has been canvassed and discussed by succeeding generations, and, on comparison with evidence from other quarters, has still much to say for itself as a statement of what actually occurred, it gains appreciably in credibility. It has justified its existence, and can claim that the burden of proof rests with those who attempt its overthrow, rather than with those who uphold it.

This principle applies to the writings which go by the name of St. John. Speaking generally, we may say that the Gospel and the First Epistle have been received as the work of John, son of Zebedee, while the Apocalypse has very widely been attributed to the same writer. These statements are merely descriptive of the general attitude. There are many exceptions, which, for the most part, are due to the critical work of recent years.

What has taken place has been a revolt against the traditional standpoint, leading in many cases to the denial that any New Testament writings are the work of the Apostle John. It will be necessary to test the data on which this denial has been made to rest : for, although the main interest of the discussion lies in the contents of the writings themselves, it is impossible to regard the question of their authorship as a matter of small moment. It *must* make a difference whether works that have profoundly affected Christian thought in every age proceed from one who stood by the side of Christ and wrote from recollection of an ineffaceable experience, or whether they are from the hand of some unknown collector of stories that were current in Christian circles long after every eye-witness of the Saviour had passed away. It is no mere question of literary or antiquarian interest. It concerns the measure of the security that we feel, when reading these writings, that we are in touch with one who knew, from direct personal experience, the mind and will of Christ.

It seems, then, to be a counsel of perfection to tell us that, as the value of the Johannine literature is determined by its power to move us and by the extent of our reaction to it, we can afford to be indifferent to the precise nature of its origin. We cannot maintain such an indifference. If the evidence at our disposal fails to produce a fixed judgment, and we have to resign ourselves to a position of indecision, we can hardly help cherishing a working faith in one or the other aspect of the question.

This attitude has to be watched, if a fair and impartial investigation is to be carried out ; otherwise, our whole historical standpoint will be rendered insecure, and our decisions be found to give no satisfaction to the candid inquirer.

It should be borne in mind that the subject is beset with special difficulties. The Johannine writings cannot

be treated, without more ado, as a coherent block of
literature—the work of one man, spread, it may be, over a
few years. The critical situation does not permit this.
In tracing their action on the formation and development of
religious thought, their joint use for convenience sake
must not be allowed to prejudge the question of their
authorship. Our employment of the term " Johannine "
for the whole of the New Testament writings which go by
that name will, therefore, be conventional, and should not
be regarded as question-begging.

Nor does this procedure need apology. With one
exception, hereafter to be alluded to,[1] the whole Church in
every quarter down to the death of Origen regarded the
Johannine writings as the work of the younger son of
Zebedee, the Apostle John. No other claimant to their
authorship had either appeared or had been suggested.
Every one concurred in assigning them to a primitive
apostle who was still living when Trajan mounted the
imperial throne.[2] This agreement is the more remarkable
from the fact that it was not immediately arrived at :
people who had not been in contact with the author hesi-
tated. The Gospel seemed to traverse those which were
already passing into assured canonical rank as true records
of what the Saviour said and did. But the hesitation soon
passed. The new Gospel was its own best defender : while
behind it stood the august figure of its reputed author, the
last of the Lord's disciples to linger on the stage. Doubts
made themselves heard after the death of Origen. The
reverent expression of the difficulties felt by Dionysius,
patriarch of Alexandria, reads like a page of the best
criticism of our own day ; and it left a permanent mark
upon the course of Christian thought.[3] But the old tradition lived on through all the centuries until the eighteenth

[1] The " Alogi," v. below, p. 31. According to Tertullian, *Adv. Marc.*
iv. 5 (cf. iii. 14), Marcion rejected the Book of Revelation.
[2] A.D. 98.
[3] Preserved by Eusebius, *H.E.*, vii. 25. Dionysius the Great, Bishop
of Alexandria, A.D. 247–265, could not bring himself to see that the
Apostle John, to whom he referred the Gospel and the First Epistle, was
also the author of the Apocalypse. His influence strongly affected

was about to close.   From that time onward, the question
has been regarded as *sub judice*.   However strong our
convictions, we cannot reckon on their being shared by
others.   The traditional view of the authorship must not
be taken for granted.   Like a besieged city, it is being
attacked on all sides ; but it would be the extreme of
dogmatism to say that it has fallen.   New material has been
brought into use.   But there has been nothing decisive,
as we shall see in the course of our inquiry.   To many
minds the difficulties, historical as well as theological,
created by the rejection of the traditional position outweigh
those which attend its acceptance.   This fact alone warrants
our *provisional* use of the old standpoint.

But there is another consideration in its favour.   Apart
from their assignment to John, son of Zebedee, through so
long a period of Christian thought, there is a very wide-
spread agreement as to the spot in which the Johannine
writings first saw the light.   Modern criticism on the whole
concurs with the judgment of antiquity in singling out the
Roman province of Asia and the great Greek city of Ephesus
as their birthplace.[1]   In that respect, the writings, widely
as the two chief branches of them differ in content and in
style, form a corpus complex indeed, but integral, with
much in common that can be set against the presence of
diversity.   Their *habitat* taken with their reputed authorship seems to allow a certain unity of treatment.[2]

But the Gospel will form the central object of our
investigation.   With its satellites—the three general epistles
—it stands complete in itself, a document of surpassing
value and interest, historically and theologically, whether

opinion all over the East.   Whereas, " in the second century, the Apocalypse was all but universally accepted in Asia Minor, Western Syria,
Africa, Rome, South Gaul " (Charles, *The Revelation of St. John*, i.,
p. xcviii.), the Apostolic authorship of the book and its claim to canonical
status were frequently rejected elsewhere for some centuries.   Its canonicity
was acknowledged throughout Western Christendom ;   and this view
gradually spread to the East within mediæval times.

[1] Dr. Burney prefers the Syrian Antioch to Ephesus as the place
of the composition of the Gospel : *The Aramaic Origin of the Fourth
Gospel*, 1922, p. 129 f.

[2] For the relation of the Gospel to the other Johannine writings,
v. below, chap. viii.

we regard it as the actual handiwork of the last surviving disciple of our Lord, or as the last of those writings which were destined to receive canonical recognition as inspired Scripture.[1]

The Apocalypse will be treated as a member of the same Johannine group; but, in view of the hesitation which still attends any attempt to determine its authorship, or its relation to the other Johannine writings, its use will be subsidiary to that of the Gospel and First Epistle.

[1] Unless we regard the Second Epistle of St. Peter as a work of the second century and therefore the last document to be admitted into the New Testament Canon under the impression that it was a genuine writing of that Apostle.

CHAPTER II

THE RELIGIOUS BACKGROUND

I. Judaism

THE Johannine writings appeared at a time of transition. The Jewish world was reeling from the effects of the war with Rome, which ended in the capture of Jerusalem and the destruction of the Temple. The Christian Church had lost, or was losing, the Apostolic witnesses of the Life and Resurrection of her Lord. Its administration had passed into the hands of those who had not known Him in the flesh.

In each case, the trial to faith and constancy was severe. What would happen to Judaism deprived at a blow of Temple and Sacrifice ? What would be the lot of the Infant Church without the presence and guidance of those who had seen the Lord ?

Under this troubled sky, lurid and ominous both for Jew and Christian, appeared the writings which tradition has assigned to the last survivor of the personal disciples of Christ. We must inquire whether they show any trace of the period of their birth, and if so, to what extent they have been affected by it, in the character and the style of their contents.

The Jew who, during the last quarter of the first century, remained indifferent to the Gospel, was thrown back on the task of accounting for the state of things. If he did not lose all hope, he had to feel his way towards such a reconstruction of his religion as should meet the necessity of the case. He must make a fresh study of the past, especially of the exile and of the oppression under Antiochus

Epiphanes. Was this overthrow in line with previous troubles, or was it a thing by itself ? Was it final ?

In the midst of this perplexity, two questions were insistent : what was to take the place of the Temple and its services ? what was to be the attitude of the nation to the Messianic hope ?

Of these the former was not so vital as we might suppose. The religious prestige of the Temple was never what it had been before the first overthrow. Rebuilt on the return from the Exile, its diminished splendour was attended by a lesser sanctity. The Holy of Holies was empty. The symbols of the Divine presence had been removed and were never restored. At the same time, the study of the prophets, soon to be placed in their completed canon, drew men's minds to the ethical rather than to the ceremonial requirements of their religion. The scorn which the prophets pour upon a round of sacrifices into which there enters no worship of heart, no devotion of the life, found a response in many a thoughtful mind. The degeneracy of the priesthood after the glory of the early Maccabean times was not without influence in the same direction. Sadducees, worldly, rationalistic, politically time-serving, had secured the succession to the high-priesthood. The old line had been broken.

The Apocalyptic writings of the first centuries before and after Christ show many a trace of this loss of esteem and regard for what had been the glory of the race. According to Enoch, the very shew-bread " was polluted and not pure." [1] In the Psalms of Solomon, the altar steps are said to have been trampled by the alien, " because the sons of Jerusalem had defiled the holy things of the Lord, had profaned with iniquities the offerings of God." [2] The Fourth Book of Ezra, a writing contemporary with the Fourth Gospel, does not even contemplate any rebuilding of Jerusalem ; but the seer has a vision of the heavenly city of which the earthly one is a symbol.[3] In II. Baruch,

---

[1] 1 En. 89, 73.

[2] Ps. of Sol. ii. 2, 3 ; cf. Amos v. 21–24.

[3] 4 Ezra x. 47 f.

which belongs to the last half of the first century after Christ, the ultimate restoration of Jerusalem is promised.[1] Elsewhere in the same book, it is said that " an offering will not again be made (from the vine) in Zion nor will first fruits again be offered." [2]

The effect of the gradual loss of regard for the Temple and its worship was further emphasised by the action of the sect of the Essenes. As a body, they held entirely aloof from the Temple and took no part in its services. The spectacle of a religious society comprising men of high moral character, when compared with the worldly Sadducean priesthood, could not fail to make a deep impression upon the public mind, and to point a way out of the general state of perplexity. Here again, the contemporary Apocalyptic writings show the direction that thought was taking.

It was felt that another means for the expression of religious faith must be sought. God had not interposed to save His Temple. To some thoughtful minds it was, therefore, not a vital necessity in the worship of His people. And, at this point, we do well to reflect on the strength of the people's faith in God and in their own place in the world in spite of the terrible experiences of the war with Rome. There was no loss of trust in the Divine governance of Israel or in its mission as the people of God.

They braced themselves to discover what God would have them do ; and they were not long in determining that henceforth a more exact and wholehearted fulfilment of the Law was the course marked out for them in the Providence of God. In this decision the influence of the Pharisees at once made itself felt. With the fall of the Temple, the Sadducees disappeared as a force in Judaism. It was the Pharisees who had brought into use the daily prayers of the Temple.[3] They had obtained seats in the Sanhedrin.

[1] 2 Baruch vi. 9 ; cf. i. 4 ; " for a time," xxxii. 2–4.
[2] *Ib.* x. 10.
[3] *V.* R. Kohler in *Jewish Encycl.*, art. " Pharisees." But in all probability, the prayers and the reading of the Law, which became so marked a feature in later Judaism, at an earlier date took their place beside the daily sacrifices in the worship of the Temple itself. " The cult of the Word of Scripture and of prayer, which had its origin in the

They were regarded as the real leaders of religion and, after the fall of the city and the state, they put themselves at the head of the new movement of legalism and so came to "shape the character of Jewish life and thought for all the future." Here again we find confirmation of what was occurring in the Apocalyptic books of the period.[1]

The pathos of the situation is extreme. Is the observance of a hard, dry legalism, which it is freely admitted cannot bring to the devotee peace of conscience or security,[2] to be the final stage of a Faith of such glorious memories? Is Rabbinism, with its commentaries, the sole outcome of the Theocracy? It has been urged in extenuation of this decline, as it seems to us, that " only thus were the pure monotheistic faith, the ethical ideal and the intellectual and spiritual character of the Jew preserved in the downfall of the old world," and that in consequence their influence for good was felt outside their own race.[3]

Doubtless the mission of the chosen people did not end with the ruin of their state; but so far, history fails to report an influence upon the world at large in any way commensurate with their past; and it is certain that while the Hope of Israel continues to centre upon the strict fulfilment of the Law, their mission will remain unfulfilled. One at least among them, " a Hebrew of the Hebrews," did not despair of the future. He admits that " blindness in part is happened to Israel." He adds, " until the fulness

---

piety of the exile, could no longer be suppressed by the sacrificial cult": F. Heiler, *Das Gebet*, 1920, p. 423.

The Synagogue, which had long served to maintain religious life in countries too distant to permit access to the worship of the Temple, became in Palestine, as in the Dispersion, a centre and home of the Faith that had once had its seat on the hill of Zion. " It was this spiritual service of Bible-reading and prayer that ' made it possible for Judaism to endure the fall of the Temple and the altar without being completely overwhelmed '": *ib.*, p. 424.

[1] 2 Baruch lxxvii. 15, 16; lxxxv. 3, " Zion has been taken from us and we have nothing now save the Mighty One and His Law"; xlviii. 22, " In Thee do we trust, for lo! Thy law is with us and we know that we shall not fall so long as we keep Thy statutes "; 4 Ezra ix. 31–38.

[2] Cf. 4 Ezra ix. 36; *v.* Box in Charles, *Apoc. and Pseud. o the O.T.*, i., pp. 554, 555.

[3] *V. Jewish Encycl.*, art. " Pharisees."

of the Gentiles be come in. And so all Israel shall be saved." [1]

In the Johannine writings, there is no such cheerful forecast to be found. In the Gospel the attitude of the Jews to our Lord is described in a spirit of stern fidelity to the actual situation.[2] In the Apocalypse, while the writer sees in vision the sealing of the servants of God, he identifies them with members of the twelve tribes and, in his description of the new Jerusalem, the gates are inscribed with the tribal names.[3] But there is nothing to show that he shares the hopefulness of St. Paul in the future of his people. He appears rather to wish to point out the continuity of the Church Universal with that of the Old Covenant. The Church is the true Israel of God although the bulk of the chosen race had not entered into it. Indeed, he records in the message to the Church of Smyrna the judgment that the Jews of that city were the Synagogue of Satan. So great, apparently, was their opposition to the preaching of the Gospel; so hard their attitude to Christ's servants.[4] However this may be, the growing antagonism of the Jews, as the first century was closing, when compared with the receptiveness of the heathen world, could not fail to open men's eyes to the fact that the future of the Church lay with the Gentile rather than with the Jew.[5]

We must next inquire into the attitude of Judaism about the close of the first century towards the Christian Church. We gather from Acts that, among the people at large, there was a kindly feeling towards the Apostles in the days following upon Pentecost. They were stirred by the events that accompanied the preaching of the Gospel, and were moved to compunction by the thought of their part in the crucifixion of the Lord. Even the priests were touched.[6] This temper of mind was strengthened by the

[1] Rom. xi. 25, 26 ; cf. 2 Cor. iii. 15, 16. But he had passed away before the fall of Jerusalem. We can only conjecture what his attitude would have been from the consideration of such passages as these.
[2] V. p. 163.   [3] Rev. vii. 4 f. ; xxi. 12.
[4] V. Swete on Rev. ii. 9.
[5] This had long ago been realised by St. Paul: Acts xxviii. 28.
[6] Acts ii. 47 ; v. 13 ; vi. 7.

high respect, felt by Jew and Christian alike, for James, the Lord's brother. There is no doubt that much of the favourable regard in which the early Apostolic Church was held was due to the lofty character and life of this saintly man.[1] This fact also throws light on the perplexing statement that, in the persecution which arose against the Church of Jerusalem at the time of the death of Stephen, " they were all scattered abroad throughout the regions of Judæa and Samaria, except the Apostles." The standing and character of James, and his known affection and solicitude for his own people, seem to have been a protection to the Apostles ; while the newer Hellenistic element in the Church of Jerusalem, which had found a spokesman in St. Stephen, was obliged to take refuge in flight.[2]

But when the martyrdom of St. James the Just, so graphically described by Hegesippus, was quickly followed by the war with Rome, and men began to trace a connection between the murder and the overwhelming troubles of the state,[3] the relations between official Judaism and the Church, which were already strained, experienced a complete breach. The complaint of the High Priest at the preaching of Christ crucified, " Ye have filled Jerusalem with your doctrine, and intend to bring this man's blood upon us,"[4] is recalled by the resentment of the authorities at the Christians' belief that the sorrows of Jerusalem were directly due to the murder of the brother of our Lord.

But long before this, the attitude of the Jews to the Church as a whole had undergone a change. The persecution of which Saul was the chief mover was quickly followed by the tumults that arose at the death of St. Stephen. For the spread of the Gospel and the enlargement of the Church beyond the borders of Judaism the first martyrdom constituted an epoch. The heralds of the Gospel, forced to leave Jerusalem, " went everywhere." [5]

---

[1] *V*. Hegesippus in Eus., *H.E.*, ii. 23 ; Jos., *Antiq.*, xx. 9, § 1.
[2] It is probable that the Twelve had not yet committed themselves to the views of St. Stephen, *v*. Acts viii. 1 ; vii. 48 f.
[3] Cf. Heges., *ib.*, Καὶ εὐθὺς Οὐεσπασιανὸς πολιορκεῖ αὐτούς.
[4] Acts v. 28 ; cf. vii. 52.   [5] Acts viii. 4.

The great cities of the Empire heard the joyful sound. But along with the spread of the Gospel there was a great increase of antagonism both to the message and its bearers. If St. Paul was here and there met with forbearance and courtesy, if curiosity and the love of novelty gave him an attentive audience, the feeling soon turned to hatred and opposition. The synagogues of the Dispersion, which at first resounded with the Name of Christ, became centres of hostility.[1] The nation at large had a sore burden upon its conscience, and there could be no full preaching of the Gospel without bringing it to mind. Hence the Jew, if not penitent, only hardened his heart against a Gospel so inseparably linked with the great crime of his people. Then, as now, the Cross was the discerner and divider of men, repelling when it did not attract.[2]

If the martyrdom of St. Stephen, with the persecution that followed it, gave the first impetus to the extension of the Church in the cities of the Dispersion, the unrest that came to a head in the martyrdom of St. James the Just led to a further diffusion of the Gospel. St. Peter had withdrawn from Jerusalem on his release from prison in A.D. 44, the year of the martyrdom of James, son of Zebedee. Antioch and Rome became successively the chief spheres of his ministry.

But in A.D. 49, five years later, he was in Jerusalem again for the council of Apostles and Elders. It is very probable that this return to Jerusalem intervened between his work at Antioch and at Rome. We do not know when St. John left Jerusalem, whether at the first retirement of St. Peter or at a much later date. He, too, was present at the Council, and it is quite possible that he remained there off and on until, warned by a foreboding of the coming troubles, the members of the Mother Church withdrew first to Pella and afterwards to more distant parts.

When the Temple and the city fell and men openly connected the disaster not only with the crucifixion of

[1] Acts xiii. 14, 50 ; xiv. 1 f. ; xvi. 19 ; xvii. 1, 5 ; xviii, 4, 12.
[2] Cf. 1 Cor. i. 18.

Christ but with the recent murder of St. James the Just, the cleavage between the Jews and the Church was sensibly intensified. We are prepared by this state of things for the singular aloofness from his own people which characterises the allusions to the " Jews " in the writings of St. John. It is possible too that, in his record of their debates with our Lord, his long experience of their opposition to the Gospel has hardened the pen with which he writes.[1]

Judaism had long been a " religio licita " in the Empire. So long as it did not make too open attempts to proselytise, the traditional tolerance shown by the Romans towards other cults gave it a certain security. To most Roman officials Christianity was for some time indistinguishable from it. Undoubtedly this was a great advantage to the Church in its early years and gave it shelter and protection, as in Corinth under Gallio.[2] But it was a state of things that could not last. The growing enmity of the Jews against the Christians opened the eyes of Roman officials to the essential difference between them. Again and again the authority of the state had to interfere in the name of mere justice. The ægis of Roman law was interposed between Christian and Jew. St. Paul saved his life at Jerusalem by recourse to the Imperial power.[3] Judaism, unnatural mother as she was, had turned against her direct and lawful offspring. It was the arm of pagan authority that was raised in their protection.

II. Palestinian Christianity

We can form no satisfying estimate of the place of the Johannine writings in the history of Christian thought without trying to trace in them the effect of the Judaic Christianity in which the writer's early life was passed.

The author of the Fourth Gospel was " a Hebrew of the

[1] But cf. Mk. vii. 3 ; Acts ix. 23, and *passim*.
[2] Acts xviii. 15.
[3] Acts xxiii. 17 f. At Cæsarea he appealed directly to Cæsar, xxv. 10, 11.

Hebrews at home in Palestine." [1] This has been proved
by investigations into the language of the Gospel and into
the writer's accuracy in description of localities.[2] The
evidence of language is far more decisive than that of
topographical knowledge. The latter could to some extent
be acquired by one who had not been brought up in Palestine, but had visited it at a much later date. Language,
on the other hand, clearly tells its own tale. The Greek of
the Gospel is that of one who has first thought out his
meaning in Aramaic and, though master of the Greek
equivalent, " forms his sentences after the example of the
Aramaic." [3] That this process is natural in the case of the
Gospel and not the result of artistic contrivance is evident
from the fact that " the Greek and Semitic forms of speech
lie so far apart that only a born Semite could write a Greek
adapted to the Aramaic. . . . No one can write in Semitic
style who does not think and speak in Semitic." [4]

Palestinian Aramaic was the language of our Lord and
His disciples. Oral teaching was in Aramaic, and when
need was felt to commit sayings or doings of the Master to
writing, Aramaic was still for a time the form that the
writing took. By far the earliest of these writings was the
collection of sayings which St. Matthew is said to have
made, probably at the time of their utterance, and which,
after their translation into Greek, formed the staple of the
discourses which are common to the First and Third Gospels.[5]
There is some ground for thinking that the substance of the
Second Gospel was Aramaic, although it was apparently
first published in a Greek dress, through which the Aramaic
occasionally asserts itself.[6] The nursery period of the

[1] Zahn, who observes that this is beginning to be admitted even by
those who reject the testimony of the Evangelist: *Neue Kirchl. Zeitschrift*, April, 1907, p. 265.

[2] Cf. A. Schlatter, *D. Sprache u. Heimat des Vierten Evangelisten*,
1902, pp. 8, 9; H. Holtzmann, *D. Joh. Evang.*, p. 15; Zahn, *op. cit.*,
March, 1908, p. 207.

[3] Schlatter, *op. cit.*, p. 9. Instances of this are given by Burney,
op. cit. passim; v. especially pp. 64 f., 69 f., 87 f.

[4] *Ib.*, p. 8.   [5] *V.* Papias in Euseb., *H.E.*, iii. 39.

[6] *V. The Rise of the Christian Religion*, p. 18, n. 1. For the theory
that Antioch, rather than Rome, was the place of its publication, *v.*
J. Vernon Bartlet, *St. Mark*, 1922, p. 35 f.

Christian Church—its first preaching and its first writing—was Judaic in language. Only as it grew in extent and in experience ; only as it came out of its Palestinian cradle, did it begin to employ the accents of a larger world and to speak in a tongue which could be understood throughout the Empire. But in thus adapting itself to its new requirements and responsibilities, it still bore traces of its earlier and more secluded state.

The Aramaisms of the Gospels are the true and unmistakable evidence of their origin. They tell of Palestine and of a time when the Church was almost wholly Jewish. This is especially true of the Fourth Gospel. The writer is plainly declared by his handiwork to be a Jew of Palestine. His claim to be an eye-witness of what he relates is supported by the linguistic phenomena of the narrative itself.

If the writer spoke the language, he also shared the life and the worship of the Palestine of the first half of the first century, and these, like the language, exercised an influence upon him which appears in his writings. If we identify him with the unnamed disciple of the Baptist, who with Andrew sought out the dwelling-place of Christ and apparently soon left following the Forerunner for the Lord, he is at once marked out as one whose mind was set on the fulfilment of the Messianic promises and who belonged to the more earnest of those who were waiting for the consolation of Israel. The fact of his discipleship with the Baptist is a proof of his discontent with the state of religion in Israel. He could not be satisfied with the traditional round of legal and ceremonial observances. He goes out to the wilderness, drawn by the fascination of the gaunt figure whose own face was set towards the dawn of a better day. This impatience with the religious life of his people is reflected in his Gospel. In his account of the different controversies in which Christ was engaged with " the Jews," we can trace the view of their hard and unspiritual attitude which he had been led to form long ago.

But he did not break with the religion of his fathers.

With his Master, he kept the feasts ; and after the Resurrection we find him going up to the Temple with St. Peter, " at the hour of prayer." [1]   When St. Paul paid his first visit to Jerusalem after his conversion, it was to see St. Peter. No mention is made of St. John.   James, the Lord's brother, was the only other leader who was seen by St. Paul.   It is probable that St. John was absent on missionary work. He was too notable a disciple not to be sought out.   When, fourteen years later, St. Paul was again in Jerusalem in order to communicate to the heads of the Mother Church the Gospel which he was preaching among the Gentiles, St. John was present as, with Peter and James, one of the " pillars " of the primitive Judaic community.   A momentous decision was arrived at.   While the heads of the Jewish Christian Church confine their labours to their own countrymen, the heathen world was committed to St. Paul and his companions.

It is significant that St. John, whose mind, if it was expressed, is not made known to us, apart from his general concurrence with what was done, threw in his lot with those who were to minister to his own people.   He remains an Apostle of the Circumcision, and it is the last glimpse that we get of him in the New Testament record.

We can imagine that the recollection of his peculiar intimacy with our Lord and of his presence at great moments of His ministry, gave him a position of great influence in the Church of Jerusalem.   If it is he to whom Papias refers as the " Elder John," it is the title which tradition would naturally assign to a ruler of a community so close in touch with the past as the Church of Jerusalem appears to have been.[2]   It is also a striking instance of the way in which a title of ordinary respect bestowed on famous Rabbis and on leading men of the Synagogue came to denote the Twelve—as we see by reference to Papias—and at length to be the fixed title of the second order of the Church's ministry.

---

[1] *I.e.* if we identify him with the younger son of Zebedee.
[2] *V.* Schlatter, *D. Kirche Jerusalems*, 1908, p. 42.

Can we trace in the Gospel the influence of St. John's Palestinian experience and of his position in the highly Jewish Church of Jerusalem? Before answering that question, we have to remember the effect which the great crime of his people in rejecting their Messiah would have on the mind of so devout a disciple. At the same time, the consequences of the war with Rome, involving the destruction of the Temple and the removal of the Christian Church from the ancient seat of Jewish worship, together with his own removal to a Greek city of Asia, hardly warrant our expecting to find much allusion to his former life. A " tradition of the elders " appears in the " six water pots of stone " at Cana.[1] The years of the building of Herod's Temple are a distinct reminiscence of the past.[2] The aloofness of Jew and Samaritan from one another and the custom of avoiding conversation with a woman in public come out in the episode of Sychar.[3] The constant allusion to the Feasts, as marking special events in the Saviour's life, betrays close touch with the actual facts.[4] The strongly marked distinction between " Jewry " and Galilee is another reminiscence ; the latter region is regarded as isolated and secluded : " Go into Judæa." " Show Thyself to the world," urge Christ's brethren as they press the need of publicity, if He would act consistently with the claims that He had put forward.[5] The entire fabric of chapter vii. is full of minute particulars which show acquaintance with Jewish ways of thinking. Customs, prejudices, difficulties, expectations of the period are all reflected here. The chapter is a remarkable instance of the life-like and historical background presented by the Jewish experience of the writer. The fact of its composition at a far later time and in the wholly different milieu of Ephesus has not suppressed the signs of its author's earlier knowledge and experience. This is especially the case with the mention of the Temple. There is

[1] Jo. ii. 6 ; cf. Mk. vii. 3. [2] Jo. ii. 20.
[3] Jo. iv. 9, 27. [4] Jo. v. 1 ; vi. 4.
[5] Jo. vii. 1, 3, 4.

every indication of precise and vivid recollection of the scenes of the incidents recorded. It was in the Treasury of the Temple that Christ proclaimed Himself to be " the Light of the World." [1] The great narthex called Solomon's Porch—a relic of the first Temple—was the place in which, at the Feast of the Dedication, He declared His essential oneness with the Father. [2] Teaching and scene are inextricably blended in the writer's mind and live again in his record. Minute touches, such as the marketing which had to be done before the Passover could be kept, show the writer's intimate knowledge of the whole situation. [3] All the details of the old life, from which he was separated more by its complete break up in the fall of city and Temple than even by lapse of time, come back to him like a flood, as, at Ephesus, he recalls for the disciples' sake his knowledge of his Master. Behind it all lies the firm rock of actual experience. It is the life of Palestine at the precise time of which he is speaking and at no other. The delicate and precarious art of literary criticism has experienced many checks in its adventurous career. It has seldom gone so far astray as when it has been invoked to pronounce that, in the narratives of the Fourth Gospel, we have a transcript of the religious experience of the Church of the early second century. That this pronouncement is a travesty of the actual state of the case is shown by the manner in which the scenes and the sayings and events belonging to them are interlaced. You cannot separate them without mangling the whole narrative.

To apply the theory of second-century Church life and thought to account for the character of the recorded incidents and teachings is to sew new cloth upon an old garment. The rent is made worse. The difficulties are increased. The fabric of the narrative is the record of a former and an actual experience. The writer belonged to the time and the mode of thought which he describes. What is new is the deeper understanding and the more

---

[1] Jo. viii. 12, 20.   [2] Jo. x. 22, 30.
                [3] Jo. xiii. 29.

spiritual apprehension of what had passed before him. His story belongs to the first half of the first century. But Pentecost has intervened between the events themselves and their committal to writing. Hence the vivid and accurate remembrance of the past.[1] Hence the elevation and the spirituality that are so often perversely assigned to the influence and the atmosphere of a later age. How far the gift at Pentecost has made itself felt in the deepening and fixing of the Evangelist's record of his early experience we cannot say with any certainty. What we do maintain is the proof, which the Gospel itself discloses, that the promised help of the Holy Spirit has done nothing to obliterate the signs of the writer's personal participation in the events that he records.

His Gospel is the work of a Jew of Palestine, who has shared the life and listened to the words of his Master. In this experience lies the chief part of the value of the writing which embodies it ; a fact strangely overlooked by those who, while alive to the extreme importance of the Gospel, assign its distinctive features to the thought of the second century.[2] They fail to see that it is a transcript from life, glowing with reality ; but like a portrait of Velasquez or Titian, conveying to the beholder far more than a formal likeness—the personality, the very being of the original. For this result, as the portrait required the genius of the consummate artist, the Gospel needed the afflatus of an inspired imagination. Those who assign it to the collective mind of an Ephesian school are the victims of a false psychology. It is not in the power of a coterie to produce a work of such transparent unity and coherence. Speaking generally of the Gospel as a whole, one mind and only one has been at work ; but the result is the effect of a youthful experience combined with the oft-repeated meditation of a prolonged life.

But we cannot form a fair estimate of the effect of his Palestinian origin, without taking account of the influence of the language and thought of the great Greek city in

---

[1] Jo. xiv. 26.   [2] *V*. p. 169 f.

which tradition says that he passed his closing years. The Jew of Palestine writes in Greek and shows his acquaintance with modes of thought and expression that lie far apart from what he had known in his youth. It will suffice at present to point out that this does not weaken the writer's grip of the early historical situation. The central Figure of the Gospel remains the Jewish Rabbi. He speaks and acts as one born and reared within Palestinian Judaism would speak and act.[1] But there is a largeness of thought and feeling which is always passing beyond the limits of his upbringing. We can detect it in the Christ of the Synoptics ; but freer scope is accorded to it in the Fourth Gospel. There is a note of universality which only emerges here and there in the earlier records. Yet it never so prevails over the other forms of thought as to obliterate their effect upon the narrative.

---

[1] *E.g.* Jo. ii. 6–9, 13–17 ; vii. 22 f. ; xiii. 13 ; xvi. 2.
Scholten takes an opposite view : " Language as well as ideas, indeed the whole ' Weltanschauung ' lying at the root of this Gospel, are so far removed from the mode of thought prevailing in Palestine and indicate so clearly the forms of the Greek Gnosis, that this writing cannot possibly have a Palestinian origin " : *D. Evang. nach Joh.*, p. 406.

CHAPTER III

Internal Evidence

THE phenomena presented by St. John, when read in conjunction with the Synoptic Gospels, are very remarkable. The first chapter of St. Mark contains a short record of a series of events of great significance and of a considerable period of Christ's ministry. The preaching of the Baptist, his baptism of our Lord, the Temptation, the call of men to discipleship, and a series of miracles are all dealt with in the compass of a single chapter. Brevity is not the only peculiarity that strikes us. The persons named are introduced without any explanation. They simply appear upon the scene. When Christ goes into the house of Simon and Andrew, the brothers who had first been called to discipleship, He is accompanied by two other disciples, James and John, the sons of Zebedee. They had been called immediately after Simon and Andrew. This personal attendance is soon found to be a settled habit with the sons of Zebedee. Again and again, in the Synoptic account, they are with our Lord on occasions when the only other disciple present is Simon Peter. This means a relation to their Master of peculiar intimacy, and a high status among His immediate followers. It is common to the whole Synoptic tradition. No feature of the Gospel history is better substantiated.

But when we take up the Fourth Gospel, which claims to have been written by an eye-witness of the Saviour's life, and, inferentially, by one who was present at critical moments of that life, we are at once struck by the contrast presented in the matter of discipleship. Simon Peter, Andrew, Philip are found again. In the Gospel proper, the sons of Zebedee are not even named. If mentioned in the appendix, it is with no more discriminating title ; the personal names of the brothers do not appear.

The most natural way to account for this strange omission is to suppose that the writer of the Gospel is to be identified with one of them and— if we listen to the voice of tradition—the younger, St. John.

This conclusion seems almost self-evident. No responsible writer would thus throw a veil over one of the chief actors in the events he is narrating, *unless that person were the writer himself*.

But, in that case, other considerations would come in to modify his procedure. The personal element in his story would make itself felt. But how and to what extent ? We may be sure that the claim of truth would not be set at nought. Accuracy of recital was all important. Filled with a deep sense of the value of his witness, he would allow no personal claim to appear. No sense of self-satisfaction must intrude, distracting attention from the central Figure. Throughout, the Gospel bears marks of the writer's sense of the urgency of the truth which it conveys, and to which he was in a position to bear witness. He will not weaken that impression in the minds of his disciples. Therefore, while his desire for self-effacement withholds mention of his name, it is not allowed to lessen the force of the witness which he is able to bear.

Accordingly, he uses a term which, if it veils, yet half reveals his identity to men who had often heard him recount the experiences of his early manhood.

To this term we must now turn our attention. Although the John of the Synoptic Gospels is not mentioned by name in the Fourth, we read there of a disciple who was with the Lord at the Last Supper and at the Cross ; who was at the empty grave, and at His appearance at the Sea of Galilee. From this close conjunction on eventful occasions, we conclude that he was an Apostle.[1] But he is five times over called the disciple " whom Jesus loved " : he was therefore singled out by Christ as the object of a special intimacy and affection, and as such would in all likelihood be one of the three who, according to the Synoptic record, stood in closest touch with their Master. But, as in the Fourth Gospel, there is no mention of John, the son of Zebedee, by name, so is there no other title assigned to " the loved disciple." This strange twofold reserve seems to point in one direction.

The son of Zebedee *is* " the loved disciple." The reserve is that of the writer himself, who claims to be an eye-witness of what he records, and whose claim is authenticated by the unknown writer of the last few words of the Gospel—perhaps an elder of the Church at Ephesus, where the Gospel first saw the light.[2]

---

[1] For, according to the Synoptics, none but Apostles were present with our Lord at the Last Supper and in Gethsemane, *v.* Zahn, *Einleit. in d. N.T.*, ii., pp. 479 f., 488, n. 12. The disciples spoken of in Jo. xviii. 1, are those said by the Synoptics to have been at the Last Supper. *V.* also Jo. xv. 27, where they are addressed as the original (ἀπ' ἀρχῆς) disciples.

[2] It is a question whether the cryptic allusion of Jo. xviii. 15, ἄλλος μαθητής can be similarly identified. B. Weiss thinks so : " The actual narrator, who in his accustomed manner introduces himself indirectly," *Komment. ad loc.* So Loisy : " Ce disciple mystérieux probablement le bien-aimé," *Le Quatr. Evang.*, p. 87. Heitmüller : " The ' other ' disciple may have been the disciple whom Jesus loved," *D. Schriften des N.T.*, p. 844. Spitta : " He only could have the interest to tell of this entrance who wrote this history and let us know by this remark that his account rested on eye-witnessing," *D. Joh. Evang.*, p. 456.

The absence of a name in this case admits of the same interpretation as the passages which speak of " the loved disciple " ; but, as Zahn says, " It might have been James," *Einleit.*, ii., p. 480. Stanton thinks he was one of the " upper classes " mentioned in Jo. xii. 42, *The Gospels*, iii., pp. 143, 144. It is quite unnecessary thus to introduce a fresh figure. Besides, to judge by the Evangelist's practice, such a figure would be named. Cf. Jo. iii. 1 ; xviii. 10, 13 ; xix. 38.

It is not reasonable to suppose that the close intimacy of our Lord with the three, recorded in the Synoptics, should have been encroached upon by the addition of another disciple, who is not once named in those Gospels. As a mere question of fitness and congruity in narration, it is wholly improbable. Psychologically and as a matter concerned with the character of our Lord's human affections, it is unlikely. The sacred ties that bound Him to the three favoured Apostles, leading Him to desire their presence in the times of His sorest need, are hardly likely to have been stretched beyond the limits assigned by the first three Evangelists. The addition of a fourth favourite, if we may use the term, is a disturbing feature in the Gospel story and brings into it a jarring note. There is

On the other hand, it has been thought by some that if the writer, although silent as to his actual name, spoke of himself as " the disciple whom Jesus loved," he showed a degree of arrogance and self-assertion that would make it highly improbable that he would have been favoured with the close affection and intimacy of Christ that he appears to claim.

Now, it will be admitted that a man's voluntary unveiling of the *arcana* of his life and character, his motives or his privileges, is apt to meet with a varied reception. To one person it appears a touching instance of candour and straightforwardness ; to another it betrays undue self-consciousness. To one it seems to spring from mere pride and vain glory ; to another it is the natural utterance of a grateful heart. We have only to think of the different construction which has been put upon many of St. Paul's references to himself to be assured that in a case of this sort, no fixed literary judgment commanding general assent can be made to stand upon such a basis.

The clear indications which are presented by the Gospel text are not to be set aside by surmises as to what the writer would be likely to feel in a matter of taste. Indeed, there are few instances in the whole range of literature in which a question of authorship is so satis-

---

only one excuse for it, and that is not a good one. It suits the attitude of certain critics and relieves them of some of their difficulties.

Loisy truly remarks that, if one took literally what is said, in the body of the Gospel, of the loved disciple, this disciple could only be one of the Twelve, *Le Quatr. Evangile*, p. 132. But why not literally true ? Both Loisy (cf. *ib.*, p. 129) and Bacon (*The Fourth Gospel*, pp. 317, 319) deny that " the loved disciple " is a disciple of flesh and blood. If a story purporting to relate history can thus be explained away in the interest of a theory, all historical narration would be impossible. Cf. *ib.*, p. 349, " This Gospel . . . is not historical but spiritual." Bacon does not explain why a spiritual phenomenon is necessarily unhistorical. Cf. E. F. Scott, *The Fourth Gospel*, p. 58, " John (unlike Philo) attaches a supreme importance to the fact." To Loisy the loved disciple is the young Church to which is entrusted the heritage of Judaism and Judaistic Christianity, *ib.*, p. 128 ; cf. pp. 125, 126.

Salome, the mother of the sons of Zebedee, was the sister of our Lord's mother (cf. Jo. xix. 25 with Mk. xv. 40, Mt. xxvii. 56) ; Christ and St. John were therefore first cousins. " According to his method, John does not name her," Lücke *ad loc.*, cf. Zahn *ad loc.* and *Einleitung. in d. N.T.*, ii., p. 460 ; and *D. Evang. des Johannes*, p. 538.

factorily solved by appeal to internal evidence as in the case before us.

Now, it is to be observed that there is no question here of a simple artifice such as that of the writers of pseudepigraphic works like I. Enoch. The silence of the Fourth Gospel in contrast with the Synoptic treatment of John, son of Zebedee, if due to an artifice, could only be attributed to a deliberate attempt to mislead. A reserve, which would be becoming in the actual writer, would be a heartless deception in one who posed in his name. In order to be taken for an Apostle and eye-witness of Christ he would be aping a scrupulous modesty, arraying his deceit in the garb of an attractive virtue. It is quite beside the mark to compare such action with that of the apocalyptic authors. In their case, the name of an ancient worthy is borrowed : but there is no attempt to carry out the illusion by pretending to the possession of special opportunities of obtaining knowledge or of certain traits of character which would deceive the reader. The work is simply placed under the shelter of a great name. Whereas, in the case of the Fourth Gospel, the writer would be passing off his goods by means of an assumption of superior virtue ; while his offence is heightened by the asseverations of truth which are so remarkable a feature of the Gospel.

But we cannot admit that a work of such spiritual depth and power could have proceeded from so tainted a source. Judged by its contents, it bears witness to its own integrity and genuineness.

The " loved disciple " is stated to have been present with our Lord on certain eventful occasions, on one of which —the Last Supper—we seem to be justified in inferring from the Synoptic narrative that none but Apostles were with their Master.[1] Now, if he were not an Apostle but an addition to the company of the Twelve in critical moments, why have we no Synoptic mention of him ?

[1] This appears in all three accounts : Mk. xiv. 17 ; Mt. xxvi. 20 ; Lk. xxii 14. The " twelve " of Mk. and Mt. are the " twelve Apostles " of Lk.

There is no apparent reason for withholding it, and the probability that a man, who stood outside the Apostolic circle and was yet so highly privileged as the Fourth Gospel declares him to be, should be entirely passed over by the earlier Evangelists, is very remote. By the side of this Synoptic omission place on the one hand the omission of John, son of Zebedee, from the pages of the Fourth Gospel and, on the other, the direct mention of the presence of a " disciple whom Jesus loved." In any ordinary investigation of authorship, it is safe to say that but one conclusion would be considered possible. The " loved disciple " of the Fourth Gospel, who, under that designation, is absent from the Synoptic narrative, and the John, son of Zebedee, of the Synoptic story, who is never thus named by the Fourth Evangelist, are one and the same person.

There is another instance of reserve, and of reluctance on the part of the writer of the Fourth Gospel to attach importance to the person of John, son of Zebedee, which points in the same direction. Throughout the Gospel, the Baptist is referred to simply as John, implying either that no other John entered into the history, or that, if there were such a man, he was of too little account to require to be distinguished from the Baptist. But that a writer, who had the Synoptic allusions to the son of Zebedee before him, could so ignore that leading Apostle as to speak of the Baptist as the only " John " who was to be thought of, is utterly improbable ; unless indeed—and this alters the whole aspect of the question—the writer *is* the Apostle.

Again, we seem to detect the figure of the Evangelist is what he tells of the earliest call to discipleship. Two followers of the Baptist hear his proclamation of our Lord as " the Lamb of God " and, impelled by a curiosity which they cannot restrain, seek to come into touch with one of whom such things are said. Their names are not mentioned. Only on the following day, when one of the two seeks out his brother Simon, is the veil so far lifted and we are allowed to know that he is Andrew. The other remains unnamed.

But a single word gives a clue to his identity. Andrew "*first*" findeth his own brother. Is this not a hint that his lead was followed by his fellow disciple,[1] that he, too, brought "his own brother" to Christ? That Andrew's fellow-disciple, who followed his example, is the narrator is evident, not only from the otherwise inexplicable neglect to mention his name, but from the fact that, in Synoptic allusions to the Apostolic company, the two sons of Zebedee are constantly found in conjunction with Andrew and his brother, or with his brother alone.

Here, then, at the very outset, the Evangelist lifts a corner of the veil which he has wrapped about his own figure. If the conclusion seems evident to the ordinary reader, it was luminous to those disciples to whom St. John handed his Gospel. May we not say that it is supported by the fact that, from the first, the ascription of the Gospel to the son of Zebedee was never disputed by Churchman or heretic[2] alike?

It is clear that, about the first decade of the second century, the Church attached the greatest importance to the authentic character of the Gospel. There is no doubt that chap. xx. 30, 31, formed the original conclusion of the book. Chap. xxi. was an afterthought written by the Evangelist, or at his instance, down to v. 24*a*. From v. 24*b* to the end we have the attestation of the elders of

---

[1] "We here read between the lines, yet clearly enough, that just as Andrew met Peter and brought him to Jesus, so his nameless companion met and brought his own brother," Zahn, *ad loc.* (Jo. i. 42), p. 131; *Einleitung in d. N.T.*, ii. p. 476. This is plainly the meaning of the passage whether we read πρῶτος or πρῶτον. And it is supported by the fact that in lists of the Apostles, the two pairs of brothers, Andrew, Peter and John, James, appear together in the first place, Mk. iii. 16–19, and=s.

[2] With one exception: the grotesque assignment of the Gospel to Cerinthus by the so-called Alogi, an anti-Montanist circle of the second century, who, in their zeal against the perversion of the Apocalypse by Montanist teachers, assigned the Johannine writings to that Gnostic heretic of the early second century, *v.* Eus., *H.E.*, iii. 28, who quotes Gaius, ἐκκλησιαστικὸς ἀνήρ as he calls him (*H.E.*, ii. 25), to that effect. "Alogi" was apparently a pleasantry of Epiphanius, *Adv. Hæres.*, li. 3; *v.* Allo, *S. Jean, l'Apocalypse*, p. clxxiv. f. Gaius himself (*fl. c.* A.D. 210), according to Zahn (*Einleit. in d. N.T.*, ii. p. 456), agreed with the Alogi in their view of the Apocalypse, but not of the Gospel, which he assigned to St. John. But *v.* Moffatt, *Introduction to the N.T.*, p. 532; *v.* below, p. 63.

the Church,[1] to whom he handed his completed work.[2]
They solemnly avow their knowledge that the writer of
the whole book, who had just identified himself with " the
loved disciple," is a true witness of the facts which he
records.[3]

The chapter forms an appendix to the Gospel proper.
It is a personal document.[4] The Evangelist had two
objects in view. One was what may be called the restoration of his friend and associate St. Peter. The other was
the removal of a curious misconception which affected the
writer himself.

After our Lord had given to the Apostle who had
thrice denied Him a pastoral charge in a three-fold form,
He proceeded to warn him of the death by which, one day,
he would " glorify God. And when He had spoken this,
He saith unto him, Follow Me." St. Peter, moved by our
Lord's solemn warning and by a dim foreboding of the
trials to which His renewed call to discipleship would
expose him, wonders if he alone of the Twelve is to experience
them. Turning about he seeth the disciple whom Jesus
loved following, and asks a question *which in itself conveys
a hint of that disciple's personality*. There would have been
little point in asking what would be the fate of a disciple
who was outside the circle of the Twelve, even if he stood

[1] The Church of Ephesus, *v.* Gutjahr, *Glaubwürdigkeit des Irenaischen
Zeugnisses*, p. 186. Zahn, *ad loc.*, n., remarks, " In the ' we ' of οἴδαμεν,
we must bethink ourselves of Aristion and Philip the Evangelist in
Hierapolis." This may be so, without excluding leaders of the Church
in which the Gospel appeared. Cf. Drummond, *Character and Authorship
of the Fourth Gospel*, p. 261, " We have here a very early attestation of
the genuineness of the Gospel, and . . . it is very difficult on any just
principles of criticism to set it aside." If the author was an Apostle,
such an attestation appears unnecessary. Its presence in the text is
probably due to controversy which arose in consequence of the character
of the Gospel.

[2] H. J. Holtzmann, *ad loc.*, p. 308, agrees with Zahn, *Einleitung in d.
N.T.*, ii., p. 493, that " there is no proof that the Gospel was ever published
without chap. xxi." It is found in the earliest and best MSS. Zahn
remarks, " That the Gospel did not circulate for a time beyond the
narrow circle for which it was composed is proved by the fact that there
is no trace of its publication without the appendix," *Forschungen zur
Geschichte des N.T. Kanons*, Teil. ix., 1916, p. 7.

[3] *V.* 24.

[4] I find that Harnack takes a similar view, *Chronologie*, i., p. 676,
n. 2.

high in the Master's regard. St. Peter wanted to know if he would have any companion in trial from among his fellow Apostles. *Would Apostleship in every case demand this sacrifice?* " Lord, and what shall this man do ? " It is hard to avoid the inference that " the loved disciple," who is here said to be the writer of the Gospel and whom we know from his presence at the last passover (just referred to) to be an Apostle, was none other than the younger son of Zebedee, whose close intimacy with St. Peter, both during the ministry and afterwards, is constantly mentioned.

The question of St. Peter at once incurs a rebuke. As though forgetful and heedless of Christ's warning and His call to discipleship, he allows himself to be diverted from the thought of his own personal responsibility to a curious questioning as to the future of another. Such curiosity our Lord characteristically checks.[1] He had foreshadowed St. Peter's future and marked out for him his course. That sufficed. The following of Christ is for each of us a personal, individual matter. We stand alone in our responsibility before God. God and my own conscience : these are the two realities with which I have to do. The case of another does not enter into the account. " If I will that he tarry till I come, what is that to thee ? follow thou Me."

But, for our present purpose, the point lies rather in the hypothetical case which Christ puts before St. Peter, together with the mistaken inference which the early Church drew from it and the correction of the mistake which the writer himself supplies. " Then went this saying abroad among the brethren, that that disciple should not die." Far and near, as the report of our Lord's words travelled, it produced a great impression. Then, one at least of His first disciples would be alive to greet Him at the παρουσία. So ran the story at the time the Gospel was being written, and the final chapter is largely devoted to dealing with it. Already in the course of the Gospel, the

---

[1] Cf. Lk. xiii. 23, 24 ; Acts i. 6–9. The tenour of the conversation is its own best proof of authenticity.

Evangelist had shown that he had departed somewhat from the idea of the παρουσία, which he had held in common with his fellow-disciples in earlier days. Now that he was old, and felt that his time was short, he will do what he can to remove a false impression : " Jesus said not unto him, He shall not die ; but, If I will that he tarry till I come, what is that to thee ? " [1]

Now, if this recital has any point and meaning, one thing is certain. " The loved disciple," who is here referred to as the Evangelist, attained a great age. He could not have been martyred in the year 44, when James, son of Zebedee, was put to death by Herod. *There would have been no mistaken inference to correct.* Side by side with this conclusion, place the fact that, at Ephesus, about the time that the Gospel was given to the Church, there lived a disciple known throughout Asia as the Elder John, who was believed to be " the loved disciple," a man of great age, an Apostle and, as was thought, one of the sons of Zebedee.

As he finally closes his Gospel, the Evangelist—or possibly those to whom he handed it—makes a solemn asseveration : " This is the disciple which testifieth of these things and wrote these things." Those who are standing by bear their own witness to it : " We know that his testimony is true." [2]

And another thing is certain. There was only one John of Ephesus who was known to antiquity as " the loved disciple " and the Evangelist. It is admitted that whether the " Elder John " be regarded as the son of Zebedee, or as an entirely distinct leader of the Church of Ephesus, who afterwards became invested by Church tradition with the personality and the attributes of the Apostle, one figure only concerns us.[3] We are thus brought nearer to a

---

[1] I find that Dr. Streeter, in a [deeply interesting chapter, deals with this aspect of the question, *The Four Gospels*, p. 474 f.

[2] xxi. 24 (cf. 3 Jo. 12). According to Wetzel, v. 24a is by the Evangelist, 24b by the recipients of the Gospel, v. Gutjahr, *Glaubwürdigkeit*, p. 186. Westcott, *ad loc.*, H. J. Holtzmann, *ad loc.*, Zahn, *ad loc.*, p. 694, Streeter, *The Four Gospels*, p. 473, assign the whole verse to the recipients.

[3] *V.* p. 64 ; cf. Holtzmann, *Evang. des Joh.*, p. 314, " The writer of

decision on the whole question. The historic facts of the case must fit the circumstances of a single person. We cannot apply those which do not seem to agree with the Apostle to an elder of the Church of Ephesus, however eminent among his brethren ; nor *vice versâ*. Thus the problem is narrowed down.

If it can be shown that " the loved disciple " of the Fourth Gospel and the Appendix, who is said in the closing verses to be the author of the whole work, and has also been identified with the Apostle John, son of Zebedee, was never at Ephesus, we must fall back upon the nebulous figure of the " Elder " ; for that a notable leader of the Asiatic Church of the name of John was at Ephesus about A.D. 100 is certain. But no one has been able to explain how it came to pass that so early as the middle of the second century (when Justin Martyn bears witness, by his assignment of the Apocalypse to the Apostle John, to that disciple's presence in Asia as a great leader of the Church) and onwards, everything that related to the Apostle was transferred to the " Elder," and in place of the son of Zebedee, the disciple of Christ, an otherwise unknown personage was clothed with the history and antecedents of St. John and credited with the Gospel.

The thing is incredible. It must have been known at Ephesus and the neighbouring cities who this John really was. The extraordinary interest which would be excited by the presence of one of the chief apostles and personal disciples of our Lord, had he been living there in extreme old age—an interest confirmed by the closing words of the Appendix to the Gospel—could never have been transferred to another John, whose antecedents would be known sufficiently well to exclude his identification with one who,

the Appendix sees in the unnamed ' loved disciple ' the long-lived John of Ephesus " ; Gutjahr, *op. cit.*, p. 188, " Surely those who were witnesses (Jo. xxi. 24b) not only spoke then, but also in the assemblies of the Church and to neighbouring presbyters ; and there must have been no one in Asia, where the Apostle John worked between 70–100 A.D., who did not know who was ' the disciple whom Jesus loved ' " ; Clemen, *op. cit.*, p. 338, " Who is this long-lived disciple ? We must find him among the two sons of Zebedee. . . . John only can be thought of."

according to the theory of E. Schwartz and others, was martyred in Palestine long years ago.[1]

Criticism possesses but one John of Ephesus with whom to operate. It appears historically and psychologically impossible to account for the belief, early as Justin Martyr and held throughout the Church of the second century, that this John was the son of Zebedee, if in reality he was another person.

The study of the indications of its authorship which the Gospel itself presents leads to one conclusion ; however it may be affected by considerations drawn from other quarters, the narrative itself, taken alone, points to a definite result. It is the work of " the loved disciple," whom, on comparison with the Synoptic narrative, we can hardly avoid identifying with the John, son of Zebedee, who is not once named in the whole course of the Gospel— an omission not otherwise to be explained.

We submit that this conclusion is the more natural. It arises out of the text itself. The internal arguments— as distinct from external factors of historical character— which are alleged against it are mainly subjective, and of a kind which fails to win general consent. They rest on psychological considerations which, if to one mind they present a certain degree of probability, do not succeed in convincing another. In these circumstances, we appear to be justified in choosing the solution which arises naturally from the narrative itself. Only the existence of some definite reason to the contrary should oblige us to revise our judgment. In the whole course of literature, there are few instances in which a work betrays the hand of the writer more clearly.[2]

[1] *V*. below, p. 75.
[2] *V*. Gore, *The Epistles of St. John*, p. 43 ; *The Holy Spirit and the Church*, 1924, p. 115, n. 3.

CHAPTER IV

THE AUTHORSHIP OF THE FOURTH GOSPEL

Tradition

UNTIL after the time of Origen, it does not appear that any doubt was felt within the Christian Church at large about the authorship of those books of the New Testament which have come down to us under the name of John. Nor was there any hesitation as to the identity of this John. He was always regarded as the Apostle, the younger son of Zebedee, a fisherman of Galilee. To him were ascribed the Fourth Gospel, the three Epistles which bear the name of John, and the Apocalypse. The grounds of this ascription are only partly known to us ; but it appears certain that they were first recognised at Ephesus, and that the decision based upon them was sooner or later accepted in all parts of the Christian Church.

The importance of this fact is hardly realised. But it surely makes a great difference in forming an estimate of the part played by the Johannine literature in the evolution of Christian thought, that we can point to the undisputed fact that that literature was referred, in all churches and by all writers who express their mind on the subject, for nearly two hundred years after its composition, to one of the chief Apostles and most intimate associates of our Lord in His earthly life. It means that the faith as therein expressed, the ideal of life as therein unfolded, the spiritual teaching as therein given, were received on the ground that they were handed on by one who had full opportunity of knowing the mind of Christ.

This consideration should be borne in mind by those

who are disposed to waive the question of authorship, as hardly affecting the issues which are at stake. Certainly, it is not the pivot of the whole matter. But it lies well within the circumference; and any fresh light that an investigation may throw upon it, should be welcomed.

Nor is the weight of this consideration lessened by the attempt to explain the ascription of authorship to St. John by depreciating the critical faculty possessed by the leaders of thought in the second century. The history of the Canon of the New Testament shows that criticism was not only being very freely exercised in the Church during that period, but that its decisions were of so sound and satisfying a character as to secure the almost unanimous approval of Christendom down to recent times.[1] It is to the keen criticism and the enlightened judgment of those early days that we owe the selection and preservation of our present Gospels from among the mass of similar literature which then abounded everywhere. If ever there were a time in the long course of Christian history when the right of criticism was claimed and exercised to the full, it was when the New Testament Canon was receiving its authoritative shape. Moreover, we are fortunately in a position to form our own estimate of the value of the critical judgments which were then being passed; we possess fragments of Gospel writings which, in their day, were read and circulated and compared with the Gospels that found their way into the Canon. In every case, comparison upholds the decisions which the Church has formed; decisions which are the more significant because they were come to in communities far separated from one another by distance and by difficulty of travelling; yet decisions

---

[1] I find that Harnack refers to this fact. " In Asia Minor for the space of two decades, a process (of criticism) was applied to the Gospels which the Church never afterwards allowed itself in the following centuries": *Beiträge in d. N.T.*, vi. 1914, p. 50. He speaks of the comparisons and reconciliations between the four Gospels which took place in Asia Minor long before the middle of the second century; men taking sides, some admitting John and rejecting the Synoptics, or one of them, and *vice versâ*; the result of the disputes being the reception of all four books: *ib.*, p. 49.

which the whole body of the Church came to confirm and to make its own.

We have therefore to remember, when we try to estimate the influence of the Johannine writings upon the expanding thought of the Christian Church, that the fire of a discoursing criticism had passed through them, and that they had emerged from the test as works which came with the authority of St. John.

But the criticism which was directed upon the writings themselves was not the only factor that led to their reception as the work of St. John by the generations that immediately succeeded. People spoke of having been in touch with disciples of Christ, and with those who had listened to His disciples. There was continuity of personal witness. The space between Irenæus and the reputed writer of the Fourth Gospel is bridged over by a single life—the life of one who had seen and conversed with both. Polycarp was a connecting link between St. John the Apostle and the period in which our four Gospels had already won their canonical rank as Scriptures of the New Covenant. And, if this remarkable connection has become known to us as evidence that we have no reason to doubt, there must have been many another link, unrecorded and forgotten, that spanned the few decades which elapsed between the writing of the Fourth Gospel and the emergence of the Johannine books into the daylight of canonical recognition. It is too often concluded that those witnesses, whose names and evidence have come down to us, are our only available source of information. Directly, this may be the case ; indirectly, it is far from the truth. Contemporaneous with the writers whom we can consult were the clergy and teachers in all the scattered churches of Christendom, whose own knowledge and testimony are reflected in the works that have survived, and whose assent can therefore be fairly relied upon.

This is a step in the argument which is seldom estimated at its true value ; yet a moment's thought will convince us that it is well worth consideration. The works of the

D

second century which we can read to-day, come to us with the authority of their writers ; *but with much more than this*. They embody the silent witness and approval of the Churches in which they originated. The link they form with the past is of no single strand. It is of many and complicated folds, and it cannot easily be broken. The effect of this state of things is cumulative ; and a criticism which ignores it at once reveals its incompetence to deal fairly with the subject in hand. In considering the value to be placed upon the opinion of Irenæus or Tertullian or Clement of Alexandria, *we have to reckon with the manifold character of the material on which they formed it*. This is especially to be remembered when the argument from the silence of a particular writer is pressed.[1] The Fathers referred to possessed not only many individual writings which have since been lost, but an acquaintance with the collective judgment of the Church, as it expressed itself in the great centres of Christian thought. It is by its singular lack of historic imagination, by its failure to place itself in the situation which obtained in the second century, that much of the prevailing criticism seems to miss the mark.

There is another consideration which may very fairly be taken into account. He who inspired the men who wrote the Scriptures did not fail those whose judgment determined their selection. The conclusions which were everywhere being formed, silently and on no arranged system, were guided by the Holy Spirit.[2] The value of the books which passed the process of sifting and discrimination bears witness to this fact. Their elevation and authority is a proof of the " inspiration of selection." To admit this is not to foreclose a question of fact by recourse to the plea of special interposition. Rather it is to take into account the actual factors of the case, and to allow them their proper place in the investigation. The presence of the Holy Spirit in the Church was a reality, and made itself felt in the judgments that were being gradually

---

[1] As by Bacon.
[2] This is fairly to be inferred from Jo. xiv. 16, 17, 26.

formed as to the spiritual value and authority of the several writings.

Parallel with this process was the accumulating mass of evidence which pointed to the authorship of the books which were finding their way into the Canon. The two processes went on simultaneously, and it is only reasonable to think that they exercised a certain influence upon one another. The belief that the Johannine books were written by the Apostle must have hastened the process of their canonisation ; while the general admission of their spiritual value predisposed men to accept such an assignment.[1]

We have also to remember that the question of authorship is, in this case, no matter of mere literary interest. The Johannine writings are too vital and epoch-making for Christianity, to permit such an attitude towards them. They make an insistent appeal for attention and consideration. Besides, the people for whom they were composed formed a close and contained body, pressed upon and hedged in by a hostile world. Writings which made so strong a demand upon belief and conduct must needs have been scrutinised and subjected to every possible trial of their genuineness and authority. It could not be a matter of indifference to the Church of the second century whether they came from an Apostolic witness of the Saviour, or were mere jetsam cast up fortuitously by the surging stream of time.

If the external evidence for the Fourth Gospel is compared with that for the first three, it will be found to suffer from a disadvantage from which the latter is almost entirely free—the difficulty of knowing whether a piece of evidence refers to the Gospel itself or to the Johannine atmosphere ;

---

[1] I find that Bishop Gore takes a similar view. " Admission to the Canon was a judgment on authenticity or apostolic authorship": *The Epistles of St. John*, 1920, p. 22. Cf. Harnack, *Beiträge*, vi., p. 25 : " It was gradually acknowledged that what was Apostolic and of the Apostolic age was paramount and classical and could not again be produced " ; E. Meyer, *Ursprung u. Anfänge des Christenthums*, vol. iii., 1923, p. 637, " The First Epistle early won canonical respect. It must have originated at the latest *c.* A.D. 100 and have quickly circulated in Asia Minor." In view of Meyer's position, this admission is significant, as the Gospel and First Epistle are by the same author.

in other words, to the body of thought existing in the traditional home of the Johannine writings. Owing to the earlier date of composition and to their difference of character, this difficulty does not arise in the case of the Synoptic Gospels.

This disadvantage, however, is counterbalanced by the fact that whereas Synoptic material is often difficult to assign to its ultimate source, there is no such difficulty to be encountered where special Johannine material is concerned. There is no one to dispute the source with the writer.

It should be borne in mind that owing to the late period at which St. John appeared—at the close of the Apostle's prolonged life, if we assume the truth of the tradition—there was ample time for conceptions which characterise Johannine literature to take root in the Churches that he influenced, and to pass into their current thought. This fact is a warning that all seemingly Johannine ideas that appear in early writers are not necessarily due to the Johannine writings. We have to guard against the temptation to refer them exclusively to that source.

Before we examine the evidence at our disposal, it may be well to think what our knowledge of the conditions of the time would lead us to expect. We are apt to make our own difficulties and problems the measure of what was experienced then, and to suppose that what is of intense interest to ourselves must have deeply affected the Church of the early second century. Silence, too, in matters of acknowledged importance is of relative, not absolute, significance. Much has perished which was being put into writing. Many things that we would give a great deal to know were of too common knowledge to be reported. After the surprise occasioned by its evident dissimilarity to the Synoptics, the authorship came generally to be regarded as certain. It was a matter too familiar to require discussion, or to need direct allusion.[1]

[1] " Early references to a Gospel which was universally acknowledged had no interest for any one unless they contained some curious or important fact." Lightfoot, *Biblical Essays*, p. 67, n. 1.

A first requirement for such an investigation as the present is a scientific use of the imagination. It is by the absence of it that so much of the Johannine criticism of the last hundred years has miscarried. We need to transfer ourselves, as far as may be, to the period and the conditions of the publication of the writings. If this were done, there would not be so many peremptory demands for express statements of authorship.

It may be provisionally assumed that the Gospel appeared about the close of the first century.[1] It pre-supposes the existence of the Synoptic account of Christ. The rest of the New Testament books, with the possible exception of the Pastoral Epistles and 2 Peter, were in the hands of the Church. One at least of the writings of the Apostolic Fathers, the Epistle of Clement, may have already seen the light. The Apostolic Age runs into the sub-Apostolic. We can draw no precise line of demarcation between them. The Didache betrays the attainment of its present shape and contents at about the turn of the century. The Epistles of Ignatius were written in the first decade of the second century.[2] It will thus be seen that we have to moderate our expectations, as we search the earliest Christian literature (outside the Canon) for reference to St. John. The streams are running parallel with one another. There is no question of derivation.

A glance over the whole field of inquiry suggests that it will tend to clearness if we distinguish between evidence that implies knowledge of the writings themselves, and evidence for their authorship. Chronologically, there is considerable difference.[3] We get citations, pointing to

[1] F. Torm observes that the generality of critics admit—independently of their views as to the genesis of the Gospel—that its composition can in no case be set later than the earliest years of the second century; *Indledning til det Ny Testamente*, Copenhagen, 1923, p. 164. Cf. Streeter, *The Four Gospels*, p. 17: "It cannot be later than A.D. 100, and may quite possibly be as early as 90."

[2] At any rate, not later than A.D. 117.

[3] For instance, Ignatius refers to "Peter and Paul" (*ad Rom.*, iv. 3), but does not mention St. John, although, as we shall see, he shows acquaintance with the Gospel; *v.* Kidd, *History of the Church*, i., p. 63. In *ad Eph.*, xi. he seems to hint at their fellowship with St. John as well as St. Paul, οἳ καὶ ἀποστόλοις πάντοτε συνῇνεσαν.

direct familiarity with Johannine literature long before we find any reference to the writer. This fact has been recently exploited to the fullest extent in the attempt to disprove the traditional view of the authorship. At the present stage it will suffice to draw attention to this procedure and to remind ourselves that the omission of an author's name, when citing his work in a society familiar with his person and history, is not only quite natural, *but does nothing to discredit the assignment of authorship when it is made later on.*

Perhaps the earliest quotation from the Fourth Gospel is made by St. Ignatius, writing to the Philadelphians while on his journey to martyrdom in the Flavian Amphitheatre at Rome, about the year A.D. 110. The allusion is clear and decisive, as comparison with the two writings shows at once.[1] Elsewhere in his Epistles, echoes of Johannine terms of speech abound; but whether derived from writings, or from prevailing currents of thought and philosophy, we cannot say. Their combined effect, on the whole, leads to the former conclusion.

Basileides, the Alexandrian Gnostic, in the reign of Hadrian, is said by Hippolytus[2] to have cited St. John i. 9. The source of the quotation is evident, and there is no reason to question the accuracy of Hippolytus in its assignment to Basileides. Thus we have clear reference to the Fourth Gospel from a period *c.* A.D. 125–140.

Another famous Gnostic teacher, Valentinus, was at

---

[1] Jo. iii. 8; Ign., *ad Philad.*, vii. 1. The exact year of his martyrdom is unknown. At the latest, it was in A.D. 117; but might have been several years earlier. He is speaking of the Spirit and goes on: οἶδεν γὰρ πόθεν ἔρχεται καὶ ποῦ ὑπάγει. If the phrase embodied a specific truth or doctrine, it might have belonged to the current teaching; it is *the choice of expression* that points to a written antecedent. With Jo. viii. 28, 29, compare *ad Mag.*, vii. V. H. J. Bardsley in *J.T.S.*, vol. xiv., p. 219: "Our study of the letters (of Ignatius) has proved not only the influence of St. John, but also that his Epistles and Gospel were already written. The hypothesis of oral influence does not account for the parallelisms."

Burney, *op. cit.*, p. 129, "The Epistles of St. Ignatius, *c.* 110, are full of Johannine theology": *v.* pp. 153 ff.

[2] *Refut. Hæres.*, vii. 22. In his citation of Jo. i. 9, we have, in the opinion of Bp. Lightfoot, the very words of Basileides, *Biblical Essays*, p. 108.

Rome a little later (c. A.D. 140–156). He, too, valued and quoted from the Fourth Gospel.[1]

"The Shepherd" of Hermas, brother of Pius I., Bishop of Rome, is probably to be assigned to A.D. 140–155. Its theology and certain verbal similarities are reminiscent of the Fourth Gospel.[2]

Polycarp, Bishop of Smyrna, used to speak, in his old age, of his "intercourse with John and the rest of those who had seen the Lord."[3] Writing to the Philippians before he had received particulars of the martyrdom of Ignatius, and therefore soon after the year A.D. 110, he asks for tidings of that saint,[4] and in his short letter shows his acquaintance, if not with the Gospel, yet with its kindred writing the First Epistle.[5]

We have the authority of Eusebius for the fact that a similar testimony to the Johannine writings was afforded by Polycarp's contemporary, Papias of Hierapolis. Like Polycarp, he quoted from the First Epistle.[6] In both of these cases, as we shall see, it is a fair inference that knowledge of the Epistle implies knowledge of the Gospel. But we can go further and from Papias' own words deduce his acquaintance with the Gospel.

It is a striking fact that the order in which he places four of the Apostles whom he names in his preface, Peter, Thomas, and the two sons of Zebedee, is the order in which they stand in St. John xxi. 2, an order which is not found elsewhere.[7] It is thought that the sayings of "The

---

[1] V. Iren., *Adv. Hær.*, iii. 4, 3. According to Lipsius, he began to teach his Gnostic doctrines towards the end of the reign of Hadrian, A.D. 117–138, v. Iren., *ib.*, i. 11, 1. Valentinus and his followers make special use of the prologue of the Fourth Gospel, v. Loisy, *Quatr. Evangile*, p. 16.

[2] With Jo. x. 7, 9, compare Hermas, *Sim.*, ix. 12, § 1. With Jo. x. 18, compare *Sim.*, v. 6, § 3. With Jo. iii. 5, compare *Sim.*, ix. 16, §§ 1, 2.

[3] Iren., *Ep. ad Flor.*, § 2.

[4] Polyc., *ad Phil.*, § 13.

[5] *Ib.*, § 7; cf. 1 Jo. iv. 2, 3.

[6] Euseb., *H.E.*, iii. 39, Κέχρηται δ'ό αὐτὸς (Παπίας) μαρτυρίαις ἀπὸ τῆς Ἰωάννου προτέρας Ἐπιστολῆς.

[7] Both Gutjahr, *op. cit.*, p. 166, and Clemen, *D. Entstehung des Joh. Evang.*, p. 381, regard this as a proof of his knowledge of the Gospel. As the latter says, "It is only to be accounted for if Papias was dependent not on the Johannine tradition, but on the Gospel itself, in which, and

Elders," preserved by Irenæus, are to be attributed to Papias.[1] If Irenæus was acquainted with Polycarp, he probably knew his contemporary Papias. In one of the sayings there is a quotation of our Lord's words in St. John xiv. 2.[2]

Less evident marks of knowledge of the Gospel have been found by some in Papias. An Argumentum or Preface to the Fourth Gospel states that, according to Papias, "the Gospel appeared, and was given to the Churches by John while he was yet alive."[3] Nor is it without significance that Papias, in his preface, declares his preference for those who record commandments derived ἀπ' αὐτῆς τῆς ἀληθείας, a specifically Johannine expression.

The cumulative effect of these traces, partly direct and partly indirect, of a familiarity with the Johannine writings possessed by Papias, is too strong to be ignored. It is heightened by the fact that Irenæus and, later on, Eusebius, who both refer the Gospel to St. John, had the complete work of Papias before them, and could not fail to be influenced by the use of the Gospel made by so early a writer, and by his knowledge of its author.[4] To many minds, the certainty that both Papias and Polycarp, friends and reputed disciples of St. John, were familiar with the First Epistle, will seem the surest proof that we possess of their knowledge of the Gospel. There is nothing to show the priority of the two writings. If it be argued that the

in which alone, the four named actually appear in this order." Cf. Lightfoot, *Essays on Supernatural Religion*, p. 193; *v.* Streeter, *The Four Gospels*, p. 451, but against his view, Lightfoot, *op. cit.*, p. 160 f.

[1] So Harnack, *Chronologie*, p. 658. *V.* Lightfoot and Harmer, *The Apostolic Fathers*, p. 549.

[2] *V.* Gutjahr, *op. cit.*, p. 166.

[3] From the tenth-century codex Toletanus, in Wordsworth and White, *Novum Test. Lat.*, i., p. 490. The Argumentum goes on to say that Papias actually wrote the Gospel at John's dictation. Jülicher regards the statement as a late legend, *Einl. in d. N.T.*, p. 323. Zahn declines to dismiss it as fabulous and compares it with the known practice of St. Paul to make use of a scribe, *Einl. in d. N.T. Theol.*, ii., p. 466; *Forsch.*, vi., p. 127, n. 1. Cf. Gutjahr, *op. cit.*, p. 173; Lightfoot, *Essays on Supernatural Religion*, p. 187.

[4] As Clemen says: "Hierapolis is after all not so very far from Ephesus," *op. cit.*, p. 402.

narrative of the Gospel facts would naturally precede their application in the Epistle, it can be replied that long before the Gospel was committed to writing, its material would have been familiar to the Asiatic Churches through the oral teaching of the Evangelist. The Epistle may have preceded the Gospel or *vice versâ*. But they form a consistent whole. In character and tone, in phraseology and idea, they are inseparable. If the Gospel speaks with the authority of an eye-witness, the Epistle claims an equal right to wield that authority among all whom the Epistle reaches.

But there is a further consideration. Those who, like Heitmüller, talk of " the rise of the legend of the Apostle John in Asia Minor " [1] and of the early substitution of his name for that of the actual writer, whether a " Presbyter John," or some unknown disciple of the Apostle, may be reminded that the Epistle acted as a safeguard and a guarantee of the Apostolic origin of the Gospel. It is clear that they were separated from one another by the briefest interval of time. They evidently arose in the same locality. They equally decline to be removed from Ephesus as their common home. To receive and acknowledge the one was to receive the other. It is futile to suggest that their origin could have remained a secret to men like Papias, Polycarp, Justin Martyr, Tatian, Polycrates, and the host of others who belonged to the Churches of Ephesus and its neighbourhood. The great personality which is suggested by both writings, the unequalled authority acquired by his experience and by his standing in the Church, makes such a theory hopeless and impossible. Too many threads of evidence—some still traceable, others that have vanished from our sight, but lay before one in the commanding position of Eusebius—converge upon the problem to make such a solution practicable.

Rather before the time when Justin was writing—the middle of the second century—there appeared, probably in Syria, the " Gospel of Peter," an apocryphal work of which

[1] In *D. Schriften des N.T.*, ii., p. 860.

we possess a few fragments.[1] They contain clear proof of the writer's knowledge of the Fourth Gospel.[2]

" The Acts of John," a writing of Leucius of the School of Valentinus (c. A.D. 150), spoke of the journeyings, περίοδοι, of St. John, and of his preparation for his death and burial.[3]

That the Fourth Gospel was known to Justin Martyr is generally admitted. He had lived at Ephesus (c. A.D. 135) and would be familiar with the tradition respecting the Fourth Gospel. His reference to the Gospels is in keeping with the early date at which he wrote. He speaks of them as " the Memoirs " written " by the Apostles and those who followed them." [4] But none of his quotations or borrowings are referred to any specific writer. His indebtedness to the Fourth Gospel and to the range of ideas of which it is the exponent, is quite evident.[5]

Like his master Justin, Tatian shows his knowledge of the Gospel.[6] He was the first to attempt the arrangement

---

[1] V. Preuschen, Antilegomena, pp. 15 f., 145 f.; Harnack, Preuss. Jahrbücher for 1893. Dr. C. H. Turner assigns it to A.D. 115–130 : J.T.S. for 1913, p. 164.

[2] With Gosp. of Pet. v. 14, cf. Jo. xix. 33 ; with v. 21, cf. Jo. xx. 20, 25 ; with vi. 24, cf. Jo. xix. 41 ; with xiv. 59, 60, cf. Jo. xxi, 1. V. von Dobschütz, D. apostol. Zeitalter, p. 14 ; Lepin, L'Origine du Quatr. Evang., p. 289 ; Grill, Untersuchungen über d. Entstehung des vierten Evang., ii. 1923, p. 396.

[3] Zahn, Acta Johannis, p. 245 f.

[4] Dial. c. Tryph., p. 199 B; cf. pp. 83 B; 195 D; 196 D; 197 C; 200 A, E.

[5] Dial., p. 186 c. " His attitude to the Gospel is reserved and uncertain. He seems to know it, but makes strikingly little use of it. . . . To him the Gospel is still not an unopposed apostolic authority": Heitmüller, Zeitschr. für d. N.T. Wissen., 1914, p. 191. E. A. Abbott in Enc. Bibl., ii., after discussion concludes " that Justin either did not know John, or, as is more probable, knew it but regarded it with suspicion." He makes the interesting suggestion that Justin " accepting the Apocalypse as the work of (Tryph., 81) the Apostle John may naturally have rejected the claim of the Gospel to proceed from the same author." In that case, Justin would have anticipated the " Higher Criticism " of Dionysius of Alexandria. Loisy has no doubt as to Justin's knowledge of the Gospel : " Sa Christologie est toute Johannique. . . . Justin emprunte au quatrième Evangile non seulement des idées dogmatiques, mais des formules, qui ne permettent pas de nier sa dépendance à l'égard de Jean." Le Quatr. Evang., p. 14 ; v. Grill, Untersuchungen, ii. p. 395. He assigns the First Apology of Justin to A.D. 152.

[6] Orat. contra Græcos, § 19 ; § 13 ; § 4, πνεῦμα ὁ Θεός, v. Jo. i. 3, 5 ; iv. 24.

of a Harmony of the Four Gospels—a step of great importance in the process of their canonical recognition. The
four are singled out from the mass of Gospel literature as
the authoritative records of the Life and Ministry of Christ,
and this took place shortly after the middle of the second
century.

Traces of the Gospel and the First Epistle are found in
the Epistle to Diognetus, a beautiful work of unknown
authorship, the earlier part, §§ 1–10, being assigned to a
date between A.D. 120–150, the latter part to the close of
the second century.[1]

In the letter addressed by the Churches of Vienne and
Lyons to the Churches of Asia in the year 177, giving an
account of those who suffered martyrdom in Gaul under
M. Aurelius, the Fourth Gospel is quoted as conveying a
prophecy of Christ.[2]

In a writing, of which Coptic and Ethiopic versions
have lately been discovered and translated into German,[3]
assigned by its editor to the second half of the second
century, "more accurately 160–170 A.D.," [4] great use is
made of the Fourth Gospel. It places St. John first in a
list of the eleven Apostles,[5] and its Asiatic home seems to
be indicated by the special partiality of the author for that
Apostle. "It was composed by an adherent of the Great
Church with a view to the controversy with the Gnostic
heresy, and especially with Docetism." "In the view of
the author, the Gospel of John is clearly the Gospel which
imparts the true knowledge of Christ."[6] This second-
century Epistle is full of interest and has an important
bearing upon the history of our Gospel.

Shortly after the middle of the century, Melito, Bishop

---

[1] With *Ep. ad Diogn.*, vi. 3, compare Jo. xvii. 11, 14 ; with *Ep.*, vii. 5,
compare Jo. iii. 17 ; with *Ep.*, x. 2, compare 1 Jo. iv. 9.

[2] Jo. xvi. 2.   The letter is preserved by Eusebius, *H.E.*, v. 1.

[3] *Epistola Apostolorum : Conversations of Jesus with His Disciples
after the Resurrection : a Catholic Apostolic Letter of the Second Century :*
C. Schmidt in *Texte und Untersuchungen*, 1919.

[4] *Ib.*, p. 402.

[5] *Ib.*, p. 201.

[6] *Ib.*, pp. 402, 225.

of Sardis,[1] and Claudius Apollinaris,[2] a successor of Papias in the see of Hierapolis, betray familiarity with the Fourth Gospel, in the scanty fragments of their writings which have survived.

About the year 175, the canonical status of the Fourth Gospel is illustrated by the fact that Heracleon, a Gnostic of the school of Valentinus, wrote a commentary upon it, which was known and used by Origen.[3]

This brings us to the period in which the evidence of familiarity with the Johannine writings, so far as it has come down to us, passes into evidence of their authorship. It is, of course, highly probable that, among the writers whom we have been citing for reference to the language of the Gospel, some at least had been not only well aware of the author's name and identity, but had recorded the fact. If we may argue from analogy, a witness of a few years later, one of whose works has survived in its completeness, Theophilus of Antioch, makes the probability almost a certainty ; for he not only quotes from the Gospel, but states that the author is St. John.[4]   This was c. A.D. 180, and he is among the first, if not the very first writer to assign the Gospel to its author, in any works that have come down to us.

In the precious fragment known as the Muratorian Canon, we have an assignment of the authorship which may

---

[1] Melito (c. A.D. 170) presented an Apology to the Emperor Marcus Aurelius.   Fragments that have come down to us show traces of acquaintance with the Fourth Gospel.   "He must have been for many years a contemporary of Polycarp," Westcott, *Canon of N.T.*, p. 220 ; cf. Lightfoot, *op. cit.*, p. 248.

[2] He clearly refers to Jo. xix. 34 ; *v.* Otto, *Corpus Apolog.*, ix. p. 487.

[3] *V.* Orig., *Comment. in S. Jo.*, ed. Bened., vol. iv. p. 66, and *passim.* Clement of Alexandria quotes Heracleon on Lk. xii. 8, to the effect that Matthew, Philip, Thomas, and many others were not called upon to make a confession of their faith before a magistrate, *Strom.*, iv. 9.   It is argued that St. John could not have been one of these.   If he escaped martyrdom, his name would have been mentioned.   He was too important a person to be omitted.   It must therefore have been the opinion of Heracleon that he died a martyr's death.   The inference is precarious.   If Heracleon shared the belief of Justin Martyr that St. John was the author of the Apocalypse, he would not be likely to include his name among those who had not been arraigned before a magistrate and called upon to confess their faith.

[4] Theoph., *Apologia ad Autol.*, ii. 22, quoting Jo. i. 1.

be dated a few years before the close of the second century. After noting the fact that Luke, the author of the Third Gospel, was not an eye-witness of Christ, the fragmentist goes on to say that the Fourth Gospel is the work of John, one of the disciples, meaning a personal disciple and therefore eye-witness of Christ, and he then gives a somewhat imaginary account of the circumstances of its composition.[1]

As the second century is about to close, the stream of evidence widens into a river.[2] Three great writers from different regions of Christendom bear their testimony to the Gospel and its authorship. Of these, St. Irenæus is the most important from his personal history and his opportunities for getting to know the facts. His great work *Contra Hæreses* was written *c.* A.D. 180–185. It abounds in quotations from the Fourth Gospel and in allusions to it. Not only have the Gospels taken their fixed and final place in sacred literature, but they are shown, by means of fanciful analogies, to be necessarily four in number. Nature and Revelation, History and Prophecy conspire to order their fourfold form. It is their destiny.

But the value of his evidence to the Fourth Gospel lies in its personal element. He was linked to the man who was universally held to be its author by one single life. As a boy, Irenæus had been a scholar of Polycarp,[3] who

[1] For the text of the passage, *v.* Westcott, *Canon of N.T.*, p. 534 f.

[2] Yet Professor Bacon speaks of " two centuries of effort (prior to Eusebius) to *authenticate* the Gospel record " : *The Fourth Gospel in Research and Debate*, p. 81 f. He speaks of this as a recent discovery. Dr. Stanton has well replied, " I believe that the ' discovery ' that during the third and early years of the fourth century the authenticity of the Gospel of St. John was still in debate and that we have evidence of a series of efforts during this time ' to authenticate the Gospel record ' is purely Prof. Bacon's own " : *The Gospels*, pt. iii., p. 129. Harnack, too, declares that in the youth of Irenæus, the Four Gospels were regarded as one work in fourfold presentation ; that is before *c.* A.D. 150 : *Beiträge*, vi., p. 48.

[3] For the probable age of Irenæus during his intercourse with Polycarp, *v.* Lepin, *L'Origine*, p. 155, n. 3. It is to be remembered that his opportunity for acquiring knowledge of the facts was not confined to his actual acquaintance with Polycarp. He had access to others whose information went back to an earlier period. People speak as if each link in the chain of witness were entirely isolated from every one except those whose names have come down to us. Cf. the letter of the Churches of Lyons and Vienne to their brethren in Asia, on the sufferings of the martyrs in Gaul : Euseb., *H.E.*, v. 1 ; *v.* Sanday, *The Fourth Gospel*, p. 61.

himself had sat at the feet of John, son of Zebedee, and other Apostles. In a letter, preserved by Eusebius,[1] he reminds Florinus of their intercourse with Polycarp, and how well he remembers the place where that Saint used to sit, his going out and coming in, his mode of life and his appearance, and how he used to speak of his familiar intercourse with " John and the rest of those who had seen the Lord." That this John was the Apostle, there can be no reasonable doubt. He is named ὁ τοῦ Κυρίου μαθητής, discipulus Domini, and is identified with " the loved disciple " and is spoken of as the writer of the Gospel. Indirectly, John is regarded as an Apostle, for Irenæus tells of his abode at Ephesus and of the fact that Polycarp, his scholar, was placed in his see of Smyrna by Apostles, presumably, therefore, by the Apostle (John) who was his teacher.[2]

It is to be observed that the assignment of the Fourth Gospel to St. John is made incidentally.[3] St. Irenæus had no need to emphasise the point ; for his opponents, the Gnostics, fully accepted it as a genuine work of Apostolic authorship. The incidental character of his testimony adds greatly to its value.

One of his contemporaries was Polycrates, Bishop of Ephesus, the eighth member of his family to exercise the

---

[1] *H.E.*, v. 20. Florinus was an early friend of Irenæus, who had lapsed into heresy.

[2] Schwartz maintains that the account by Irenæus of Polycarp's intercourse with John " is contradicted by the silence of Ignatius in his letter to him and of his letter to the Smyrneans," as though the failure of a writer to mention in a short letter an event distinctly recorded by another writer sufficed to render it improbable : *Zeitschr. für d. N.T. Wissensch.*, 1910, p. 91. On the other hand, Bousset remarks, " This is in fact a witness of the most important kind, which seems to me to hold its ground against all that modern criticism can allege to the contrary " : *D. Offenbarung des Joh.*, p. 39.

It is strange that some have denied that Irenæus, by the term μαθητής, could have meant John the Apostle ; for he shows clearly that the John whom he calls ὁ τοῦ Κυρίου μαθητής is that Apostle. Thus, speaking of the elders who consorted with John " the disciple of the Lord " in Asia, he adds, " Certain of them saw not only John but other Apostles also " : *Adv. Hæres.*, ii. 22, 5. After speaking of the Church of Ephesus as founded by St. Paul, he states that John remained with them until the time of Trajan, and that it is a true witness to the tradition of the Apostles " : *ib.*, iii. 3, 4.

[3] Cf. *Adv. Hæres.*, iii. 16, 5 ; i. 8, 5 ; iii. 1, 1.

episcopal office. In a letter to Victor, Bishop of Rome, written about A.D. 190, he speaks of the loved disciple as John, a martyr and teacher, and says that he fell asleep at Ephesus. Now, as bishop of that see, succeeding in it some of his own kinsmen, Polycrates must have been in a position to identify without the shadow of a doubt the teacher of whom he is writing. He is the " John who lay upon the Lord's breast . . . both a martyr and a teacher. This man fell asleep in Ephesus." [1]

St. Clement of Alexandria, writing c. A.D. 190–200, quotes the Fourth Gospel and the First Epistle as the work of St. John.[2] In a fragment preserved by Eusebius, he describes the origin of the Gospel.[3] He refers to the Four Gospels of our Canon as " handed down to us by tradition." [4]

---

[1] Ap. Euseb., H.E., v. 24, Ἔτι δὲ καὶ Ἰωάννης ὁ ἐπὶ τὸ στῆθος τοῦ Κυρίου ἀναπεσών, ὃς ἐγενήθη ἱερεὺς τὸ πέταλον πεφορεκώς, καὶ μάρτυς καὶ διδάσκαλος· οὗτος ἐν Ἐφέσῳ κεκοίμηται. The expression ἱερεὺς τὸ πέταλον πεφορεκώς is evidently symbolical. It was not a Jewish High Priest, as the meaning of the priestly plate or badge seems to denote, who reclined on the Saviour's breast at the Last Supper. Had so remarkable an incident occurred, it would not have been left to a writer of the end of the second century to record it, and that in a passing reference. The phrase, as it stands, does not admit of a literal interpretation. It is a graphic indication of the writer's lofty estimate of the person and the rank of the John of whom he is speaking. He sees in him one who in the Churches of Asia held much the same position as the High Priest in Israel ; and at the same time the idea serves to mark his sense of the continuity that existed between the ancient Church and the Church of Christ. Everything that was of permanent value and significance in the old passed on into the new. When, too, it is remembered that the same kind of language is applied by Epiphanius to St. James, the Lord's brother, it becomes certain that the remark of Polycrates cannot be cited to prove that the Gospel could not have been written by the son of Zebedee; v. Epiph., Hær., lxxviii. 14.

[2] Clem. Alex., Strom., v. 12 (Jo. i. 18) ; Pædag., i. 6 (Jo. vi. 53) ; ii. 15 (1 Jo. v. 16, 17) ; iii. 6 (1 Jo. ii. 18, 19) ; Pædag., iii. 12 (1 Jo. ii. 3).

[3] Hypotyp., vii., in Euseb., H.E., vi. 14.

[4] No evidence against the Johannine authorship can be derived from the obscure remark of Clement, Strom., vii. 17, that the teaching of Christ's Apostles was ended in the time of Nero, for in Quis dives Salv., 42, the same writer speaks of the Apostle John as living at Ephesus, after his release from Patmos, and establishing bishoprics in neighbouring cities, τοῦ τυράννου τελευτήσαντος, i.e. on the death of Domitian, A.D. 96. Besides, in Strom., vii. 17, Clement is dividing the teaching of the Gospel into periods corresponding to the reigns of Emperors, Christ Himself teaching in the time of Tiberius, the Apostles, " as far as the ministry of Paul " (μέχρι γε τῆς Παύλου λειτουργίας), finishing theirs in the time of Nero.

Tertullian, writing in the first decade of the third century, quotes the Gospel and the First Epistle, and regards them as the work of the Apostle John.[1]

Before we pass from the witness borne by such tradition as has come down to us, it is well to consider the opinion of one who, living a century later than Clement, had before him, besides the scanty remains of those Greek writers which we possess, many writings that have perished.

After the author of the Book of Acts, Eusebius was the first historian who attempted to trace the fortunes of the Church of Christ, as it spread from the Upper Room at Jerusalem throughout the Roman Empire. We learn from his own words that he was a close student of the literature at his disposal. He weighed and compared the value of the sources of his information,[2] and we have to thank him for preserving priceless extracts from his stores of knowledge that would otherwise have been lost to us.

Now Eusebius, while expressing himself as doubtful about the authorship of the Apocalypse,[3] had no doubt as to the validity of the general judgment of the Church that the Fourth Gospel was the work of the Apostle. The importance of this fact is evident. It means that he found nothing in the writings which he could consult— such as the complete work of Papias, or in the Apocryphal Gospels, of which we possess slight fragments—to cause him to reject the universal tradition. He is in full agreement with Irenæus, Clement, Origen, Dionysius of Alexandria, as to the identity of the Evangelist and St. John the Apostle and as to his prolonged life at Ephesus. With the material at his disposal, and the possession of collateral

---

[1] After speaking of the Apostles as authors of the " Evangelicum Instrumentum," he says, " Denique, nobis fidem ex Apostolis Joannes et Matthæus insinuant; ex Apostolicis, Lucas et Marcus instaurant " : *Adv. Marcion.*, iv. 2, p. 414 A, B. He regards John as author both of the Apocalypse and the First Epistle, *De Præscrip. Hæret.*, xxxiii., p. 214 B ; *De Anima*, xvii., p. 276 C. But in his many quotations and references to the Fourth Gospel, Tertullian seldom stays to name the author. He takes it for granted that he is too well known to need mention. But *v. Adv. Prax.*, xv., xxi., xxiii., xxvi. ; *Adv. Marcion.*, iv. 35, p. 452 B.

[2] *V. H.E.*, i. 13 ; ii. 25 ; iii. 36 ; iv. 5.

[3] *H.E.*, iii. 25, 39 ; *v.* Procksch, *Petrus und Johannes*, 1920, p. 110.

ines of tradition, he must have known whether there was
any foundation in fact for the existence of a state of things
which would at once negative both his own view and that
of the authors whom he quotes. Had he been aware of
such a situation, we can be assured, from our knowledge of
his historical method and his care for accuracy, that he
would have mentioned it.

We may at any rate be certain that, if St. John the
Apostle had suffered martyrdom at an early date, and had
therefore never lived to a good old age at Ephesus, Eusebius
must have been aware of it. He would not have concurred
in the statements of the early writers whom he quotes.
He would not have assigned the Gospel to the son of
Zebedee. It is difficult to avoid the force of this consideration, when we try to estimate the value of the tradition.

We have traced the steps by which the Fourth Gospel
came to be generally recognised and quoted, first as a
writing of authority ; somewhat later as of Apostolic
authorship and more definitely as the work of John, son of
Zebedee.

To contend that the absence of any definite assignment
to him before the last quarter of the second century renders
that assignment untrustworthy is to misunderstand the
situation.

In the first place, we have at our disposal a mere
fraction of the literature of the early and middle years of
the century. Much which may have contained specific
allusions to the author has perished. Secondly, it took
time for the Gospel to become known beyond the community in which it originated. In the third place, it is
certain that a Gospel presenting features so unlike those
that had already established themselves in the confidence
of the Church did not at once gain an equal position of
authority. And there is another consideration which is
much lost sight of. The personal identity of the author
was too well known in Ephesus and the neighbouring
churches to make it probable that his name would require
mention whenever his words or his actions were referred to.

E

A guarantee that certainty was obtainable is supplied by the state of parties which already existed in the Churches of Asia. The fact that the Gospel was quickly welcomed and employed by Gnostics in the interest of their peculiar doctrines, and that they never disputed its assignment to the Apostle, would make the great Church all the more alive to the necessity of proving its genuineness. In the controversies that arose, each side would anxiously inquire into the origin of a writing to which each appealed. Any flaw in the evidence would be seized at once. The Fourth Gospel was not one of those New Testament writings which took its place in the growing Canon without demur. All the more trustworthy on that account is the witness to its authorship when at length it meets us a few years later, for it is a witness that has been put to the test.

And the evidence, when it comes, is copious and diverse. This fact should, we think, be taken into account by those who complain of the earlier absence of direct testimony. The ascription to the son of Zebedee is found at the close of the second century in every quarter of the Church, making it probable that each community had arrived at the one conclusion independently through a long chain of unbroken tradition. Facts have a way of establishing themselves by the mere force of their occurrence. The separate links in the process were too many and of too heterogeneous a character to permit misapprehension. The theory that a transfer was effected, and that a writing which is known to have been produced in Ephesus by a man named John, came in course of time to be everywhere referred to the son of Zebedee, and this by a complete mistake—that Apostle having been martyred long before the date of the Gospel—makes too great a claim upon our credulity. The conditions under which Christians of the second century had to live in the midst of a hostile world made such a state of ignorance or indifference impossible. Apostolic authority, direct intercourse with Christ, were factors of too great moment, especially in such times of stress, to remain subject to doubt. When the writer of the Gospel handed his work to the Church—a large and intelligent community—there were too many concerned in its reception, and too close an investigation of its contents took place, to make it possible that any confusion or uncertainty could arise as to his identity. In such a matter, the misapprehension of an individual would be speedily corrected by the knowledge of the rest of the community. The presence—or the absence—of one of the leading Apostles of our Lord could not become and remain a matter of uncertainty in the Church of Ephesus.

This, then, is our reply to the contention that the lateness of the direct ascription to the Apostle deprives the tradition of historical value. The silence of earlier decades is no proof that such ascription had not already been made. But even if the literature of the period had contained no reference to the Gospel's Apostolic authorship, this omission would not suffice to disprove the conviction, which was universal before the century closed, that the John of Ephesus, who wrote the Gospel, was the son of Zebedee, the Apostle and eyewitness of our Lord. From the first, when the Gospel left the hands of its author, the facts must have been too well known to need recalling. Every member of the Church knew to whom the Gospel was due. Moreover, it contained what, to people of the time, was a clear indication of its origin. Every one could see through the transparent veil which " the loved disciple " had drawn round him. External report was met by the disclosures of the book itself.

As a pure question of literary history, apart from other evidence, the general tradition which we find in being at the close of the second century is too widely and too deeply founded to be set aside on any ground except that of the fact—if fact it can be called—that the son of Zebedee was never at Ephesus in his old age. But this is a matter which requires separate investigation.

CHAPTER V

PAPIAS

IT is hardly too much to say that, next to the inspired writings of the New Testament, the most precious existing relic of Christian antiquity is the fragment of a work of Papias, Bishop of Hierapolis,[1] which we find embedded in the text of Eusebius.[2] The work[3] from which it was taken was written in the early years of the second century. Eusebius appears to have regarded its authority as depending rather upon its early date than upon the intelligence and force of the writer.[4] He quotes from the preface a passage in which Papias states the method which he adopted in getting to know what had actually been reported by disciples of the Lord as to His teaching.[5]

Before discussing the interpretation of this famous and much-debated passage, there are one or two considerations of a general character to be noted.

The phraseology is obscure and awkward to a degree almost unparalleled in any passage of importance. The result is that no scheme of interpretation that has hitherto

---

[1] *Flor.*, c. A.D. 100–140.

[2] *H.E.*, iii. 39.

[3] Λογίων Κυριακῶν ἐξεγήσεις. With this term for the Gospels, Λ. K. compare the expression of Dionysius of Corinth (c. 170), τῶν Κυριακῶν Γραφῶν : Euseb., *H.E.*, iv. 23.

[4] σφόδρα γάρ τοι σμικρὸς ὢν τὸν νοῦν : *Ib.*

[5] The words of Papias are as follows :—Οὐκ ὀκνήσω δέ σοι καὶ ὅσα ποτὲ παρὰ τῶν πρεσβυτέρων καλῶς ἔμαθον καὶ καλῶς ἐμνημόνευσα, συγκατατάξαι ταῖς ἑρμηνείαις, διαβεβαιούμενος ὑπὲρ αὐτῶν ἀλήθειαν. . . . Εἰ δέ που καὶ παρηκολουθηκώς τις τοῖς πρεσβυτέροις ἔλθοι, τοὺς τῶν πρεσβυτέρων ἀνέκρινον λόγους· τί Ἀνδρέας ἢ τί Πέτρος εἶπεν ἢ τί Φίλιππος ἢ τί Θωμᾶς ἢ Ἰάκωβος ἢ τί Ἰωάννης ἢ Ματθαῖος ἢ τις ἕτερος τῶν τοῦ Κυρίου μαθητῶν, ἅ τε Ἀριστίων καὶ ὁ πρεσβύτερος Ἰωάννης, οἱ τοῦ Κυρίου μαθηταί, λέγουσιν. Οὐ γὰρ τὰ ἐκ τῶν βιβλίων τοσοῦτόν με ὠφελεῖν ὑπελάμβανον ὅσον τὰ παρὰ ζώσης φωνῆς καὶ μενούσης.

been applied to it is free from difficulties. Neither of the two chief and opposing renderings is without a measure of inconsistency. Neither is to be taken offhand as the only possible account of the writer's meaning. But, in spite of its ambiguity, the passage, when taken at its face value, without reading into it preconceived opinions of our own, is capable of affording a meaning which is not only supported by evidence from other fields of research, but is actually required by the structure of the passage itself.

Another preliminary consideration is the approximate date of Papias himself and his literary activity, for he uses terms of age and time in his narrative.[1] He belonged to the second generation of Christians. His book was probably written in the second or third decades of the second century [2]; certainly not so late as Harnack suggests, 145–160. The description of him by Irenæus as ἀρχαῖος ἀνήρ,[3] would be quite inappropriate to one who had lived so near his own time.

All these indications of the early date of Papias explain his meaning in the passage before us.

Now, it is to be noted that Papias has two classes of people in view in this passage, the "elders" who were

---

[1] οἱ πρεσβύτεροι, οἱ τοῦ Κυρίου μαθηταί.

[2] E. A. Abbott, in *Enc. Bibl.*, ii., col. 1818, speaks of *c.* 115–130 A.D. as the date at which he was investigating and writing. "John was attaining, but had not yet attained, recognition as an Apostolic Gospel," *v.* B. J. Kidd, *History of the Church*, i., p. 64.

Sanday favours a date so early as A.D. 100, and places Papias at the point where the second Christian generation was passing into the third. Westcott's place for him is also in the second generation. The very title of his work, "Interpretations of the Oracles of the Lord," rather than "of the Gospel," points to an early stage of the process of canonisation. For, as Harnack has pointed out, the Gospels were known as one work in a fourfold presentation (and not otherwise) in the youth of Irenæus, *i.e.* before A.D. 150: *Beiträge zur Einleitung in d. N.T.*, vi., 1914, p. 48. Indeed, the attitude of Papias (gathered from his own words and from the title of his book) towards the Gospels points to a stage of canonisation earlier even than that of Justin Martyr, not to speak of Irenæus. He has more respect for what he has learned from the utterances of Apostles than for what he has read in books. The Gospels are being read critically. They have not yet attained their canonical rank. As authorities, they are not yet on a level with the law and the prophets.

All these considerations point to the probability that Papias stood very near in time and, perhaps, in personal relation to the Apostles.

[3] *Adv. Haer.*, v. 33, § 4.

actual disciples (Apostles) of Christ, to one or two of whom he had listened in early days, and whose teaching he " well remembered," and *their* disciples, whom he was accustomed to catechise and question if they came his way,[1] when he was deprived of access to the elders themselves, probably through his removal to Hierapolis.

But then he goes on to intimate that he is also dependent (such is the sequence of his thought) on informants for knowledge of what (apparently) other " disciples of the

---

[1] *It is the Apostles themselves* whom Papias calls " Elders," not their followers (παρηκολουθηκώς τις τοῖς πρεσβυτέροις), as Brooke, *Epistles of St. John*, p. 166; Charles, *Revelation of St. John*, i., p. xlii., and others affirm. This is clear from the language of Papias himself; for, τοὺς τῶν πρεσβυτέρων λόγους is expanded into τί 'Ανδρέας ἢ τί Πέτρος εἶπεν, κ.τ.λ., and through that epexegetical clause τῶν πρεσβυτέρων is identified with τῶν τοῦ Κυρίου μαθητῶν. Cf. Zahn, *op. cit.*, p. 221 f., " The indirect interrogatives (τί εἶπεν) and the relative sentence co-ordinated with them (ἅτε . . . λέγουσιν) expound τοὺς τῶν πρεσβυτέρων λόγους. V. Jerome, *De Viris Illustr.*, 18. So, too, Bousset, " By the presbyters Papias understands those of the first generation of Christians who could speak of the Lord out of their own intercourse with Him": *Die Offenbarung des Johannis*, p. 37. Zahn points out that " Eusebius himself is the classical witness for the correctness of this interpretation which he disputes: ' Papias acknowledges that he received the words of *the Apostles* from their followers (τοὺς τῶν πρεσβυτέρων λόγους παρὰ τῶν αὐτοῖς παρηκολουθηκότων)." . . . He substitutes τοὺς τῶν ἀποστόλων λόγους for the τοὺς τῶν πρεσβυτέρων λόγους of Papias," *op. cit.*, ii., p. 222; *v.* Lepin, *L'Origine du Quatr. Evang.*, p. 136; Gutjahr, *D. Glaubwürdigkeit des Iren. Zeugnisses*, p. 90. Cf. Otto Procksch, of Greifswald, *Petrus und Johannes*, 1920, p. 110, " In the same sense that Andrew, Peter, and other Apostles are πρεσβύτεροι for Papias, so also is John, so that one cannot so understand πρεσβύτερος as to obtain two figures of John."

A fruitful cause of the misunderstanding of the fragment of Papias has been the confusion of his language, when speaking of οἱ πρεσβύτεροι, with that of Irenæus. *They do not mean by that expression the same men.* Papias uses the term of Apostles (" disciples of the Lord ") only. Irenæus, who lived long after and to whom Papias himself would seem an " ancient man," uses it of disciples of Apostles. The mistake has been in reading the later language of Irenæus back into that of Papias; *v.* Iren., *Adv. Hæres.*, ii., 22. 5; v. 5. 1; v. 33. 3; v. 36. 1, 2. Thus Mommsen, speaking of communications of Apostles made to Papias through their disciples the presbyters (such is his interpretation of the passage), adds, " Harnack has rightly referred the sayings of the Apostle John, communicated under a similar designation (presbyters) by Irenæus, to these collections, and to the writings of Papias." He regards the presbyters of Papias and of Irenæus as the same people: *Zeitschr. für d. N.T. Wissen.*, 1902, p. 156. But *v.* Lightfoot, *Essays on Supernatural Religion*, p. 145. Dr. E. A. Abbott says, " In attempting to decide between these two views (whether ' Elders '=Apostles or their followers) it will probably be felt that . . . the expression ' I inquired into the words of the Elders, what said Andrew, etc." affords almost irresistible evidence for the former." But he then tries to explain it away: *Expositor*, 1895, p. 337 f.

_ord " are even now saying [1]—Ariston and the Elder
ohn—men still alive and teaching, though not where he
ould have immediate access to them, or he would not have
o depend on others for his information.[2]

At this point, we are faced with a problem which, like
o many matters of controversy, is due to carelessness or
bscurity of language—perhaps to the poverty of intelli-
ence with which Papias has been charged. What does he
nean to convey? That there were two Johns, whose
estimony about Christ was open to him—the John, son of
Zebedee, the Evangelist [3] (whom he names among the
Apostles Andrew, Peter, Matthew), and another John
whom he names together with Ariston? If that is his
neaning, he has done all that language can do to hide it.
By his use of terms, he shows that the John of the latter
clause is the John of the former. Each is called a disciple
of the Lord, the usual but not exclusive designation of an
Apostle. Each is called an Elder, the expression which
Papias uses for men who were indisputably Apostles of
Christ in the full sense of the word. But he distinctly bars
Ariston from inclusion in this inner circle.[4] A disciple he

---

[1] λέγουσιν, pres. tense. Mommsen, on the strength of the words οἱ
οὗ Κυρίου μαθηταί failing in the Syrian text, thinks them an interpolation
after ὁ πρεσβύτερος Ἰωάννης. But, as Gutjahr remarks, " those words are
genuine and to be taken as of direct disciples of Christ. Papias has heard
hem both ": op. cit., p. 122. V. Clemen, Die Entstehung des Johannes-
vangeliums, p. 408.

[2] " Men who, like Papias himself, had been in the past in intercourse
with disciples of Jesus still living, Ariston and John, or who were still
n an intercourse with them which was denied to himself ": Zahn, op.
it., ii., p. 222. " Papias must be considered as a personal disciple of
he Apostle John ": Procksch, Petrus und Johannes, p. 110.
The identification of τῶν πρεσβυτέρων with τῶν τοῦ Κυρίου μαθητῶν
(v. p. 60, n. 1) is not affected by the fact that the term μαθητής is presently
applied to Ariston, who was certainly not what τῶν . . . μαθητῶν in the
earlier clause denoted, " disciples " who were also Apostles (Andrew,
Peter, etc.). μαθηταί is a generic term not confined to Apostles, but
meaning, as in the New Testament, personal followers of Christ. In this
passage of Papias, the term πρεσβύτερος, which is withheld from Ariston,
s applied to men who are known to be Apostles. Is not the John who is
called both πρεσβύτερος and μαθητής (like the John of the former clause)
the Apostle?

[3] σαφῶς δηλῶν τὸν εὐαγγελιστήν, Euseb., ib., § 5.

[4] As Zahn points out, μαθητὴς τοῦ Κυρίου " clearly means not merely
a Christian but a personal disciple of Jesus ": Einleitung, ii., p. 210.
Yet, it is to be noted, he is not called πρεσβύτερος. " John, in noteworthy

was ; but not in the sense in which Papias applies the term
to the primitive college. Of this varied use of the word
disciple to express the relation of His followers to our Lord,
there are many instances.[1] In the present case, " the
Elder John " as a " disciple " is clearly parted from
Aristion by receiving an additional designation—one which
identifies his rank with that of the men who stand in the
former clause.

We therefore seem to have no alternative but to interpret the awkward language of Papias as implying that the
Elder and disciple John of the second clause is the John,
Elder and disciple, of the first. What to some reads as the
description of a different person, is but a clumsy way of
saying that the Apostle, who belonged to the earliest band
of Christ's followers, although, in the former clause he is
ranked with Andrew and Peter, as able to supply testimony
from the first days as they were, and with Matthew, as
himself an Evangelist, is (now regarded from a fresh point

distinction from Aristion, receives just that title which we should expect
for a head of the Church of Jerusalem (*e.g.* ' Presbyter ' Hillel, Gamaliel,
or ' the old presbyters,' a fixed ' Titulatur ' in Jerusalem)." " To the
presbyters belong, before all, the Twelve, the members of the original
community " : A. Schlatter, *D. Kirche Jerusalems*, 1908, p. 42 ; *v.* Zahn,
Einleitung, ii., pp. 210, 221.

[1] Μαθητής is the regular term for an Apostle in the Synoptic Gospels.
Where " Apostle " is used, it is always in the plural—of the Twelve, not
of a single Apostle—as in Mt. x. 2 ; Mk. vi. 30 ; Lk. vi. 13, and elsewhere. In Jo. xiii. 16, the context shows that the singular ἀπόστολος is
used simply of a messenger in relation to him who is sending him ; not
in the special sense of an " Apostle." In agreement with this Gospel
practice, a frequent designation for an Apostle in writers of the second
century from Papias to Irenæus is μαθητής, as in the passage under consideration. For Irenæus, *v. Adv. Hær.*, ii. 22. 5 ; cf. Zahn, *Einleitung*, ii.,
p. 488.

In view of this wide use of μαθητής for " Apostle," it is strange that
Dr. Charles speaks of it merely as " a title which does not exclude apostleship " : *Revelation of St. John*, i., p. xxxix. " The question why John
is chiefly designated by Irenæus merely as ' disciple of Christ ' is answered
by the fact that he employs a favourite designation of the author of the
Gospel " : Gutjahr, *op. cit.*, p. 4. Besides, as Gutjahr points out, Irenæus
twice speaks of John as an Apostle, *Adv. Hæres.*, i. 9. 2 and 3. He also
contrasts him with " other Apostles," ii. 22. 5, and numbers him among
Apostles, iii. 3, 4. Cf. Zahn, *Einleitung*, ii., p. 455 : " The former
designation (μαθητής) is the more natural one, since the composition of a
Gospel is not the special function of an Apostle, and since it is essential
for the significance and trustworthiness of a Gospel that the author has
been an eyewitness of the Gospel history, but not that he was ' Apostle.' "

of view) still living and giving forth his testimony.[1]   It is
the two points of view that cause the obscurity of the
whole passage.   Papias is thinking of St. John's fellowship
and joint experience with the men of the first age, and that
dominates the language of the former clause.   But as soon
as he has put his sentence into writing, he bethinks him of
the fact that that Apostle's testimony is still to be had.
His life bridges the period of transition from the first days
down to the time when Papias himself is writing ; and as
he writes, the contrast between the distant past and the
present, leads him to break up into two clauses (and thereby
confuse the issue) what belongs to the life of one man.

That this is the true interpretation of the passage is
confirmed by the fact that, down to the death of Origen, a
second John living and teaching in Asia Minor (as the John
of whom Papias writes was universally believed to have
done) was unknown throughout the Church.   Men like
Irenæus, who had the whole work of Papias in their hands,
knew of only one—the son of Zebedee.   It was not until
Eusebius, fastening on a remark of Dionysius of Alexandria,[2]

---

[1] I find that O. Bardenhewer takes a similar view, *Geschichte der
altkirklichen Literatur*,[2] i., 1913, p. 446 ; so, too, Gutjahr, *op. cit.*, p. 123.

Gutjahr draws attention to the fact that the silence of all Church
historians before Eusebius is against the existence (separate from the
Apostle John) of a " presbyter John." Dionysius of Alexandria could
only appeal to two μνήματα in Ephesus. *He had no other John to suggest
worthy of mention* in Apostolic or sub-Apostolic times. He knew nothing
of a separate " presbyter John," *op. cit.*, p. 112. Cf. Bousset, *D. offenbarung des Joh.*, p. 38, " Papias is no witness for the admission of two
Johns of Asia Minor. Irenæus, too, in any case, knows of but one John
of Asia Minor. And this John was an eye-witness of our Lord's life."

Ib., p. 39, " Those who disputed the genuineness of the Apocalypse,
the Alogi and Gaius, appear to have known nothing of a second John.
Otherwise they would certainly not have clutched at the doubtful expedient
of assigning the authorship of the book to Cerinthus." Cf. Lepin, *op.
cit.*, p. 154.

[2] In Euseb., *H.E.*, vii. 25, referred to *ib.*, iii. 39. 6. The expression
of Dionysius is μνήματα, " monuments " or " memorials," not " graves "
as it is often rendered. There might well have been two such memorials
in so large a city as Ephesus, dedicated to so great a light of Asia as
St. John. Cf. Jerome, *De Vir. Illustr.*, ix., who speaks of " duas
memorias " ; *v.* Zahn, *Acta Johannis*, clv. ; H. J. Holtzmann, *D. Evang.
d. Joh.*, p. 19, " The two Johns in Asia and their graves are a product of
the aversion to the Apocalypse which was shared by Dionysius and
Eusebius. It must not be attributed to the Apostle." *V.* Bousset,
D. Offenbarung Joh., p. 40.

Allo remarks that Gaius and the Alogi, who attributed both the

that two memorials bearing the name of John were in existence at Ephesus, began to distinguish in the preface of Papias another John than the Apostle, that the idea was suggested that Papias was speaking of two distinct men, introducing an historical situation unknown to the communities among which John of Ephesus had lived and worked.[1]

It is therefore safe to affirm that a person, unknown to the writers of the century that succeeded his reputed career, is not to be suddenly called into existence by the art of an ecclesiastical historian, who is vainly endeavouring to interpret the clumsy and obscure language of a writer whom nevertheless, from his early date and means of accurate knowledge, he feels bound to cite. *There is no historical evidence for a second John of Ephesus.*

Papias knew of only one ; but, in distinguishing between

Gospel and the Apocalypse to Cerinthus, serve as witnesses to the ancient tradition : " on n'avait pas encore découvert ' l'autre Jean.' Et les deux écrits demeuraient toujours associés dans la confiance ou la défaveur ": *S. Jean, l'Apocalypse,* p. clxxvi. But as to Gaius and the Gospel, *v.* Charles, *op. cit.,* i., p. c.

[1] Zahn does not hesitate to say that " the elder John owes his existence (*i.e.* as a distinct individual) to the critical notes and arts of Eusebius ": *Einleit. in d. N.T.,* ii. p. 490. Salmon, *Introduction to the N.T.,* pp. 279, 291, takes a similar view. " John," says Zahn, " belongs to both groups of Christ's disciples, whose words Papias inquired about from their disciples. Hence the repeated mention of him. The result is merely an awkwardness of style on the part of Papias ": *ib.,* p. 222. Bousset writes, " It is certain that Papias speaks not of two Johns in Asia Minor —the apostle and the presbyter—but of one John whom we are to look for as a near neighbour of Papias in space and time. Of a second John the second century and the first half of the third know nothing ": *Enc. Bibl.,* i., p. 198. Cf. *Id., D. Offenbarung des Joh.,* p. 39 ; p. 40, " There was only one John of Asia Minor. If we admit this, we can understand how the John of the Apocalypse could be referred to without any distinction, as the great John known to all." Cf. Lepin, *L'Origine du Quatr. Evangile,* p. 133, " . . . ce fait singulier que Papias est présenté par Eusèbe comme auditeur de Jean le presbytre, par Irénée comme auditeur de Jean l'apôtre, et que seul l'apôtre apparait bien connu dans les Eglises d'Asie-Mineure au second siècle, tandis que le presbytre semble to talement ignoré." V. Burney, *op. cit.,* p. 152.

It is to be noticed that the passage of Papias contains another linguistic indication that the John of the former clause is the John of the second. Instead of employing the disjunctive ἤ by which he separates the names in the former clause, he uses the copulative τε, as though linking the John of the second clause with the John of the former, ἅτε Ἀριστίων καὶ ὁ πρεσβύτερος Ἰωάννης, κ.τ.λ. I find that Bousset takes a somewhat similar view : " The τε connects the sayings of Aristion and the Elder directly with those of the remaining Apostles as sayings of the same class ": *D. Offenb. des Joh.,* p. 37, n. 1.

the information brought to him about the earlier teaching of the Evangelist and Apostle, and the reports of his present teaching, he unwittingly gives rise to the suspicion that he is speaking of two different men.

This view is strengthened when we compare the language of Eusebius in another context with that of Georgius Hamartolus in a fragment referred to below.[1] Georgius is evidently indebted to Papias for his information; for it is to Papias that he presently refers for the perplexing statement that the Apostle and Evangelist was put to death by Jews—perplexing, if it is Papias who is his authority for the statement that John, the sole survivor of the Twelve and the author of the Gospel, was released from Patmos and allowed to dwell at Ephesus. Besides, he actually goes on to say, " the well-informed Eusebius also says in his history of the Church, ' to Thomas was assigned Parthia, to John Asia, with whose people he dwelt and died at Ephesus.' " [2]

But there is another passage which goes to confirm our interpretation of the language of Papias. Polycrates, Bishop of Ephesus, writing to Victor, Bishop of Rome, about A.D. 190, speaks of " John who lay on the Lord's breast and was a priest wearing the πέταλον, a martyr and a teacher, as having fallen asleep in Ephesus." [3] Irenæus, the contemporary of Polycrates, writes in a similar strain. He is speaking of our four Gospels : " Afterwards, John, the disciple of the Lord, who also used to lie upon His breast, himself also gave forth the Gospel, while he was dwelling at Ephesus in Asia." [4]

Here, it is to be noticed that Irenæus is in full accord with the Bishop of Ephesus of his day as to the life at Ephesus of the Evangelist, whom he calls John, and whom he identifies with " the disciple whom Jesus loved." Like Papias, if he it was, who was the authority of Georgius on the question, he speaks of John as the Evangelist. Like Papias, he calls him ὁ μαθητὴς τοῦ Κυρίου. Like Papias, and like Polycrates, he places him in Ephesus.

[1] Chap. vi.   [2] Euseb., H.E., iii. 1.   [3] Ibid., iii. 31.
[4] Adv. Hær. iii. 1, 1.

From these comparisons, it is difficult to avoid the conclusion that only one John was known by the ancient Church to have lived at Ephesus, identified by writers of the second century, who had ample means of ascertaining the facts of the case, with " the beloved disciple," the Apostle and Evangelist. The various writers, writing as they did with different purposes, bring out different aspects in which their subject is viewed. *But it is clear that they are all speaking of the same man.* He is the John of the primitive community, too well known for it to be necessary to refer continually to his parentage [1] ; sometimes styled " disciple," sometimes " Apostle," and as the last survivor of the Twelve, or again as a witness and teacher ; as one very near to the heart of Christ, and as the writer of the Fourth Gospel.

But granted that, from the true interpretation of the words of Papias cited by Eusebius, and from comparison with the statements of other early writers, we may conclude that there was but one John of Ephesus who was known to antiquity, can we be sure that he was the John of general Christian tradition, the son of Zebedee—the writer of the Gospel ?

The answer is not so simple as might appear. It is true that the tradition of the universal Church, from about the middle of the second century down to recent times, has replied in the affirmative. But some,[2] who can find but

---

[1] Corssen makes the surprising statement that Papias could have known nothing of the origin of the Fourth Gospel, *Zeitsch. für d. N.T. Wissensch.*, 1907, p. 222 f. Cf. B. Weiss, *Evang. des Joh.*,[7] p. 8 ; Gutjahr, *op. cit.*, pp. 183, 185, *v.* above, p. 46.

" It is certain," says Harnack, " that Papias himself was acquainted with the Apocalypse and the Fourth Gospel—we knew this of the Apocalypse long ago and, as regards the Gospel, it must be clear to every one who looks upon the First Epistle of John and the Gospel as an unity " : *Chronologie*, i., p. 658.

[2] Thus Bousset, *Encycl. Bibl.*, i., col. 198. Although Bousset has seen that Papias and Irenæus knew of only one John of Ephesus, he somewhat perversely argues against his identity with the Apostle from the use by Irenæus of the term μαθητής in speaking of him. But this is the term which Papias applies to Apostles in the Eusebian fragment of his preface, *v.* above, p. 58. Besides, Irenæus himself, in the passage immediately following one in which he calls St. John τῷ τοῦ Κυρίου μαθητῇ (*Adv. Hær.*, ii. 22. 5), styles him " Apostle " : " Quidem autem

one John of Asia in the confused language of Papias, decline to call him the Evangelist. We are told that " Papias was a disciple of John the Presbyter "—the one " John of Asia." Yet the term " presbyter " we owe to Papias, and according to him the presbyters in the context are Apostles.

Now, where the judgment of scholars of equal learning and penetration differs so profoundly as in the problem before us, the more reasonable course seems to lie in the consideration of the earliest parallel evidence. Generally speaking, we may say that, as a whole, it points very decidedly to the son of Zebedee. Two men of the name of John are known to Scripture and to the history of the first two Christian centuries as men of light and leading—the Baptist and the son of Zebedee. And when we come to look for indirect evidence, we do not look in vain. According to Eusebius,[1] we have the assurance of Hegesippus, a contemporary of Papias, who flourished A.D. 155, that after the Apostles passed away, a conspiracy of godless error set in. But he had just been saying that until the death of Symeon, Bishop of Jerusalem in the reign of Trajan, the Church was pure. This leads us to infer that the Apostolic band survived, at least in the person of its last member, until the age of Trajan. Who should this last survivor be but the Evangelist St. John, who, according to the Coislinianus fragment of Georgius Hamartolus, based as we inferred upon Papias,[2] was sole survivor of the Twelve and living at Ephesus in the reign of Nerva ; and who, according to Irenæus, " abode in Asia until the times of Trajan " ? [3]

There is also the indirect evidence which is to be derived from the study of Eusebius. His own belief was that to John, son of Zebedee, Apostle and Evangelist, was assigned

---

eorum non solum Joannem, sed et alios Apostolos viderunt." In citing them as authorities for the life or words of Christ, an early writer would naturally think of their *discipleship* rather than of their *Apostleship*. The former title involved a more personal relationship to their Master than the latter, and it was this personal connection which gave weight to their evidence, *v.* above, p. 62, n. 1.

[1] *H.E.*, iii. 32.   [2] *V.* above, p. 65.   [3] *Adv. Hær.*, ii. 22. 5.

Asia as the sphere of his Apostolic ministry, and that he lived and died in Ephesus.[1]

Indirectly, Justin Martyr is a witness for bringing John the Apostle to Asia, if not to Ephesus. He was living in Ephesus A.D. 135, about the time of his conversion ; and he states that John the Apostle was the author of the Apocalypse. Now, whoever wrote the Apocalypse was a leading teacher and light of the Churches of Asia Minor.[2] We have therefore the assurance that—in the knowledge of Justin—John the Apostle had lived, presumably at Ephesus, but certainly in Asia Minor. Justin could not have been ignorant of the fact, if such a personage had actually lived there.[3] The point is this. Justin, in virtue of his literary judgment as to the authorship of the Apocalypse and of his possession of local knowledge, certifies to the presence of John, son of Zebedee, in Asia Minor. If John had not been there, he could not have been the author of the Apocalypse, a work which contains ample evidence that the writer had lived among the people to whom he wrote.[4] But that is exactly what Justin says was the case. In his Dialogue with Trypho, he speaks of " a certain man among us named John, one of the Apostles of Christ, in the revelation which was imparted to him." [5] We have, therefore, the assurance of a man who was living and teaching

---

[1] *H.E.*, iii. 1, εἴληχεν . . . Ἰωάννης τὴν Ἀσίαν, πρὸς οὓς καὶ διατρίψας ἐν Ἐφέσῳ τελευτᾷ. Cf. iii. 23, where he cites Irenæus and Clement of Alexandria to the same effect.

[2] As Bousset says, " The Epistles of the Apocalypse testify definitely enough to a John who occupied such a position in Asia that, if the mere name of John were mentioned, no doubt could arise as to who was intended." *D. Offenbarung des Johannis*,[5] p. 36. On the question of authorship of the Apocalypse and its relation to the Fourth Gospel, *v.* below, p. 97 f.

[3] Dr. Charles, who admits that " the author of Revelation was evidently the chief authority in the Ephesian Church," ignores this indirect evidence of the presence of the Apostle, which can be fairly drawn from Justin. *Revelation of St. John*, i., p. xlv. Bousset admits it, but proceeds to minimise its force, *D. Offenbarung des Joh.*, p. 42.

[4] Harnack goes so far as to say, " I will not dispute the fact that Justin held the Fourth Gospel to be apostolic and Johannine ; his testimony as to the assignment of the Apocalypse to John the Apostle appears to me to be equally valid for the Gospel ": *Chronologie*, i., p. 674 ; cf. p. 680.

[5] *Tryph.*, 81.

at Ephesus about A.D. 130–135, that John, son of Zebedee, had been there among them and that at a period hardly more than a generation ago.[1]

That the John of Asia who wrote the Epistles to the seven Churches of Ephesus and the neighbouring cities was not only fully acquainted with all the local circumstances, but was conscious of possessing an almost unlimited authority over the Christian population, is evident from the letters themselves. But he makes no claim to have founded the Churches. That was the work of other men ; of St. Paul, who had spent two whole years at Ephesus and with such success that so careful an historian as St. Luke does not hesitate to assert, somewhat rhetorically, that all the people of Asia heard the word of the Lord Jesus, both Jews and Gentiles. According to 1 Tim. i. 3, St. Paul, on departing to Macedonia,[2] left Timothy to continue and safeguard his work. The two men were " the apostles and religious chiefs of Asia." [3] So far, St. John had not yet come upon the scene, or St. Luke would not have failed to mention him. It is most probable that, at the beginning of the war with Rome, when the Church of Jerusalem withdrew from the city, John, if he had not already left Palestine, went northward and finally settled at Ephesus. When the Apocalypse was written, the Churches of Asia had been long enough in existence for their faith and zeal to have lost much of its first ardour.[4] The allusions to this fact in the Epistles point to a date for the composition of the Apocalypse towards the close of the century. It would be strange if the hardships of his

---

[1] Cf. Zahn, *Einleitung*, ii., p. 454. Lepin is justified in saying, " La tradition du séjour Éphésien de Saint Jean, reconnue si générale et si ferme au dernier quart du second siècle, paraît établie déja en Asie-Mineure, autour de 155, et à Éphèse même, dès autour de l'an 130." *Op. cit.*, p. 153.

[2] Acts xx. 1, 3.

[3] Allo, *Jean l'Apoc.*, p. ccx.

[4] Cf. Acts xx. 29, a passage quoted by H. Holtzmann, *Einleitung in d. N.T.*, p. 470, and by Schmiedel, *Offenbarung, Briefe des Johannis*, p. 6, as an argument against the presence of St. John at Ephesus. But v. Zahn, *Einleitung*, ii., p. 583. St. Paul's prophecy was soon to be fulfilled in the rise of Docetism and the Cerinthian heresy.

exile at Patmos did not exert some influence upon St. John's language as he upbraids the Churches for their spiritual decline. He writes as one who knows that his authority will be fully recognised. It suffices to name himself John. There was but one outstanding figure in the Churches of Asia so named, and the tradition of Ephesus, as voiced by Justin Martyr barely forty years later, styles him the Apostle, son of Zebedee.

Not only does the seer speak with authority, he writes with complete knowledge of the circumstances of each Church that he addresses. This knowledge had been gained during the years of his ministry among them. When that ministry was interrupted by the decree of exile, and when it was renewed by his release from Patmos, the stir that must have been aroused in Ephesus and the neighbouring cities made it impossible for any one who, like Justin Martyr, came upon the scene a generation later, to be uncertain as to his identity. Taken in conjunction with the other strands of evidence that bear upon the point, it becomes very difficult to imagine that in the express language of Justin Martyr we have nothing but the record of an early mistake, by which the Apostle St. John was substituted for a John of whom we have no knowledge until his hypothetical existence meets us as a venture of Eusebius.

The memory of a whole community of Churches, which had been exposed to cruel persecution and whose sufferings had been interpreted and illuminated by the presence and ministry of an eyewitness of Christ, could not have so played them false ; could not, we may add, have so confused the minds of all who came in after years to inquire upon the spot the occurrences of that momentous time. The requirements of certain critical theories as to the history of the Johannine writings cannot be allowed to set at nought a method of interpretation which in any other historical inquiry would be admitted as sound and reasonable.

The importance of Justin's evidence in the Johannine controversy is manifest. It entirely negatives the contention of recent critics [1] that the assignment of the Fourth Gospel to St. John was the work of the last quarter of the second century, and that it was chiefly due to the influence of Irenæus. On the contrary, we can go much farther back for the data on which the question of authorship rests. The presence in Ephesus of John, son of Zebedee, the reputed author, was known to Justin about A.D. 135 ; while the Gospel itself was known to him as one of those which had been written by Apostles and followers of Apostles.[2] We have not to wait for Irenæus in order to obtain evidence for its Johannine authorship.

To sum up the result to which this discussion seems to lead. As there was but one John of Ephesus known to antiquity, so, notwithstanding the obscurity of his language, one John only is named in the preface of Papias. The evidence for the sojourn of John, son of Zebedee, in his old age at Ephesus is trustworthy ; and the Gospel which was assigned to him by the consentient voice of antiquity saw the light in that city or its neighbourhood. It may therefore be fairly concluded that the John whom Papias twice mentions in the fragment was none other than the Apostle of our Lord, " the loved disciple " and the author of the Gospel which has always borne his name. The argument is necessarily complicated by the nature of the evidence at disposal, and by the divergence of view on the part of those who have dealt with it. As a literary judgment, lacking, as is usual in such cases, the material which would be needed for complete demonstration, it will probably continue, as in the past, to meet with opposition. Nothing but the discovery of fresh documentary evidence will suffice to set the question wholly at rest. But the burden of proof lies with the opponents of the traditional belief in the authorship of the Gospel. Its rejection raises greater difficulties than it solves. That this appears throughout our discussion of the fragment of Papias may, we think, be admitted.[3]

---

[1] Such as Bacon. [2] *V.* above, p. 48.

[3] Like Dr. Charles, *The Revelation of St. John*, i. p. xliii., Canon Streeter assigns the Gospel and the Epistles to the shadowy figure of John the Elder : *The Four Gospels*, pp. 432, 460.

CHAPTER VI

THE ALLEGED MARTYRDOM OF ST. JOHN

THE criticism which rejects the Johannine authorship of the Fourth Gospel and the Epistles which bear the Apostle's name is mainly subjective, and depends upon the weighing of probabilities—such as the supposed impossibility that they could have been written by a fisherman of Galilee. But within the last half century we have been confronted with what has appeared to some to be a solid ground for this view.

In addition to the extracts from the lost work of Papias, which have been preserved by Eusebius, we now possess a statement attributed to Papias by two mediæval Chroniclers who appear to have had access to his work, and whose fragmentary remains have recently been discovered.

The first fragment was published in 1862. It belonged to the Chronicle of Georgius Hamartolus, a Byzantine monk of the ninth century,[1] and to a manuscript which differs from the numerous manuscripts of the same writer, which have been preserved, in respect of an important reading.[2] But not only does this reading stand alone, unsupported by the rest of the MSS.; it is followed by a

---

[1] *V.* Lightfoot and Harmer, *The Apostolic Fathers*, p. 519; A. Preuschen, *Antilegomena*, p. 94.

[2] Codex Coislinianus, Paris, 305, (Ἰωάννης) μαρτυρίου κατηξίωται. All the other known MSS. of Georgius read ἐν εἰρήνῃ ἀνεπαύσατο. "The Coisl. MS. of Georgius is the oldest MS. that bears his name, but it does not give the original form of his *Chronicle*, but an edition of the same. . . . Apart from the fact that, if several editions of a writing omit a passage and only one gives it, it is antecedently more probable that this one has inserted it rather than that all the rest have left it out, the narrative of the other MSS. has the advantage of consistency, while the narrative of Coislinianus is inconsistent in itself." C. de Boor, *Texte u. Untersuchungen*, v. 2, p. 177. *V.* below, p. 74.

misquotation from Origen, who is cited to the same effect, viz. that John suffered martyrdom.[1]

But Georgius makes another statement. Notwithstanding the assurance of the great majority of the MSS. that John ἐν εἰρήνῃ ἀνεπαύσατο, he says that John (according to Papias) ὑπὸ Ἰουδαίων ἀνῃρέθη, while the excerpt ends by quoting Eusebius to the effect that John received Asia as his sphere of ministry, spending his life there and dying at Ephesus.[2]

This farrago of contradictory statements very naturally failed to produce much impression.

When, a few years later, a fragment of a MS. of the eighth or ninth century was found, containing a similar reference to Papias, a more serious view began to be taken as to what Papias really said in his perished work. Many have come to think that it contained a statement that John, son of Zebedee, ended his life as a martyr.[3]

But these two fragments which purport to report what Papias wrote need close investigation. The Codex Coislinianus version of the passage in Georgius Hamartolus makes three definite statements as to the fate of the Apostle and Evangelist St. John, ἐκ τῶν δώδεκα μαθητῶν· that he was judged worthy of martyrdom; that he was killed by Jews; that, according to Origen, he suffered martyrdom. Georgius, in confirmation of his statements, cites our Lord's forecast of suffering, " Ye shall drink of My cup and be baptized with the baptism with which I am baptized," and appeals to the truthfulness of God which, in consequence of this assurance of Christ, would require a martyr's death

---

[1] Orig. *in Matt.*, iii. (ed. Bened.), p. 719. Georgius states that " the learned Origen, in his interpretation of the Gospel of Matthew, affirms that John was martyred (ὅτι μεμαρτύρηκεν Ἰωάννης)." But the words of Origen are as follows: after saying that Herod killed James, the brother of John, with the sword, ὁ δὲ Ῥωμαίων βασιλεὺς, ὡς ἡ παράδοσις διδάσκει, κατεδίκασε τὸν Ἰωάννην μαρτυροῦντα διὰ τὸν τῆς ἀληθείας λόγον εἰς Πάτμον τὸν νῆσον. According to Origen, the " martyrdom " of John was not that of death, but of living testimony in the island where, as Origen goes on to say, it appears that he saw the Apocalypse.

[2] Euseb., *H.E.*, iii. 1.

[3] " The martyrdom of John and James rests on the sure and impregnable witness of Papias and the Syrian Martyrology." Schwartz, *Z.N.T.W.*, 1910, p. 89 ; Charles, *The Revelation of St. John*, i., p. xlvi. f.

from His disciple.[1] But it is only reasonable to suppose
that the death at the hands of Jews was more likely to be
carried out at Jerusalem than elsewhere, and Georgius
speaks of it in conjunction with the martyrdom of James,
the other son of Zebedee, which certainly did take place at
Jerusalem. Yet, what do we find elsewhere in this same
fragment ? Not only do all the MSS. except Codex Coislinianus read (for μαρτυρίου κατηξίωται) ἐν εἰρήνῃ ἀνεπαύσατο,
but Georgius actually tells us that John was recalled by
the Emperor Nerva from the island (Patmos) and allowed
to live at Ephesus, and that, being the only survivor of the
Twelve, he wrote his Gospel. Finally, he quotes Eusebius
as saying that John received Asia as his sphere of work,
making his abode and dying there.[2]

Yet we are asked to believe that out of this contradictory set of circumstances comes the fact that Georgius
found in the second book of the work of Papias the statement that John, Apostle and Evangelist, as Georgius
believed him to be, was put to death by Jews (presumably)
of Jerusalem.

But we turn to the other fragment which is thought to
make the evidence of Georgius doubly sure.[3] It belonged to
an Epitome which some think was based on a perished work
of the fifth century by Philip of Sidé in Pamphylia.[4] Like

---

[1] Mk. x. 39.   [2] H.E., iii. 1.
[3] V. L. Jackson, The Problem of the Fourth Gospel, p. 143.
[4] An epitome of entirely uncertain origin, but supposed to be derived
from a late (fifth century) work of an obscure chroniclist, which has
entirely perished, is a poor authority to be set against the evidence of a
writer like Eusebius, who not only had before him the work of Papias
from which the fragmentist quotes, but had access to sources of information which, through lapse of time, were no longer accessible to him. It
is only necessary to mention this conflict of opinion to make it clear that
the opponents of the traditional position do not hesitate to form literary
judgments which, in any ordinary controversy, would at once be rejected.
     It is to be noted that we do not possess two independent authorities
for the statement by Papias that John suffered martyrdom at the hands
of the Jews, but one. Both Georgius and Philip of Sidé (if the fragment
is derived from him) use the same terms in describing Papias' work,
Κυριακῶν λογίων and ἐν τῷ δευτέρῳ λόγῳ, showing that one of the copyists
was indebted to the other for his knowledge of what Papias had said ;
v. Lepin, op. cit., p. 115. Dr. Kidd appears to hold a similar view ;
Georgius is clearly borrowing from Philip of Sidé. Hist. of the Church,
vol. i., p. 63. As he says, " these assertions (as to a statement of Papias)
when examined melt away," ib. E. Meyer speaks of Philip of Sidé being

Georgius, the fragmentist quotes from the second book of
Papias, to the effect that " John the Divine and James his
brother were killed by Jews." [1]   He had already said that
Papias had been a disciple of John the Divine and a companion of Polycarp.[2]   Here, again, we meet with a conjunction of circumstances that do not seem to agree.   If
Papias of Hierapolis was a companion of Polycarp and with
him a disciple of St. John, this double relationship must
have been brought about in Asia, in the same country in
which Georgius, basing his information on Papias, regarded
St. John as living and dying.   So far, then, is the tran-
scriber of Philip of Sidé from confirming the statement of
Papias as handed down by Georgius that he only brings a
similar array of contradictory material, which makes it
still more difficult to think that Papias ever made the
historic statement that is imputed to him.   For, in
describing Papias as friend of Polycarp and disciple of John
the Divine, the fragmentist is no doubt saying what Philip
of Sidé found in the work of Papias ; and the Asiatic residence which seems required to form this connection puts an
early martyrdom at Jerusalem entirely out of the question.[3]

But Georgius asserts that the truth of God is pledged
to the fulfilment by martyrdom of Christ's saying to the
sons of Zebedee, " Ye shall drink of My cup." [4]   He has

repeated by Georgius : *Ursprung u. Anfänge des Christenthums*, vol. iii.,
1923, p. 634.   The historian Socrates, who was nearly contemporary with
Philip of Sidé, describes his work as " without chronological sequence."
H.E., vii. 27.

[1] Ἰωάννης ὁ Θεολόγος καὶ Ἰάκωβος ὁ ἀδελφὸς αὐτοῦ ὑπὸ Ἰουδαίων ἀνῃρέθησαν.
The term ὁ Θεολόγος, here said to have been applied by Papias to St.
John, is a much later title of the Apostle.

[2] " À la manière de G. Hamartolus . . . il établit un rapport étroit
entre Jean l'Apôtre et l'évêque d'Hiérapolis." Lepin, *op. cit.*, p. 110.

[3] Yet Schwartz asserts that " it must be regarded as historic fact
that James and John were put to death in 43 or 44 at the order of
Agrippa."   " Über den Tod der Söhne Zebed," in *Abhandl*[n]. *der Königl*[n].
Gesellschaft der Wissen., 1904, p. 5.   If Schwartz takes his stand on
Papias to prove the early martyrdom of St. John, we can confront him
with evidence clearly based on the same writer to the effect that John
lived and worked and died at Ephesus at a much later date than that to
which Schwartz assigns his martyrdom at Jerusalem, *v.* below, p. 80.
Unlike Schwartz, Charles suggests a later date, " before A.D. 70," for the
supposed martyrdom, *op. cit.*, i., p. xlix.

[4] Mk. x. 35 f.   Schwartz considers that " if this claim is taken seriously,
then not only is the conclusion unavoidable that they have both died as

persuaded himself, like some modern scholars, that red martyrdom is the only explanation of Christ's words. But these same modern scholars regard the prophecy as a *vaticinium ex eventu*,[1] and are puzzled to account for its origin, since the opinion that John, son of Zebedee, outlived all the other Apostles and died peaceably at Ephesus was a tradition soon to become generally diffused throughout the Church.[2]

And this brings us to what is perhaps the greatest difficulty that besets upholders of the " red " martyrdom of St. John. If he did indeed suffer as a martyr at Jerusalem, the fact must have become everywhere known in the Church. If, as Schwartz thinks, he was put to death at the same time as his brother, we may be certain that St. Luke would have said so. But he is silent [3] ; and in a few years the tradition of his long life and peaceful end has become a fixed possession of the Church in every quarter.[4]

Now, we cannot believe it possible that a martyr whose triumphant end, they say, Christ Himself had foretold, would have been robbed of his crown by men like Irenæus, who claimed to have heard the truth about him from

---

martyrs, but the seat on both sides will only be explained if they have left the earth at the same time and together," *ib.*, p. 4. " The oracle in Mark seems an unanswerable ally (Bundesgenosse) for the statement of Papias (that both brothers were martyred)," *ib.* Heitmüller considers it " unnecessary to take Mk. x. 35 f. as meaning that John was killed at the same time as James, but in any case before A.D. 70." *Zeitschr. für die N.T. Wissensch.*, 1914, p. 189.

[1] Not so Charles, who " accepts the words as an actual prophecy of Christ, and one that was fulfilled in actual fact " : *The Revelation of St. John*, i., p. xlv.

[2] Cf. Clemen, *D. Entstehung des Joh. Evang.*, p. 432.

[3] Cf. Lepin, who points out that St. Luke, by speaking of James as the brother of John, excludes John from martyrdom : Acts xii. 2, *op. cit.*, p. 111. E. Schwartz has the boldness to assert that a late correction has removed the name of St. John from this passage. *Zeitschrift für d. N.T. Wissen.*, 1910, p. 99.

[4] F. Spitta, referring to the view of E. Schwartz (suggested by Wellhausen, *Evang. des Marcus*, p. 90) that John was martyred, says that the difficulty of Wellhausen (*Evang. des Joh.*, p. 100) is the best refutation of his own and Schwartz's view of the end of John ; " How could the saying that John would not die arise if he and James were the first martyrs among the Twelve ? What has happened that such an event could be completely forgotten ? " *Zeitschrift für d. N.T. Wissenschaft* for 1910, p. 58 ; cf. Lepin, *L'Origine*, p. 121.

actual witnesses.[1] And if he had died a martyr, is it not highly improbable that, *in order to secure the fulfilment of Christ's prophecy*, the legends of the poisoned cup and the boiling oil would have been framed ?[2] It is clear that those who felt that actual martyrdom could alone satisfy the Saviour's forecast were perturbed *by the fact that it did not take place*, and they cast about for some makeshift to ensure its fulfilment ; as though his reputed sufferings in the stone-quarries of Patmos and his long life at Ephesus failed to constitute a μαρτυρία for Christ that should adequately answer to His prophecy.[3]

[1] " Apart from the improbability that the Jews in Ephesus would have martyred this old man, it would then be inconceivable that all native tradition in Asia (Leucius, Irenæus, Polycrates, etc.) can only speak of a peaceful ending of this John. The Church of Asia would have robbed its greatest saint of his martyr's crown on no conceivable ground. . . . Here we have an *argumentum e silentio omnium* against which one strives in vain ": Zahn, *Forschungen zur Geschichte des N.T. Kanons*, vi., p. 149 f. J. P. Badham asks, " Would an Apostle who perished so early have been chosen as a peg to hang these documents (the Johannine writings) upon ? Could the author of the Fourth Gospel have come forward as impersonator or literary executor of an Apostle so long dead ? ": *Amer. Journal of Theology*, 1904, p. 542. Cf. C. Clemen, *Amer. Journal of Theology*, 1905, p. 656, " The conclusion cannot be drawn from Mk. x. 39, that, at the time of the writing of Mark, John had died a martyr "; A. Harnack, *Theol. Liter. Zeitung*, 1909, p. 10, " This pretended fact (alluding to Wellhausen's theory of John's martyrdom) rests, apart from Mk. x. 35 f., on two questionable arguments, while it has half a dozen of the strongest arguments against it "; C. Clemen, *D. Entstehung des Joh. Evangeliums*, p. 438, " People later on might well have made John a martyr, but they certainly would not have robbed him of his martyr's crown."

[2] " Romam . . . ubi Apostolus Johannes posteaquam in oleum igneum demersus nihil passus est, in insulam relegatur ": Tert., *De Præscrip. Hæret.*, 36, p. 215 A ; *v.* Salmon, *Introd. to N.T.*, p. 374.

[3] Clemen remarks, " In Papias we have the oldest passage in which Mk. x. 39, might have had an influence ": *Amer. Journ. of Theol.*, 1905, p. 651.
Georgius in his *Chronicon* cites the text immediately after his excerpt from Papias, but this does not prove that Papias himself connected the prophecy with the death of John. It is to be noted that the future tenses of Mk. x. 39, πίεσθε and βαπτισθήσεσθε are changed into " can drink " . . . and " can be baptised " in the Syr^sin. Syr^c. versions. J. Weiss considers that the object of this change was " to set aside an inconvenient and, in the view of the translator, an unfulfilled prophecy of Jesus " and that " this text is also a sign that the Syrian translator had already adopted the tradition that John did not die a martyr's death ": *Zeitschr. f. d. N.T. Wissen.*, 1910, p. 167.
Chrysostom, who refers to the prophecy as implying martyrdom *In Matt. Homil.*, lxv., speaks elsewhere of the long life of St. John, and remarks καὶ γὰρ Ἰάκωβος ἀπετμήθη μαχαίρᾳ καὶ Ἰωάννης πολλάκις ἀπέθανε, his life was a martyrdom: *De Petit. Filior. Zebedei* vol. i., p. 637, Gaume.

We seem, therefore, to be driven to the conclusion that, whatever Papias handed down in his perished work respecting John, son of Zebedee, he made no mention of martyrdom. Had he spoken of it, his narrative would have left its impress upon the literature of the second century, for even if, as Eusebius supposes, he was not an actual disciple of St. John, as a contemporary of Polycarp, he was in a position to acquire direct knowledge of the Apostle's fate. Knowledge that was accessible to Papias, and was employed by him, would be reflected in the thought and tradition of the subsequent decades. So far as these have come down to us, they contain nothing to show that the martyrdom of St. John was ever a recognised fact in the early Church. Had it been known, we cannot account for the general belief, of which we so soon get proof, that the son of Zebedee passed to his rest in a calm old age at Ephesus.[1] That belief could never have arisen in spite of the fact that Christ's prophecy was fulfilled by his actual martyrdom by Jews, *if fact there were*.

To judge by the argument of Georgius, the saying recorded by St. Mark appears to have deeply impressed the chroniclers, and to have found an echo here and there in Martyrologies.[2] But in every case, these isolated refer-

[1] Harnack concludes that what Papias said must remain undecided (dahingestellt), *Chronologie*, i., p. 666. K. Clemen, who has recently investigated the matter, thinks that "Papias has related nothing about a martyrdom of John in Jerusalem": *D. Entstehung des Johannes Evang.*, pp. 442, 438.

[2] The question of the martyrologies has been investigated by Dr. J. H. Bernard in *The Irish Church Quarterly*, 1908, p. 58 f. Harnack, reviewing his article, says of the oldest Calendar, the Syrian of A.D. 411, "What a strange Calendar which would have us believe that Stephen was martyred on Dec. 26, James and John on Dec. 27, Peter and Paul on Dec. 28, while for a long while other days of martyrdom had been current in the Church for James, Paul, and Peter!" Referring to Gregory of Nyssa (*Migne*, xlvi., cols. 789, 725), he adds, "The matter is clear. The ancient customary Feast of Peter, James, John, and Paul following Stephen was originally no Martyr Feast; but the Choir of leading and Christ-witnessing Apostles must be celebrated after the Proto-martyr. . . . To reckon John among the martyrs was no difficulty, as the legend of the oil-bath was widely spread in the Church. Bernard has explained the paradoxical insertion in the Syrian Calendar." *Theol. Literaturzeitung*, 1909, p. 11. Cf. C. Clemen, *Amer. Journ. of Theol.*, 1905, p. 644, "This evidence (Syrian Martyrology) is surely too late to deserve credence." Dr. Stanton, after reviewing the evidence, sums up against the reliability of what was a

ences to martyrdom seem to be due to no other cause than
a wish to account for the accuracy of the forecast attributed
by St. Mark and St. Matthew to our Lord, *as they interpreted
it*. They are not to be put, for a moment, in comparison
with the universal belief of the second century, that St. John
lived and died in a peaceful manner at Ephesus.[1] To do
so would be to reverse the processes of historical criticism
and to set a higher value on the late and the vague in
testimony, than on the early and the definite.[2]

We may therefore conclude that whatever difficulties
stand in the way of our assigning the authorship of the
Fourth Gospel to the son of Zebedee, a statement of Papias
is not one of them ; for the accounts of what he is reported
to have said upon the subject contain a context which puts
his early death by martyrdom at Jerusalem entirely out of
the question. The very chroniclers, who refer us to Papias
as having made such a pronouncement, show that they

Syrian translation from a Greek original. *The Gospels as Historical Documents*, iii., pp. 113 f., 121, 122. Cf. Kidd, *History of the Church*, i., p. 64,
" As Stephen is loosely called an Apostle, so St. John is spoken of as a
martyr in the wider sense of a witness, not necessarily unto
death " ; *v*. F. Torm, *Indledning til det Ny Testamente*, p. 122. He
compares the change of the day commemorating the translation of the
bodies of St. Peter and St. Paul from the catacomb of San Sebastiano
to the day of commemoration of their martyrdom, June 29, with what
has occurred in the case of St. John. *V*. L. Pullan, *The Gospels*, p. 304 f.

[1] " From the middle of the second century this knowledge (of his
martyrdom) vanishes. Yet, it is to be noticed that here and there later
on, traces of the old report occur." Heitmüller, *Zeitschr. für d. N.T.
Wissen.*, 1914, p. 190. If it were *knowledge*, not an attempt to explain
Mk. x. 35 f., it is incredible that it would have so vanished from the mind
of the Church. " The view of the early death of John is incorrect ; it
had no existence during the Apostolic age. What has afterwards been
said and written cannot prevail (aufkommen) against the clear witness of
the New Testament." Spitta, *op. cit.*, p. 58.

Gutjahr, after discussion of the question, sums up as follows : " However the matter stands, so much is evident, that the statement of Georgius
and of the excerpt (of Philip of Sidé) said to proceed from Papias, can in
no case be appealed to against the Asiatic residence of John." *Op. cit.*,
p. 111.

I cannot agree with Dr. Charles when he says : " A myth can arise
in a very few years. Hence it is not strange that such writers as Hegesippus (*ob. c.* 180), and subsequent writers as Irenæus, Tertullian, Origen,
have lost all knowledge of the early martyrdom of John the son of
Zebedee " : *The Revelation of St. John*, i., p. xxxvii. n. 2,

[2] " It is quite an unhistorical caprice to prefer the ostensible witness
of Papias to the chorus of witnesses on the other side " : Harnack in
Theolog. Literaturzeitung, 1909, p. 10.

were in possession of information which made it wholly improbable that Papias said anything of the kind.

For the context of the report, *clearly based on the same author*,[1] declares that, so far from dying a martyr in the forties, St. John lived on after release from Patmos and wrote his Gospel and lived at Ephesus (so Georgius), Papias having been his disciple with Polycarp (so Philip of Sidé), presumably in the neighbourhood of Hierapolis.

A further proof that Papias could not have made the alleged statement is furnished by the attitude of Eusebius. He had the work of Papias before him ; and whatever his judgment of that writer's mental capacity, he could hardly avoid attaching weight to his evidence on so plain a question as the residence of St. John at the close of the first century in his own neighbourhood at Ephesus. Had Papias—so far from testifying to the presence of St. John at Ephesus— actually stated that the Apostle was martyred, before the first century was half over, at Jerusalem, the fact must have influenced the historian and been reflected in his own work. Indeed, we may say that he could not have made the statements [2] as to the long career of St. John which he does make.[3]

---

[1] I find that Lepin takes this view of their dependence on Papias : *L'Origine du 4ᵉᵐᵉ Evang.*, p. 112.

Not only does a comparison of what these two writers definitely assign to Papias with what they have evidently derived from him, reveal striking contradictions, as we have already seen ; but, it is to be observed that by the earlier writer (Philip of Sidé ?), the authority himself, who is quoted for the martyrdom of St. John, seems to be regarded with a certain amount of suspicion. He charges Papias with erroneous statements about the millenium ; and adds, " he also relates other marvellous things." We can detect the same opinion of his authority's poorness of intelligence, which Eusebius had so bluntly confessed ; and yet, out of the mass of inconsistencies contained in these fragments, we are asked to reverse the judgment of the Church of the second century, and indeed of all responsible writers down to the end of the eighteenth century. We are to credit the son of Zebedee with a martyrdom at Jerusalem, of which no authentic trace is to be found—apart from shadowy hints assigned long afterwards to Papias ; the very writer, whose statements, in the context of what is quoted from him, negative the assertion that he ever spoke of the martyrdom of St. John. This method of procedure, if applied to any question of ordinary literary interest, would be universally repudiated.

[2] Euseb., *H.E.*, iii. 1 ; iii. 20, 23.

[3] In reply to L. Jackson's view that Georgius and the de Boor frag- mentist confirm one another, Stanton suggests that both are derived from Philip of Sidé, who is known to have been unreliable : *The Gospels*, pt. iii., p. 112 n. ; cf. Lepin, *op. cit.*, p. 115.

And what is true of Eusebius is true of Irenæus. As a pupil of Polycarp, the friend and companion of Papias, he was in a position to know all that the Bishop of Hierapolis could tell of St. John. It is evident that nothing reached him from that source as to an early martyrdom of the Apostle, whom he designates by the Gospel title μαθητής, and by the phrase " the disciple whom Jesus loved " : for, as he says, " John the disciple of the Lord gave forth his Gospel, while dwelling at Ephesus." [1]

There is another consideration. The deep respect and homage paid in the Early Church to red martyrdom makes it impossible to believe that if St. John had died a martyr's death, the fact could have been either suppressed or could have so faded from the memory of the Church that responsible writers like Irenæus and historians like Eusebius, with the literature of the second century before him, show no trace of it, and, indeed, report a condition of things which puts the martyrdom out of the question.

And, finally, there is what has been called " the clear witness of the New Testament." [2] It knows nothing of an early martyrdom of the younger son of Zebedee. Not only is the silence of St. Luke inexplicable on such a theory, but his description of James as " brother of John," in his account of the martyrdom of the former, draws attention to the historic fact that the younger brother was untouched by the persecutor.[3] Five years later he was present at the Council at Jerusalem, a pillar of the Church, joining with St. Peter and St. James, the Lord's brother, in assigning to St. Paul the Gentile world as his sphere of missionary work.[4] Henceforth his name disappears from New Testament history.

---

[1] *Adv. Hær.*, iii. 1. 1. An avowal is made by Schmiedel, " It must be conceded that the unacquaintance shown by all Church fathers down to the time of Philip of Sidé (or his excerptors) with the statement of Papias now in question is very remarkable " : *Enc. Bibl.*, ii., col. 2510. Yet he can speak on the same page of " the result obtained from Papias " !

[2] F. Spitta, *Zeitschr. f. d. N.T. Wissen.*, 1910, p. 39.

[3] Acts xii. 2. Dr. Stanton has rightly characterised the unworthy suggestion of Wellhausen that St. Luke " here suppressed some names, perhaps only a single one," *op. cit.*, iii., p. 119.

[4] Gal. ii. 9.

But if our identification of St. John with the loved disciple is justified, he is referred to in a later writing in terms that seem to preclude the possibility of an early death by martyrdom. A purely conditional saying of Christ was interpreted to mean that " that disciple should not die " ; and a rumour to this effect went abroad among the brethren, a rumour which must have quickly died a natural death, if an early martyrdom of the disciple had actually taken place.[1]

We can therefore appeal to the narrative and to the implications of Scripture itself, against the theory that the career of St. John was brought to a close by his martyrdom at the hands of the Jews.

[1] *V.* Spitta, *op. cit.*, p. 58.

CHAPTER VII

MEDIATING THEORIES OF AUTHORSHIP

A MEDIATING position is assumed by some who, while rejecting the extreme view that the hand of an eyewitness is not to be discerned in the Gospel, are yet unable to admit that it is the actual work of one of the original Apostles. They acknowledge much that points to an eyewitness: many of them believe that John passed the last years of his life at Ephesus. But they find it difficult to imagine that the work as it stands proceeded, in his extreme old age, from an Apostle who in early manhood was a fisherman of Galilee. So, in spite of tradition, they transfer the authorship from the Apostle to a disciple of an Apostle; from the original witness to one who had so far become imbued with his mind and teaching that he was enabled to write a Gospel, startling indeed in the novelty of its presentment, yet so true to the historical situation, that the Church of the place of its birth and, later on, the Church Universal, gave it recognition as a genuine work of St. John, and, after a time, *admitted it as such* into the Canon of Scripture. And this transference from master to pupil is effected airily and confidently, without heed to the moral difficulties [1] which to many minds are involved in their theory; quite apart from the extreme improbability that, at about the close of the first century, or the first two decades of the second, an unknown

[1] " Moral " because in a way, unexampled in Scripture, the writer appeals for belief to the fact that with his own eyes he saw what he records: a claim which, by no stretch of imagination, can be fairly satisfied by the supposition of a faithful adherent who, writing under the eye of the Apostle, and on the strength of his intercourse with him, appropriated his experiences and posed as the personal disciple and eyewitness of the Christ Whom he had never seen.

disciple lived at Ephesus, who was capable of such an achievement as the creation of the Fourth Gospel.

One form of this theory supposes a Johannine *Grund-schrift*—material supplied by the Apostle—which has been edited by one of his adherents at Ephesus.[1] The idea is attractive in so far as it admits a strong Johannine element [2] —a foundation of Apostolic testimony. But when it is applied to the actual contents of the Gospel and, at the same time, confronted with the circumstances of its reception by the Church, it fails to meet the situation.

For, the marked distinction presented by the Gospel between its record of Christ's sayings and that of the Synoptics remains, and the theory at once creates fresh difficulty. An editor would hardly have presumed to run counter to the Synoptic tradition. The contrast is not removed, and the existing difficulty is increased. We know that the Gospel had at first to contend for its acceptance by the Church, so new and revolutionary did it appear.[3] What would have been its chance of reception if it was known to have come from one who was neither a disciple of Christ nor an eyewitness, but one who, on a certain basis of information supplied by such an authority, gave forth a version of the Gospel which deviated so widely

[1] *V.* Wendt, *D. Lehre Jesu*, p. 41 ; F. Spitta, *D. Joh. Evangelium*, *passim ;* Wellhausen, *Erweiterungen u. Änderungen im vierten Evang.*, 1907, p. 38, and elsewhere ; Id., *D. Evang. Johannis*, 1908, *passim.* Wellhausen has been effectively answered by Zahn in the *Neue Kirchliche Zeitschrift* for 1911, *v.* pp. 38 n., 41, 44. As to Spitta's attempt to prove extensive re-editing of the Gospel, *v.* Zahn, *ib.*, p. 114 n.

[2] This is the case with Spitta, *op. cit.* Harnack, who draws a distinction between the Apostle and the "Elder John," has made the notable admission : "That in some way John, son of Zebedee, stands behind the Fourth Gospel cannot be denied (in Abrede gestellt werden), and accordingly our Gospel would have to be considered as a Gospel of John the Elder, according to John the son of Zebedee " : *Chronologie*, i., p. 677. *V.* J. Chapman, *John the Presbyter*, pp. 74, 75, "The Apostle has been expelled with a pitch-fork, *tamen usque recurret.*" *Ib.*, p. 77, "Harnack's view is bound to come round to the traditional one, if it is logically carried out." *V.* C. R. Gregory who, after saying, "The aged son of Zebedee is possible as author, and I still hold to him," adds, "If this Gospel is repeated, 'interpolated,' and completed, so may all have been done by John himself. No one else is needed for it." *Wellhausen und Johannes*, 1910, pp. 65, 66.

[3] *V.* p. 114.

from that which the Church had already received ? Yet, as a matter of fact, it *was* accepted very soon in the region of its origin, and a little later in every part of the Church.

Besides, the theory of this disciple's authorship has to account for a condition of things in the Church of Ephesus which is hard to credit. So fresh and revolutionary a presentation of events would largely depend for its acceptance upon the question of its authorship. It would require the highest possible credentials. The attribution to Cerinthus, absurd as it appears, is an echo of questionings that arose in the first half of the second century. But Justin Martyr, whose assignment of the Apocalypse to St. John is a proof that he knew of that Apostle's residence in Asia Minor, shows acquaintance with the Fourth Gospel ; and, as he never cites any Apocryphal Gospel, it is fair to conclude that he placed the Fourth Gospel on a par with the other ἀπομνημονεύματα τῶν ἀποστόλων which he quotes. If this was his opinion of its value and authority, it is only likely that the view, which we know to be prevalent about thirty years afterwards as to its authorship, was shared by himself.

Now, where debate and questioning appear to have quickly manifested themselves in the traditional home of the Gospel, we may be certain that the claim of an author who so strongly asserted both his truthfulness and his competency to bear witness, would be minutely examined. Opponents would not be put off by the assurance (which seems so satisfying to some modern critics) that a work which contained the teaching of an Apostle *as reported by a pupil* could be described as the actual production of his Master. Where so much room for contention was presented by the contrast with the Synoptic record, the question of Apostolic authority would be weighed with the utmost care. If a disciple of the Apostle, and not the Apostle himself, wrote the Gospel, and if it met in some quarters with doubt and hesitation, how are we to account for the fact that in a few years, its ascription to St. John was an universal tenet of the Church ? The doubts and misgivings that arose would be made the most of by the opponents of practices or of opinions which appealed to the Gospel, or to its reputed author, for sanction. Moreover, in a community hedged round by an unsympathetic world, and so driven in upon itself, as was the Church of Ephesus at the turn of the century, it could not have remained a secret whether the Gospel were Apostolic or a summary and report of Apostolic teaching.

It is thought by some that the assignment to a pupil or adherent eases the situation : that we get rid of the difficulty that is felt in attributing such a masterpiece of religious thought to one who long years ago had been a fisherman of Galilee, and who shows in style and phraseology that in old age, and we know not how long before, he has become familiar with modes of thought far removed from what he had known in Palestine. To this end a lay figure has been conceived and clothed with attributes which to the critic appear to be out of the reach of the Apostle. When we ask for evidence of the existence of this highly gifted person, or try to trace his presence in the Gospel as it has come down to us, there is nothing to be found ; while the problem, if such it is thought to be, is only rendered more difficult of solution. For, if it is wonderful that one who for over two years had, at the most impressionable period of life, the advantage of daily and hourly intercourse with Christ, and had developed qualities, as we may suppose, of love and insight that won His affection, should have been able in his maturity to recall and write the Gospel ; how far more incredible it appears that some unknown scribe, who had never had these advantages, should have written it !

So far, then, from contributing to the solution of the problem of authorship, this theory increases the difficulty. Not merely does it deprive the traditional author of his claim on the gratitude of Christendom for what is felt by many to be the Gospel which gives the truest picture of our Lord in His life on earth. It requires us to imagine the existence, at a period singularly destitute of men of the highest gifts, of one who, without the advantage of belonging to the inner circle of the Apostleship, or even perhaps to the band of the primitive disciples, surpassed all the rest in knowledge and grasp of his great subject, and yet remained unknown in the Church in which he lived, and unrecorded in any writing that has come down to us.

Here, as in so many of the other aspects of the Johannine question, the traditional position is beset with less difficulties than the theories which oppose it.

The Gospel, on the strength both of its contents and of the external evidence of its history, comes to us as the work of an actual follower of our Lord. Nothing short of direct proof of the contrary can negative this position.[1] And this is not forthcoming.

But efforts are made to compensate for the lack of proof by the substitution of probabilities so handled that they claim the force of actual fact.

Here we get into the sphere of psychology, a science which, it must be remembered, deals with data that do not readily admit of accurate tests. Its conclusions, therefore, are not such as would be *necessarily* accepted by reasonable people. It is not an exact science. All it can do is to furnish us with suggestions, based on a more or less wide induction, as to how a person is likely to act in such and such circumstances. But the extraordinary variety, not to say opposition, of opinions thus formed shows how carefully the historical critic should proceed when he has recourse to its help. There is always the possibility that a factor hitherto unknown, or unnoticed, has entered into the complex of the conditions which we are trying to probe. Allowance has to be made for distance in time, for the effect of climate and social circumstances, for the many things which may have crossed and modified

---

[1] " I have never faltered in the conviction that the testimony of an eyewitness lies behind this Gospel." C. H. Turner, *The Study of the N.T.*, 1920, p. 34. I cannot agree with Dr. Stanton in thinking that " the framer of the statement at xxi. 24 . . . was betrayed into exaggeration when he attributed the composition of the Gospel to an immediate disciple of Christ." *The Gospels*, pt. iii., p. 146.

G

the action of the forces which have determined the result,
so far as it has become known to us.

It is true that the bearing of psychology on the question
of the authorship of the Gospel has, as yet, received very
inadequate treatment. But on few questions have opinions
which are closely connected with psychology been so
dogmatically expressed. Negative conclusions have been
drawn in spite of positive evidence to the contrary which,
whether definitely relying on psychological considerations
or not, are clearly in very close touch with them. Quite
apart from tradition and from the conclusions which would
naturally be drawn from the Gospel itself, the question
has been summarily foreclosed by appeal to what is after
all a mere surmise : " whoever wrote the Gospel, it could
not have been the son of Zebedee." The personal status
and circumstances of the Apostle, and the conditions under
which it was written, are thought to exclude such a
possibility.

Now, it may be conceded that we are justified in the
resort to psychology for the solution of a question of
disputed authorship up to a certain point. But there is a
limit to its use. At the most, it can furnish us with a
certain degree of probability. But this is not enough for
some. They claim far more than probability for conclusions which are based on nothing more sure than psychological grounds. They will tell you that they are quite
sure that a writer, who said this or refrained from saying
that, could not have been the man to whom tradition,
taken in connection with the writing in question, has
consistently pointed.

Now, this mode of reasoning treats psychology as a
science, whose laws not only hold good in all circumstances,
but—what is more to the point—are in every case ascer-
tainable. Take one or two instances of the way in which
it is applied.

The self-designation of the writer as " the disciple
whom Jesus loved " is thought to render it incredible that
he should have been an Apostle and one of the inner group

admitted to a special degree of intimacy and trust. Now, we find that when this incredibility is tested, it appears to rest upon nothing more solid than a subjective estimate of probabilities, an estimate likely to be reversed by the next person who deals with the question.[1]

No one can say how far the devout, emotional elements of such a character as the writer would overbear the ordinary dictates of self-repression and reserve, when he came to record his recollections of a wonderful experience. Nor can we flatter ourselves that we possess the data required for entering fully into the conditions then prevailing. Certain factors at once suggest themselves : the gratitude of a favoured disciple ; the feeling of awe produced by the gradually awakened consciousness that, in those far off days, he had in a sense more true than was the case with Enoch, " walked with God " ; and then, as he struggles to overcome, for the purpose of his written testimony, the natural reluctance to speak of self in such a connection, there is the hint that would quite suffice to prove to his converts and adherents that he spoke of what he had seen and heard—the mention of " the disciple whom Jesus loved " ; a security for the good faith and certainty of one who repeatedly shows that, above all things, he claims the right to be implicitly believed, because he *knows*. It is clear that if, as we gather from the Gospel itself, this disciple was the author, there must at once have arisen in his mind, as he sat down to write, a conflict of varied emotions.

The tendency to dogmatise must therefore be held in check. We have certain fixed data, together with some high probabilities, from which to draw our conclusions ; while in the background there is a steady and consistent current of tradition of which account must be taken. Seeing that from the point of view of psychology, com-

---

[1] Cf. Clemen, *D. Entstehung des Joh. Evang.*, p. 469, " With many others, I do not see why John should not in all humility so style himself (" loved disciple "), if he has really been adjudged worthy of this position by Jesus." Kreyenbühl compares St. Paul's " I live, yet not I, but Christ liveth in me."

pletely opposite verdicts are passed upon the writer's self-designation, it is evident that it cannot be made a ground for rejecting the Johannine authorship.

Another objection, based to some extent, like the first, upon psychological considerations, asserts that the Gospel as a piece of literature is beyond the capacity of a fisherman of Galilee.[1] Here, again, we have a matter of opinion, incapable, like the former objection, of anything like proof.

Now, in the first place, it rests upon a mistaken view of the conditions of life in the Palestine of the first century. There was nothing in the family life or social position of Zebedee to make it unlikely that his sons, who on growing up joined him in his business, could have had a fair education. If St. Paul, by trade a tent-maker, could from his far-off Tarsus, repair to Jerusalem to be educated by the great Rabbi Gamaliel, what was there to prevent a son of a capitalist and employer of labour by the sea of Galilee from receiving some amount of training so near at hand as Jerusalem from the religious teachers of his people? The fact that he was in a position to go out into the wilderness to the Baptist and for some time to put himself at school with him, shows that his circumstances were easy.[2] And, if he is to be identified with the " other disciple " who was known to the High Priest, it is fair to argue that the disposition of meditative receptiveness combined with fervour of spirit that attracted the affection of our Lord, must have proved attractive to his earlier teachers, contributed to his opportunities for gaining knowledge, and led to that measure of intimacy with members of the hierarchy to which the Gospel refers.

When, to the probability of these early occasions for training in the religious heritage of his own people, are added the later advantages of contact with the thought and language of a great city like Ephesus, our case is greatly

[1] *V.* H. Holtzmann, *D. Evang. des Joh.*, p. 20; E. F. Scott, *The Fourth Gospel*, p. 37; P. Gardner, *The Ephesian Gospel*, pp. 54, 71.
[2] *V.* Headlam, *The Life and Teaching of Jesus the Christ*, p. 176, " All these first disciples were men of substance and position."

strengthened. Bearing in mind the fact that, between the two intellectual stages of his career—the Judaism of Palestine and the Greek environment of Ephesus—had come first the discipleship of the Baptist, and then the discipleship and close intimacy of Christ, it is hard to see why it is more likely that another than he wrote the Gospel that bears his name.

But, at any rate, to maintain that the social condition of John, son of Zebedee, as it is described in the Synoptic narrative, would prevent him from receiving a good education, or make it unlikely that he could become acquainted with members of the high-priestly family, is to carry modern notions of what is customary into an age in which they were unknown. The pursuit of a trade was then no bar to intercourse with leading members of the community, nor did it hinder a man from access to the thought and learning of the day. Like Christ, St. John both surprised and offended people by the possession of gifts of mind and character to which they thought he had no rightful claim.[1] He was not a professed Scribe. He had not studied the Law as it was expected of one who took upon himself to come forward prominently as a teacher. Yet they could not help wondering at the influence which he and St. Peter exercised, and it was observed " that they had been with Jesus "[2] " Unlearned and ignorant men " they might have been, if judged according to the rigorous standard of the schools. Yet again and again, history records that it is not always the man who has been trained in accordance with the most approved methods of his time who leaves the deepest mark upon its life and thought. At any rate, our knowledge of the conditions and habits of life of the Palestine of the first century, and of a great city of the Empire like Ephesus, does not enable us dogmatically to rule out the possibility that a work like the Fourth Gospel could have been written by the son of Zebedee. On the contrary, when taken in connection with the external

[1] With Acts iv. 13, cf. Jo. vii. 15.
[2] Acts iv. 13.

evidence and with the argument which can be legitimately drawn from St. John's close intimacy with Christ, so far from being impossible, his authorship attains a high degree of probability. What is quite certain is that a negative conclusion is not to be reached merely on psychological grounds.

To sum up—the appeal to psychology and to social considerations appears to fail when it seeks to prove that, if the designation that he was the loved disciple was applied to himself by the writer of the Gospel, he could not have been the Apostle whom the Synoptic narrative describes as a close intimate of Christ ; and when it categorically denies that the Gospel could have been written by one who long before had been a fisherman of Galilee. It is not that the use of such a mode of arguing is illegitimate, but that, from its very nature, its appeal has too diverse an effect upon different minds to produce anything like general acceptance ; quite apart from the fact that, in the case in point, rebutting evidence is forthcoming.

The suggestion which has been worked out by Hugo Delff, of Husum, that the author of the Gospel was a John not of Galilee, but of Jerusalem, has proved attractive to some.[1] According to this theory, he was a member of the family of the High Priest, who on the outbreak of the war with Rome retired to Asia Minor, and was there known as John the Elder.

If it appears to simplify certain difficulties in the traditional position, it raises objections which to some minds would be fatal to its adoption. It introduces as " the loved disciple " a person of whom we have no further knowledge and, be it noted, on such an occasion as the Last Supper, when, so far as we know, only Apostles were present. This disciple, unknown, or at least unmentioned, by the Synoptic writers, is regarded by Delff as the author, apart from certain interpolations, of what he calls " the specially historic and original source of our knowledge of

[1] Professors Sanday and, more recently, C. H. Turner and C. F Burney.

Christianity." [1]   The indications which the Gospel itself presents [2] that the disciple was intimate with the High Priest and that, if we press (unduly) the meaning of τα ἴδια,[3] he was living in Jerusalem, have seemed to favour the theory. It is also urged that the various measures taken by the Sanhedrin—their secret sitting and the issue of orders for the arrest of Christ—could only be known by one who was intimately connected with members of the Council; while the learning and literary capacity shown in the Gospel are not what one would expect from a Galilean fisherman.[4]

Against these considerations, the objections are many and weighty, while the points which appear favourable admit of a different construction.

To take the first argument. Such intimacy with the High Priest as the Gospel implies does not require relationship to explain it.[5] Acquaintance with the High Priest or with his *entourage* would suffice. It was an occasion when, in the excitement caused by the arrest, access to the αὐλή would not be difficult for one who was known to the authorities. Then, as to the home to which " the loved disciple " took the bereaved Mother. There is nothing to imply that he possessed a house in Jerusalem at the time : what is meant is that where he made his home, that was the home of Mary. There is no indication in the text that the disciple was already a householder in Jerusalem. As to

[1] *D. vierte Evang.*, 1890, p. 1.

[2] Jo. xviii. 15, taking ἄλλος μαθητής as identical with the loved disciple, and therefore the author of the Gospel, as Delff thinks, *D. vierte Evang.*, p. 87, n. 1 ; so Loisy, " Il est très probable que ce disciple est le bien aimé." *Le Quatrième Evang.*, p. 128 ; Zahn, " In Gethsemane, as at the Last Supper, only Apostles were present." *Einleitung in d. N.T.*, ii., p. 480. That this was the case appears from Jo. xv. 27. *V.* above, p. 27.

[3] Jo. xix. 27 ; but cf. xvi. 32. *V.* Zahn, *ad loc.*, p. 593, n. 39, and *Einleitung in d. N.T.*, ii., p. 490, n. 17.

[4] Delff, *Neue Beiträge zur Kritik des vierten Evang.*, p. 3.

[5] On the meaning of γνωστός, Jo. xviii. 15, *v.* Zahn, *op. cit.*, ii., p. 491. Stanton thinks he was one of the upper classes named in Jo. xii. 42, a disciple, but not openly. According to Scholten, *D. Evang. des Johannes*, p. 379, a Galilean fisherman (if ἄλλος μαθητής is identified with John, son of Zebedee) could not have been an acquaintance of the High Priest. B. Weiss replies, " it is hard to see why not." *Evang. des Joh.*[7], p. 27 ; *v.* above, p. 90.

the other indication of the priestly connection of the author on which Delff relies—his knowledge of the proceedings of the Sanhedrin—it does not appear to have occurred to him that the writer could have had every information on these points from Nicodemus or Joseph of Arimathæa, at any time subsequent to the Resurrection.[1]   Then is it so evident, as Delff supposes, that a fisherman of Galilee could not have acquired the knowledge of Jewish thought and custom which was possessed by the writer of the Gospel ?   Apart from opportunities for instruction that he may have had in early youth, the friendship of members of the Council would have enabled him to acquire the information which is disclosed by the Gospel.   At any rate, we have no means of determining the extent of the advantage which this unknown " John of Jerusalem," if there was such a person, would have had over the fisherman of Galilee in general culture and in knowledge of the times and customs of which he wrote.

If the points favourable to Delff's theory are by no means conclusive, what is to be said of the objections ?

The writer's references to the ruling powers in Jerusalem are expressed in terms which are far more natural on the lips of a Galilean Jew than of one closely connected with the Jewish hierarchy.   They all show his complete detachment from his people as a whole ; but they also point to an attitude towards the authorities which seems to indicate that he regarded them with entire lack of sympathy.

All this is more easily explained on the theory that the writer was a Galilean, whose acquaintance with the conditions of life and thought in Jerusalem was acquired in the first instance in early youth, by occasional visits in the company of his Master, and, afterwards, by actual residence in the capital.[2]

But, there is one fatal objection to the theory.   If this John of Jerusalem is to be identified as " the loved

---

[1] This same remark applies to Delff's contention that Jo. xii. 42, 43, could only be affirmed by one who belonged to the aristocracy of the nation : *D. vierte Evang.*, p. 2.

[2] Cf. Jo. iii. 1 ; x. 24 ; xviii. 14 ; xix. 38.

disciple " and the writer of the Gospel, the situation which arises is inexplicable. In the Synoptic narrative the Apostle John, son of Zebedee, is presented as one of the three leading members of the Apostolic company. With his brother and St. Peter, he is in the closest touch with our Lord at times when other disciples are excluded.[1] In the Acts, he appears again in association with St. Peter, and later on as a pillar of the Mother Church of Jerusalem. But when we turn to the Fourth Gospel, apart from the passing allusion in the appendix, his name is never mentioned.

How is this to be accounted for on the supposition that the author of the Gospel was a John of Jerusalem, " the loved disciple," *but not the son of Zebedee?* We could only imagine that he harboured a personal antipathy or jealousy against the Apostle, unless he took the view that he was of too little importance to be worthy of mention. The former attitude would have excluded him from the special favour of Christ : in the latter case he would appear to be unacquainted with the actual state of affairs, and would have lost credit as an eyewitness of the events which he records.

But apart from these considerations, the theory requires a condition of things in the Churches of Asia which is quite improbable—a state of ignorance as to the identity of its great teacher which shows an attitude of complete indifference and apathy in a matter of general concern to all who cared for the truth of the Gospel. It means that the Bishops and Presbyters of those Churches, in which this great light of Asia taught and among whom he ended his days, did not know whether he was one of the original Apostles and witnesses of Christ, or an otherwise unknown person, who by some strange chance became invested with the Apostle's gifts and authority, to which he had no claim.

To the present writer a better solution of the problem —the silence as to John, son of Zebedee, in the Gospel which bears his name, contrasted with the place assigned to him in the Synoptic Gospels and in the Acts—is to regard him as " the loved disciple " and the author of the book.

[1] At the raising of Jairus' daughter; at the Transfiguration; in Gethsemane.

CHAPTER VIII

THE RELATION OF THE FOURTH GOSPEL TO THE OTHER JOHANNINE BOOKS

THAT which Christian tradition has agreed to put together, criticism has largely tended to put asunder. While the Gospel and First Epistle are generally, and the Second and Third Epistles by many,[1] assigned to the same writer, there are few who can be found to identify him with the author of the Apocalypse. It is admitted that the differences of material, point of view, style and language, make it difficult to bring all the works within the closing years of the life of one and the same man ; while the evidence as a whole requires us to assign each of them to the last decade of the first century, or the first decade of the second. If, as some think, the date of the Apocalypse could be placed in the reign of Vespasian, an interval of time sufficient to account for certain differences of treatment and language would be gained. But the evidence, both external and internal, is against it. The tradition that the Seer experienced his visions towards the end of the reign of Domitian [2] is met by the state of things which is disclosed by the book itself.

Many years must have rolled over the Churches of the province of Asia before they presented the picture of decline which meets us in the letters of the Seer. The Apostle and Evangelist of Asia was St. Paul. There is no trace of any other figure of commanding authority until a

---

[1] *E.g.* Jülicher, *Einleitung* [5], p. 241 ; Charles, *The Revelation of St. John,* i., pp. xxxiv., xli. ; Grill, *Untersuchungen,* ii., p. 398.
[2] Iren., *Adv. Hær.,* v. 30. 3, quoted by Eusebius, *H.E.,* iii. 18. 3. For recent discussions of the date, *v.* Charles, *op. cit.,* i., pp. xci. f. ; Allo, *S. Jean, l'Apocalypse,* pp. ccii. f.

good many years have passed. It is unlikely that the
' John '' of the Apocalypse arrived in Ephesus before
A.D. 67–70. The book itself is its own witness that it
belongs to a period not far removed from the close of the
first century.

The question of its relation to the other strain of
Johannine writing—Gospel and First Epistle—can therefore get no material help from the supposition that a considerable space of time separated their composition. If
they are the work of one man, he wrote them within ten
or fifteen years. A comparison of the points of agreement
and of dissonance can be drawn up [1]: but even then
opinion will be divided. A certain measure of probability
may be arrived at, and with this we must be content until
fresh evidence of a positive character comes to light.

To clear the ground, certain data may be specified.
(1) There was only one John of Ephesus who was a commanding personality in the Churches of Asia. In our
investigation, we have no other of that name with whom
to operate.[2] (2) All the Johannine writings in their
present form belong to the turn of the century, A.D. 90–
110. (3) Ephesus or its immediate neighbourhood is the
scene of their promulgation. It was there that they all
came into the hands of their first readers.[3]

With these conclusions in mind, Gospel and Apocalypse
may be laid side by side and the resulting impression be noted.

The difference in material and in language is evident at
a glance, and is admitted by every one. As to material,
this is perfectly natural, for the object of the two writings
is very different ; and, if the Greek differs profoundly, one
may expect a change of style where the subject-matter in
each case is so unlike.

But the difference of subject does not explain the fact
that, of two writings attributed to the same author and
published within the space of a few years, one is full of
solecisms while the other is written in fairly good Greek.

---

[1] *V.* Charles, *op. cit.*, i., pp. xxix. f.
[2] *V.* p. 62.   [3] *V.* p. 68.

The reason is more likely to be found in the respective circumstances of their composition. The Seer of the Apocalypse was in a state of ecstasy when the visions were vouchsafed to him. He " was in the Spirit." If he recorded them with his own hand, the mental strain must have been intense and, like an impressionist in art, he would be more careful to convey the truth of his vision of reality than to attend to niceties of language ; and on reading what he had written he may have felt indisposed to revise and amend. Or, again, if he dictated the substance of his book and, in the fervour of his soul, fell at times into strange and uncouth forms of speech, his amanuensis would hardly dare to check or correct the inspired current of thought with which he was dealing.

Wholly different circumstances attended the composition of the Gospel. There was entire absence of the storm and stress of spirit out of which, as from a volcano in eruption, flowed the wonderful imagery of the Apocalypse. With his own hand, or with the help of another, the writer is setting down the oft-recalled experiences of his youth. He is telling once again the story of the Saviour's life on earth. He goes back to actual facts, as he remembers them. The tones of the Saviour's voice still ring in his ears. The words in their Aramaic form are indelibly impressed on his mind. Leisurely they assume the Greek dress in which he had so often clothed them. There is no need to hurry. Calmly and coherently the story is unrolled.

As we think of these differences—not only of subject-matter and aim—but of the circumstances in which each writing saw the light, does it seem possible that, widely as they diverge, they came from one and the same author ; that, at any rate, the incongruity is not so great as to put such a conclusion entirely out of the question ? The difficulty is no doubt formidable, and to some it will continue to be decisive.

But, greatly as they differ, the two works disclose a very intimate connection. There is a similarity of thought, which is not to be explained by their nearness to one another in time or place of origin. If the metal has come out, at white heat, from the same crucible, it has been poured into moulds of varied shape. Differ as they do, Apocalypse, Gospel and Epistle abound in parallels of conception and of language, that indicate the existence of a close fellowship or circle, if not the action of a single individual. Indeed, there are resemblances so close that a circle or school of thought will hardly account for them ; more especially if we consider the intensely personal note which is struck in each class of writing—the note of an individual experience, in each case emphasised in a degree peculiar to these writings.[1]

The force of the resemblance is heightened by the extreme dissimilarity of purpose and aim of the two writings. Underlying the necessary differences, there is constantly to be found an element of likeness which points to a single source. If the action of the dissimilarities is centrifugal, that of the resemblances is centripetal ; and when the circumstances are taken into account, the latter influence is to some minds the more powerful one.

The resemblances of language and phrase appear upon the surface, and are therefore, at first sight, the more striking. It is surely significant that each kind of writing —Apocalypse, Gospel, and First Epistle—begins with a preface setting forth its substance or purpose ; a sign that in each case there is a high sense of the value of method. Still more remarkable is the harmony of thought which pervades the three prefaces. In each is found the great conception of the Λόγος. In the Apocalypse, the term refers to the Gospel, the revelation of God as a body of truth [2] ; in the First Epistle, τοῦ λόγου τῆς ζωῆς as interpreted by its context, καὶ ἡ ζωὴ ἐφανερώθη, can hardly be denied a personal meaning, pointing to the Risen Christ as He revealed Himself to His disciples.[3] The Gospel prologue forms the highest stage of the ascending scale, καὶ Θεὸς ἦν ὁ Λόγος. From the Word as the expression and declaration

---

[1] Rev. i. 1, 4, 9 ; Jo. xix. 35 ; xxi. 24.
[2] ὃς ἐμαρτύρησε τὸν λόγον τοῦ Θεοῦ, i. 2.   [3] Cf. Lk. xxiv. 39.

of God's will for man in the Apocalypse, we pass through the Word as the manifestation of Divine Life to the Word as a Person Who is with God and is Himself Divine. The connecting link of thought is strong and cannot be broken. Christ is in Himself the Gospel which He came in flesh to exemplify and proclaim. The closeness of the train of thought seems to betray the action of a single mind.[1]

The prefaces of the three writings present another similarity. They each insist that the Word, however revealed, whether as Gospel, or as Person, was intended to be, and was, apprehended by man. The John of the Apocalypse " bare record of . . . all things that he saw." The writer of the Epistle declares that " the Life was manifested and we have seen it." The Fourth Evangelist claims the same experience : " The Word was made flesh . . . and we beheld His glory." [2] Here again is a likeness of idea too close and striking to be mistaken. It points to the probability that when we compare the threefold experience, we have to do with the product, not of a circle or school of thinkers, but of one mind. As a literary judgment, apart from historical or doctrinal considerations, this view is almost self-evident.

From this it follows that the truth conveyed in each preface is based on personal experience. In his anxiety to drive the point home, the writer of the Epistle allows himself to use the language of tautology, and his care for certainty comes out just as strongly in the Gospel.[3]

There is another similarity in the thought of the three prefaces which should be noticed. Each is concerned with an actual unveiling, a revelation, of Jesus Christ. In the Apocalypse, Christ is both the object and the medium of what is made known.[4] In the Epistle He seems to stand before us, as before His disciples, in the glory of His Resurrection life.[5] In the Gospel, He appears as one of us.

---

[1] V. below, p. 106.
[2] Rev. i. 2, cf. v. 19 ; I Jo. i. 1, 2 ; Jo. i. 14.
[3] Jo. xix. 35.   [4] Rev. i. 1.
[5] I Jo. i. 1, αἱ χεῖρες ἡμῶν ἐψηλάφησαν. Cf. Jo. xx. 27 ; Lk. xxiv. 39. The writer " emphasises the visibility and *tangibility* of the incarnation of the Logos as in Jo. i. 13–16." Bacon, *The Fourth Gospel*, p. 456 ;

In each case the disclosure was perceived by the bodily sight of the recipient of it. The Seer of the Apocalypse narrates "what he saw." [1] It was a direct revelation. In the Gospel and Epistle, the disclosure is made to the writer in conjunction with his fellow-disciples. But in addition to the appeal to bodily sight made by the Incarnate Word, there was given a revelation of His Person which could only be appropriated by faith and contemplation. The Evangelist expresses it as the glory of the Only-begotten of the Father; the writer of the Epistle connects the revelation with the manifestation of Eternal life. In the Apocalypse, Christ is seen in glory. In each case, it is clear that bodily sight brought with it something that could only be apprehended by the eye of faith. Only, this admission that spiritual perception was involved must not be allowed to weaken our grasp of the all-important fact that Christ was seen as Man among men by those who bore witness to Him.[2]

From this comparison of the prefaces to the three works it is difficult to avoid the conclusion that a single mind—if not responsible for the writings as a whole—was, at any rate, the force that lay behind the school or group in which they had their origin.

A striking coincidence of thought and phrase is found on comparing the witness of the Baptist in the Gospel—"Behold the Lamb of God which taketh away the sin of the world"—with the reiterated designation of the exalted Christ as

---

Lepin, *op. cit.*, p. 278; Sanday, *The Fourth Gospel*, p. 76. But E. Meyer seems to regard the person of the Christ, Who revealed Himself to the author of the Apocalypse, as not that of the historic Jesus. He says "it is quite impossible that this book was written by any one who had come even casually (vorübergehend) in contact with Jesus Himself; for the man Jesus is here not only put in the background by the supernatural Christ, but entirely disappears behind Him": *Ursprung u. Anfänge des Christenthums*, vol. iii., 1923, p. 636. But, as many instances of correspondence show, the exalted Christ of the Apocalypse is the Christ of the Gospel and the First Epistle, *v.* Rev. i. 5, 18; xix. 13; xxii, 16. Cf. Baumgarten in J. Weiss, *D. Schriften des N.T.*, ii., p. 866.

[1] ὅσα εἶδεν, i. 2.

[2] Holtzmann rightly insists on this: ἐθεασάμεθα, Jo. i. 1, must be understood literally, according to 1 Jo. i. 1–4. It is the equivalent of ὁρᾶν. *D. Evang. des Johannes*, p. 44. *V.* Wendt, *D. Evang. des Joh.* E.T., p. 231; cf. Iren., *Ad Florinum* in Euseb., *H.E.*, v. 20.

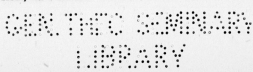

" the Lamb of God," or " the Lamb," in the Apocalypse. In the first chapter of the Gospel, the Baptist directs the attention of his disciples to Jesus as He walked towards him on two successive days. " Look well. This Man, whom you see walking, like any other man, before your eyes, is one Who, in His own person, is playing the same part that is played by the sacrificial lamb through all the religious history of your people."

To us the idea seems to be thrown out abruptly. A lamb is a strange designation for a young man in full strength and vigour. But to the hearers, " the Lamb of God " at once called up in their minds thoughts of momentous periods in their past, of Divine intervention, of sacred custom, of deep religious experience. They would think of the answer of Abraham to Isaac's questioning —" My son, God will Himself provide a lamb for a burnt offering." [1] What Isaac *seemed* to Abraham at that moment, Jesus was actually to the prophetic eye of the Baptist as He walked in the desert country beyond the Jordan. They would think, too, of the lamb which since the deliverance from Egypt had formed the feast commemorative of that great act of God. Hence, the words of the Baptist as he pointed to Christ, would not sound so strange as we might suppose. The phrase itself, in the mouth of a religious teacher, could only be interpreted in accordance with Old Testament analogies. It could only awaken thoughts of pardon and deliverance ; and to those who waited for the consolation of Israel, it spoke of the Messianic hope.

One disciple of the Baptist, at least, treasured and, long after, recalled for others the startling phrase ; if, indeed, it was the younger son of Zebedee who, with Andrew, approached Christ with the question, " Rabbi, where dwellest Thou ? " And it is not without significance that St. Peter who, though not present on the second day of the Baptist's declaration, was brought to Jesus by his brother in consequence of his own personal experience following upon that

[1] Gen. xxii. 8.

declaration, received a lasting impression of its extreme importance. In his Epistle, he writes of Christ as " a Lamb without blemish and without spot." [1] The reference is clearly to the same Old Testament types, and rested equally upon the witness of the Baptist. We may be certain that both writers were lastingly impressed by their experience of Christ as interpreted by the Forerunner, and as identified by him with the actual fulfilment of their people's ancient hope.

When we turn to the Apocalypse, the recurrence of the conception of Christ as the Lamb of God is found to be one of the most striking features of the book. Ἀμνός does not occur. The word used is always the diminutive Ἀρνίον.[2] The idea is the same, and the likeness of thought to the Gospel witness of the Baptist is remarkable. True, it is to Christ, not in His humiliation, but in His exaltation ; to Him, Who said to His servant John, " I am He that liveth and was dead : and, behold, I am alive for evermore," [3] that the title is applied. But it is in virtue of the conceptions of sacrifice and atonement which it suggests that the term is chosen to denote the Lord of Glory. " I beheld, and lo . . . stood a Lamb as it had been slain." He is " the Lamb slain from the foundation of the world." The redeemed " have washed their robes and made them white in the blood of the Lamb." [4]

With this insistence on the sacrifice of the Lamb and on the redeeming power of His blood compare the Gospel account of the Baptist's words, " the Lamb of God which taketh away the sin of the world," and the effect of his proclamation on the earliest group of disciples. In each case, the main idea is that of redemption. In each case it is the deliverance from sin, wrought by the sacrifice of the Lamb, that fires the imagination and influences the action of the disciples to whom the revelation was made. Its effect on the Apocalyptist is evident from his abundant use of the idea as supplying a title and a motive for adora-

---

[1] 1 Pet. i. 19.   [2] Rev. *passim.*   [3] Rev. i. 18.
[4] Rev. v. 6 ; cf. verses 9, 12 ; xiii. 8 ; vii. 14.

H

tion. Its effect on Andrew and his fellow-disciple appears first in their turning to Christ and sojourning with Him, and then in their subsequent transference of discipleship from that of the Baptist to Him Who had been proclaimed as the Lamb of God.

But what is the actual relation of the two expressions of thought—that of the Baptist as, according to the Gospel, he looked on Jesus as He walked, and that of the Seer as he looked upon the glorified Christ ? The earlier must be regarded as spoken in an ecstasy of prophecy. The latter came to the Seer in a vision. Much depends on the meaning of ὁ αἴρων τὴν ἁμαρτίαν τοῦ κόσμου.[1] Whatever the effect on the faithful Israelite of the offering of the sacrificial lamb, in the one offering of the Servant of Jehovah on the Cross, the sin so borne is regarded as taken away.[1]

The fundamental thought of the Baptist (as narrated in the Gospel) and of the Apocalyptist is the same—that of forgiveness through the sacrificial offering of One Whose death would suffice for the world's redemption. If the unnamed disciple who heard the Baptist speak was the Evangelist, we might expect to find traces in his writings of the effect of the Baptist's proclamation. As far as the Gospel is concerned, the question of sin and its pardon plays a very small part. The writer's gaze is fixed throughout on the Saviour Himself. His Person, rather than His work, is the absorbing subject. But in the First Epistle, where the needs of the writer's disciples are considered, the question of forgiveness is a leading one.[2] Sin and its pardon, its utter incongruity with the life and calling of a child of God, its entire opposition to God's will—all these conceptions come out with startling emphasis and show that the writer's sense of the sinfulness of sin is as strong as that of St. Paul. He employs the language of one who,

---

[1] Jo. i. 29 ; cf. 1 Jo. iii. 5, ἐκεῖνος ἐφανερώθη ἵνα τὰς ἁμαρτίας ἡμῶν ἄρῃ. It was the complete healing of the sick and the casting out of devils that led the Evangelist to see in Christ's action a fulfilment of the prophecy, " Himself took our infirmities and bare our sicknesses." " To bear " was to take away. Mt. viii. 16, 17 ; Is. liii. 4.

[2] 1 Jo. i. 7–ii. 3 ; ii. 12 ; iii. 4, 5 ; iv. 10.

f he " heard John speak," was deeply and permanently impressed by what he said.

When we turn to the Apocalypse, we find that the forgiveness of sin is a dominant conception, and if we identify the writer with the Evangelist, or a member of his group, it will seem to us like the echo of the Baptist's proclamation. The Seer has no sooner begun the story of his visions than he breaks into praise of " Him that loved us and washed us from our sins in His own blood." [1] " The accuser of our brethren " is overcome by them through " the blood of the Lamb." [2]

But, besides the passages which connect forgiveness with " the blood of the Lamb," " the Lamb " is the title given by the writer of the Apocalypse to Christ as the object of the worship of heaven, and as sharing with the Father the glory ascribed by the redeemed to the author of their salvation. The language employed is varied, and is very remarkable. The redeemed are " the firstfruits unto God and to the Lamb." Those who have " gotten the victory over the beast " sing the song of the Lamb. The victorious Lamb is " King of kings and Lord of lords." The union of Christ and His Church is described as " the marriage of the Lamb." The Holy City has need of neither temple nor luminary, for the Lord God Almighty and the Lamb are the Temple of it," and " the Lamb is the light thereof." [3]

Now, this language is remarkable. The Seer is possessed with the belief that, in his visions of heaven and of the heavenly life of the exalted Christ, he is allowed to see the ultimate triumph of the Cross. Hence the identification of His Person with the Lamb slain in the foreknowledge of God before the foundation of the world, symbolised and foretold in the Passover, pointed out by the finger of the

[1] Rev. i. 5, 6 ; cf. his report of the Song of the Redeemed, v. 9, " Thou wast slain and hast redeemed us to God by Thy blood out of every kindred and tongue and people and nation " ; v. 12, " Worthy is the Lamb that was slain."

[2] Rev. xii. 10, 11.

[3] Rev. xiv. 4 ; xv. 3 ; xvii. 14 ; xix. 7, 9 ; xxi. 9 ; xxi. 22, 23.

Baptist. This language of the Apocalypse, if it stood alone, would be hard to explain. It is accounted for at once when we turn to the Fourth Gospel and think of the impression made upon the writer by the words of the Baptist, remembering too that Apocalypse and Gospel alike had their literary home in Ephesus. " The Lamb gathers up into itself and displays symbolically all those conceptions of self-sacrificing love which centre in the Cross and appear in the Christian life, so far as it is lived in correspondence with the will of Christ.

" The Lamb " as set forth in the Apocalypse, is expressive of power as well as self-sacrifice. In his war with the ten kings, the victory is with the Lamb : " the Lamb shall overcome them, for He is Lord of lords and King of kings." [1] The vision of the victorious Lamb of God is thus in complete agreement with the mind of the Christ of the Fourth Gospel, when on the eve of the Cross He said, " Be of good cheer. I have overcome the world." [2]

From this comparison it is difficult to avoid the conclusion that the Seer and the Fourth Evangelist have breathed the same atmosphere and that the similarity of conception and terminology even points to a single mind, as in each case the ultimate, if not the direct, source and inspiration of the language used.

Again, the use of " the Word " as a personal term for the Only-begotten Son is characteristic of both writings, and—except in the First Epistle—is found nowhere else in the New Testament. In the Apocalypse its use strikes us as tentative and relative. He is " the Word of God." When the prologue of the Gospel came to be written, the expression is absolute and used with all boldness. Christ is thus named directly : " and the Word was with God, and the Word was God." In the Apocalypse, the Word is conceived rather as belonging to God, as a possession of His. In the Gospel it receives a full, personal meaning. The Word is God. There is thus a distinct development of thought. The Word is not merely the expression of

[1] Rev. xvii. 14.   [2] Jo. xvi. 33 ; cf. Rev. iii. 21.

God's mind: He is God conceived as Self-expressing. This evolution of idea wears the look of the process of a single mind. It may have been imparted to disciples and by them employed in the writings before us. But the step itself was taken by one mind, and that, as we believe, was the mind of John of Ephesus.[1]

Speaking generally of the conception of Christ's Person in the two writings, the traces of development do not hide the essential agreement. The glory of the Only-begotten Son, as it appeared to the Evangelist, had already shone upon the eyes of the Seer. The former pronounces Christ to be God unequivocally.[2] In the hearing of the Seer, the heavenly hymn of praise to the Father upon the Throne is directed also to the Lamb.[3] In each case, Godhead is ascribed to Christ equally with the Father, but in the subordination which is natural to Sonship and derivation of being, when set side by side with the absolute and underived Being of the Father. The Christology of the two writings is in complete agreement; only what is implied in the Apocalypse is declared openly in the Gospel. And this unfolding is, from the nature of the two works, just what we should expect. The dominating figure of the Apocalypse is the exalted Redeemer, Christ, the Lamb of God, Who was slain and is now "alive for evermore." The Christ of the Gospel is the Incarnate Word; and the true nature of His Person as it was manifested in His earthly life, is the main subject of the Gospel.

A less evident instance of agreement is furnished by the use of water as a symbol of Divine Grace, both in the Gospel and the Apocalypse.[4] The thought goes back to the Old Testament[5] and to Jewish Apocalyptic.[6] It was, therefore, part of the religious terminology of the first Christian century. Hence it cannot be alleged in proof

---

[1] V. above, p. 99.   [2] Jo. i. 1.   [3] Rev. v. 13; vii. 10.

[4] Jo. iv. 10, 13, 14; Rev. vii. 17, ζωῆς πηγὰς ὑδάτων· xxi. 6; xxii. 1, 7.

[5] Is. lv. 1; Ps. xxxvi. 9, πηγὴ ζωῆς; Prov. x. 11; Jer. ii. 13; πηγὴν ὕδατος ζωῆς, xvii. 13.

[6] 1 En. xvii. 4.

that its use in two separate writings shows identity c
authorship. But, the phrase in its various forms is
striking one ; and the fact of its use in two writings whic
emanated from the same place seems to show the choice c
a single mind. The least that can be said is that it form
part of a mass of cumulative evidence which points in tha
direction.

The similarity of idea which subsists between the Gospe
and the Apocalypse is not maintained by their languag
and phraseology. So great is the divergence that, to man
minds, it presents an invincible barrier to identity o
authorship. One man, it is said, could not have writte
within the space of the few years that separate the tw
works.

While fully admitting the difference, it cannot b
allowed to settle the question offhand. In the first place
the divergence of language is counterbalanced by the stron
similarity of idea which has been referred to. Unity o
thought is not obliterated by diversity of language
Secondly, it was to be expected that writings of so differen
a character and purpose, composed under such different con
ditions, would show marked contrast in style and language
The visions of the Apocalypse have the appearance of direc
impressions made upon a mind in a state of ecstasy—
impressions which the Seer regards as God-given, and
therefore to be imparted to the Church in a form as nea
as possible to the original communication. This account
for the literal transference of such terms as $\dot{\alpha}\pi\dot{o}$ $\dot{o}$ $\ddot{\omega}\nu$ $\kappa\alpha\grave{\iota}$ $\dot{o}$ $\ddot{\eta}$
$\kappa\alpha\grave{\iota}$ $\dot{o}$ $\dot{\epsilon}\rho\chi\dot{o}\mu\epsilon\nu os$ [1] from mind to page. The original clothing
of the impressions which he received kept its form as h
translated it into the Greek of the Churches for whom h
wrote. The sharpness of the outline must not be sacrificed

[1] Rev. i. 4. Zahn points out that " if a writer employs $\dot{\alpha}\pi\dot{o}$ with th
genitive thirty or forty times, but only once with the nominative, a
here, it is clear that his object is to let $\dot{o}$ $\ddot{\omega}\nu$, $\kappa.\tau.\lambda.$ be recognised as an in
declinable proper name, a paraphrase of the name of Jahveh " : *Einl
in d. N.T.*, ii., p. 629, n. 7. Cf. Charles, *The Revelation of St. John*, i.
p. 10, " The Seer has deliberately violated the rules of grammar in orde
to preserve the divine name inviolate from the change which it woul
necessarily have undergone if declined."

in the interests of language. The solecism is allowed to remain. If he revised his first notes, he shrank from tampering with what at the moment seemed the truest transcript of his experience. It had become too sacred for change either by his own, or by a scholar's hand. Rough-hewn, as by the quarryman of Patmos, it must not be smoothed away by the culture of Ephesus. His experience was too recent and too vivid to be thus dealt with. Somewhere, in such considerations as these, lies the secret of the stylistic idiosyncrasies of the Apocalypse.[1]

When, some years later, the Gospel and First Epistle came to be written, the circumstances were different. If the writer was the same man, the resident at Ephesus knew Greek better than the prisoner of Patmos. The narratives of the Gospel and the homiletics of the Epistle were cast in a totally different mould from the vision-pictures of the Apocalypse. There was also nothing to hinder the employment of an amanuensis. The Greek of the Gospel is still that of one whose native language it was not. Whether it had a written Aramaic original, or was merely the Greek transcript of the author's thought, the air of Palestine breathes through every page. The Evangelist lives his life there over again, and his Master's words come back to him in their Aramaic form. The Gospel, if not a translation of a first Aramaic draft, is at least the embodiment of an unwritten store of recollections, too deeply engraved in the writer's mind and too often recalled in teaching to lose the sharpness of their outline.

To sum up what has been said : The relation of the

---

[1] Dr. Charles thinks that the grammatical differences make the assumption of a common authorship of Gospel and Apocalypse "absolutely impossible" unless a very long interval intervened between their dates, an interval which he does not accept, *op. cit.*, i., p. xxix. On the other hand, Burney remarks, "The case against identity of authorship of the Gospel and the Apocalypse can certainly not be maintained upon the ground of style. The evidence is all in the other direction." *The Aramaic Origin of the Fourth Gospel*, p. 152. "Though Dr. Charles holds that the author of the Apocalypse was not the author of the Gospel, the description which he gives (*The Revelation of St. John*, i. p. xliv.) of the characteristics of the former is applicable . . . to the latter" : *ib.*, p. 150.

three chief Johannine writings is too intimate to be disproved by the divergence of their language and style. The divergence is in part explained by the nature of their contents. Its significance will be estimated variously by different minds ; but on principles of sound and rational criticism it should not prevent our seeing in these writings the inspiration, if not the actual workmanship, of one remarkable mind.[1]

---

[1] Charles, who regards the Gospel and the Apocalypse as by different authors, admits that " the two writers were related to each other, either as master and pupil, or as pupils of the same master, or as members of the same school." *The Revelation of St. John*, i., p. xxix. ; cf. *ib.*, p. xxxiii. E. Meyer puts forward the strange theory that " a third John is the author of the Apocalypse ; he was in exile in Patmos and has apparently written in Ephesus . . . the author cannot be identical either with the Apostle or the Presbyter " : *Ursprung und Anfänge des Christenthums*, vol. iii., p. 636. Like Bousset, *Encycl. Bibl.*, i., col. 197, and Burney, *The Aramaic Origin of the Fourth Gospel*, p. 152, Meyer regards Rev. xxi. 14 as excluding the Apostolic authorship of the book of Revelation, *ib.*, p. 637. But here, as in the case of St. Paul's references to his Apostleship, the question turns upon psychological considerations. There is nothing in this claim for the Apostolic College, *as a whole*, of a position in the Church universal which corresponds with that assigned to them by our Lord Himself, to make it presumptuous for the author to advance it, if he were himself a member of the College. Cf. Mt. xix. 28 ; Lk. xxii. 30.

CHAPTER IX

THE FOURTH GOSPEL AND THE SYNOPTIC GOSPELS

Narrative.

No one can begin to study the Fourth Gospel without at once coming into touch with the first three. Great as is the dissimilarity of the two great strands of Gospel narrative, there is also a likeness both of aim and method, which persists, and which warrants the inclusion of the four writings under the designation of "The Gospel"—the message of Salvation, once, during the Saviour's lifetime and for some years onward, forming the substance of the spoken Word, afterwards, of the Word committed to writing, as the first preachers and hearers were beginning to pass away.

Reference to the Synoptic Gospels is required from the fact that, as is generally admitted, they lay before the Fourth Evangelist as he set to work upon his own.

This is clearly shown by points of agreement both in subject and in language.[1] It is confirmed by tradition [2] and by the probability amounting almost to certainty that a person so fully in touch with Church life as the writer of the Fourth Gospel would have access to the earlier ones.[3]

---

[1] Cf. (allowing for difference of treatment) the Baptism ; the feeding of the five thousand ; the cleansing of the Temple ; the entry to Jerusalem ; the Crucifixion and Resurrection, not to speak of the many resemblances of phrase and idea which run through each Gospel.

[2] Cf. Clem. Alex., *Hypotoposes* in Euseb., *H.E.*, vi. 14, Τὸν μέντοι Ἰωάννην ἔσχατον, συνιδόντα ὅτι τὰ σωματικὰ ἐν τοῖς Εὐαγγελίοις δεδήλωται, προτραπέντα ὑπὸ τῶν γνωρίμων, πνεύματι Θεοφορηθέντα, πνευματικὸν ποιῆσαι Εὐαγγέλιον. Cf. Euseb., *H.E.*, iii. 24.

[3] As we might expect, from the close association of St. John with St. Peter, to which the Gospels and the Acts bear witness, the correspondence of St. John with (Petrine) Mark is most noticeable. But his knowledge of St. Luke is also very evident. With Mk. ii. 11, cf. Jo. v. 8 ;

Can we discover from internal evidence the writer's attitude towards them? Was it one of 'servitude or independence?

It has come to be regarded almost as an axiom, that if the accounts of the Synoptics differ from the Fourth Gospel, it is the latter authority that must give way. The reasons alleged for this decision are the earlier date of the composition of the Synoptics, the more concrete and matter-of-fact character of their contents and the corroboration thought to be afforded by three converging strains of evidence.

But these reasons require investigation. In the first place, an early date is not an unfailing safeguard of accuracy. The best evidence is often found to be that which is based on reflection upon what has occurred, or has been reported to have occurred, rather than on an immediate and impulsive transfer of impression to writing. This is especially the case where the fact in question involves much more than what appeals to the bodily senses. We have only to think of the Person Who forms the subject of Gospel narrative to be able to realise this.

Secondly, it is true that the first three Gospels often give a plain, literal account of things, and this is a characteristic mark of their value. They represent our Lord as He appeared to the people, without trying to conceal their misapprehensions; they give the actual impression with no attempt to correct it [1]; whereas, in the Fourth Gospel, Christ is seen through a medium of devout, long-pondered thought. Yet, true as this contrast is, it does not cover the

with Mk. vi. 33–43, cf. Jo. vi. 1–14; with Mk. xiv. 3, 9, cf. Jo. xii. 3; with Mk. xi. 9, cf. Jo. xii. 13; with Mk. xiv. 54, 67, cf. Jo. xviii. 18, 25. Likeness to St. Luke is slight until we come to the Resurrection narratives. St. John agrees with St. Luke against Matt. and Mk. in placing Christ's appearances to the disciples in Jerusalem instead of Galilee. With Lk. xxiv. 24, cf. Jo. xx. 3–9; with the two angels at the tomb, Lk. xxiv. 4, cf. Jo. xx. 12; with Lk. xxiv. 36 ff., cf. Jo. xx. 19, 20, 27; 1 Jo. i. 1. There are slight points of contact between St. Matthew and St. John, in which St. Mark frequently shares. Wendt is probably right in saying that "a literary connection between the Synoptics and John must be acknowledged." *Das Evang. des Johannes*, E.T., 1902, p. 47; cf. J. Moffatt, *Introd. to Literat. of N.T.*, 1912, p. 533 f.; Streeter, *The Four Gospels*, pp. 396 ff., *v.* below, p. 136 f., Harnack, *Chronologie*, i. p. 680.

[1] For instance, "Son of Joseph," Lk. iv. 22. But this is true also of the narrative parts of the Fourth Gospel, Jo. vi. 42.

whole ground of comparison. The Synoptics are not wanting in signs of reflection upon the material of their narratives.[1] The First and Third Gospels appeared quite late enough to admit of the existence of such a medium of reflection. On the other hand, the Fourth Gospel frequently records the bare historical facts.[2].

Then, the plea of corroboration by a triple strain of evidence is not so effective as is supposed. St. Mark is, as a rule, the solitary authority in incident and action reported by the three writers.[3] The other two repeat, certainly adding their *imprimatur*, but seldom showing any sign of independent sources of information in these sections. The claim of three against one is therefore not to be substantiated throughout. Besides, if the Fourth Evangelist was indeed an eyewitness, his evidence, though later in publication, was direct, whereas St. Mark was dependent upon St. Peter.

Therefore, in estimating the comparative claims of the Fourth Gospel and the group of three to trustworthiness, where they seem to conflict, we are not justified in starting with an unconditional bias in favour of the latter.

The points of difference vary in importance. Some are thought so conclusive that St. John is at once put out of court. In other cases, his representation is allowed to have made good its claim to acceptance.

One or two considerations should here be borne in mind. If the Three lay before the writer of the Fourth, any disparity that presents itself to us, must have appealed with equal—if not greater force—to himself. He revised, amended, added, omitted, with his eyes open—a fact much lost sight of by recent criticism. Besides, for this task, he was in possession of knowledge to which we have no access.

Disparities of representation would be clear also to the

---

[1] *E.g.* Mk. vi. 52 ; ix. 6 ; xv. 10.

[2] *E.g.* Jo. i. 49, " Thou art the King of Israel," a mode of address most unlikely when the Gospel was written. Or, again, things said of Christ which the writer faithfully records, while fully conscious that they were mistaken : Jo. vi. 42 ; vii. 41.

[3] The long interpolation, Lk. ix. 51–xviii. 14, is an exception. So also the birth narratives of the First and Third Gospels.

disciples and adherents to whom he handed his work. From what we know of its gradual acceptance by the Church, it seems that the process of canonisation was not completed without a struggle. The fact of its success points to the probability that its first readers had access to stores of collateral information, which accounted for disparities and removed the obstacles to its reception, which at first presented themselves.

It should also be borne in mind that, at its appearance, the first three Gospels were already in process of obtaining quasi-canonical rank. Along with the Pauline Epistles, they were being read in the services of the Church, and were gradually attaining the status of " the Law and the Prophets." [1] This fact heightened the responsibility of the new writer, and increased the gravity of any attempt that he might make to amend or correct them.

Now, it is no answer to these considerations to say that the peculiar and definite object of St. John released him from attention to historic accuracy. He had no wish to be released. If words mean anything, he claims to write true history with the best guarantee for such accuracy—his presence when the history was being made—a fact of which he makes a great point, in a way, too, which is unexampled in Gospel writing.[2]

That he had a theological purpose in view is evident from his own statements ; but so had St. Mark [3] ; yet, in each case, it is interwoven with facts of actual occurrence *and is based upon their certainty*.

That, in carrying his purpose into effect, the Fourth Evangelist, either made no effort, or was unable, to rid his mind of the mode of thought of his own time, and that,

[1] Perhaps the earliest indications of this process are the allusions of Papias to Gospel writings, which are preserved by Eusebius, *H.E.*, iii. 39. By the time that Papias wrote, they had become of such account in the Church as to deserve to be explained and interpreted in a work of five books. This was in the early decades of the second century.   The Gospels alluded to are the Second and the First : *v.* Westcott, *Canon of the N.T.*, p. 77 n. 1 ; Loisy, *Le Quatrième Evangile*, p. 130.

[2] Jo. xix. 35 ; xx. 30, 31 ; cf. xxi. 24.

[3] Mk. i. 1.

consequently, his portrait of Christ is drawn according to the views prevailing, say, at the close of the first century, or in the early decades of the second, has not been proved.[1] But what does emerge, on a close study of the text, is the fact that we have the inestimable advantage of seeing our Lord as He appeared to a witness, who lived long enough to be able to apprehend the full meaning of what he had seen and to check his conception by the reasoned experience of the Christian Society.

This delay, if we may so call it, in the issue of the final Gospel was providential. The earlier Evangelists were hardly in a position to do what St. John has done, even if they had the spiritual force and capacity which the task required. In his own person he was the fulfilment of the promise which he alone has recorded : " (The Holy Spirit) shall bring all things to your remembrance." Christ lives and breathes in the Fourth Gospel, because " manifested in remembrance," reflected from the faithful mirror of a mind at once accurate and devout.

To return to the question with which we started. What precisely was the attitude of mind of the Fourth Evangelist towards the Gospels that lay before him as he wrote his own ? It cannot be answered in a word. He had probably made use, in teaching, of the *corpus* of tradition which lay behind them, so that when going over certain portions of the ground, as he came to write, he would hardly discriminate between the written and the oral substratum.

This would account for some of the deviations in the material common to himself and the three. His attitude is rather that of a man who is familiar with an earlier presentation of his theme, but, so far from being in any way tied to it, moves with complete freedom and independence ; so much so, that on occasion he does not hesitate to differ, and, what is more, expresses no concern at the difference. So sure is he of his own position that he adapts and corrects

---

[1] Yet it is a commonplace of " liberal " criticism, supposed only to need statement in order to be accepted : cf. *e.g.* Loisy, *Le Quat. Evang.*, p. 129 ; Heitmüller in J. Weiss, *D. Schriften des N.T.*, ii. pp. 702, 705 ; E. F. Scott, *The Fourth Gospel*, p. 300 ; *v.* below, p. 169.

without assigning a reason, confident that the group of adherents to whom he handed his finished work would look for none. They knew who he was that wrote it.

I believe that this is a fair description of the state of things as a whole ; but we must look closer into detail.

There are traces of familiarity with the Synoptic tradition either as enshrined in the Gospels themselves, or as presupposed by them ; a knowledge which our author does not permit to fetter his own narrative ; but which serves as a useful criterion, when we come to investigate his trustworthiness. One or two instances will suffice for our purpose.

Take the story of John the Baptist. Much has been made of the difference between the Synoptic and the Johannine Baptist.[1] In the latter case the sole object is said to be the glorification of the Messiah ; while the earlier Gospels present the Baptist as concerned rather, by the preaching of repentance and the administering of baptism to his converts, to be the herald of the coming kingdom. It is true that in the Fourth Gospel the emphasis is laid upon the Person of Christ rather than upon the details of the Baptist's own preliminary work and preparation for Him ; but the two accounts do not so conflict as to lead us to reject the one, if we accept the other.[2]

The Fourth Evangelist is clearly aware of the earlier account and feels free to give what he conceives to be the predominant feature of the situation ; while later on he inserts a note to guard those who, like himself, were familiar with the Synoptic narrative, from supposing that Christ's public ministry only began when that of the Baptist had ended in his imprisonment.[3] If he strongly emphasises the

---

[1] V. Heitmüller in D. Schriften des N.T., ii. p. 732. But the Messiah-ship comes out quite plainly in Matt. iii. 11, 12. It is not confined to the Fourth Gospel.

[2] It is only natural that when the Fourth Evangelist began to write, interest in the figure and work of the Baptist (already fully described by the Synoptic writers) should have subsided.

[3] Jo. iii. 24, οὔπω γὰρ ἦν βεβλημένος εἰς τὴν φυλακὴν Ἰωάννης, a silent correction of deductions which might be drawn from Mk. i. 14 ; Matt. iv. 12 ; cf. Acts x. 37 ; xiii. 24 ; Euseb., H.E., iii. 24 ; Zahn, in Jo., p. 213 ; Einl. in d. N.T., ii. p. 509 ; H. S. Holland, Philos. and the Fourth Gospel, p. 154.

prophetic element in the sayings of the Baptist, we remember that nothing could be stronger than our Lord's testimony to his prophetic standing.[1]   This is to be taken into account when we consider those features of the Baptist's witness to " the Lamb of God," which are peculiar to the Fourth Gospel.[2]

A typical instance of the peculiar relation of the Fourth Evangelist to his predecessors in Gospel writing is presented by the miracle of the Feeding of the Five Thousand—the only incident reported by all four writers before they come to the story of the Passion.   Here, again, there is knowledge of the Synoptic version, but independence of it.   The main facts are the same throughout ; yet the later writer inserts individual touches—difference of initiative, the presence of the lad, the detail of the barley loaves, the specifying of names of Apostles more directly concerned, consequences of the miracle—which clearly betray the independent knowledge of an eyewitness, who recalls the events of a momentous day.[3]   Then follows, what is characteristic of the plan and purpose of the Fourth Evangelist, a discourse in the Synagogue of Capernaum, in which He Who had been working the miracle proclaims Himself to be the true bread from heaven, without which life could not be.   The miracle and the teaching are woven together in the writer's mind.

One more instance will suffice for the present.   It shall be taken from the narrative of the Passion.   Here the Fourth Evangelist is in close touch with the Synoptic tradition, fully aware of it, yet still holding himself free to give his own version of what happened and to amend the

---

[1] From " Q," Matt. xi. 7 f. ; Lk. vii. 24 f.

[2] Jo. i. 29, 36 ; cf. p. 101 f.

[3] Jo. vi. 1-16.   In view of the disparity of details combined with agreement in the main course of events, we cannot go with Heitmüller, when he says, " His (the Fourth Evangelist's) dependence on the Synoptic tradition is unmistakable."   D. Schriften des N.T., ii., p. 772.   Westcott, in loc., and Zahn, in loc., p. 321, are of the opposite opinion ; as the latter remarks, " John moves with a certainty and an independence of the older Gospels, which find their most natural explanation in the fact that here we have the narrative of an eyewitness."   Cf. Sanday, The Authorship of the Fourth Gospel, p. 122 f.

earlier one. It is generally allowed that the dates of the
Last Supper and of the Crucifixion are correctly given in
the Fourth Gospel ; the first hours of Nisan 14th, beginning
from sunset of the 13th, for the Supper ; the closing hours
of the same day (=Friday afternoon) for the Crucifixion,
about the time when the Paschal Lamb was being sacrificed
in readiness for the Feast after sunset.[1] The Synoptic
tradition identifies the Last Supper with the meal at which
the Lamb was eaten, and places it in the early (evening)
hours—not of the 14th, but of the 15th of Nisan.

That this version of the story is incorrect appears even
from the Synoptic narrative itself. In spite of the recorded
precaution of the Sanhedrin against an arrest of Christ on
the Feast Day,[2] it actually informs us that it was on the
Feast Day that the arrest, the trial and the Crucifixion
took place.

That this could not have been the case, we again have a
Synoptic assurance in St. Mark's account of the hasty
removal of the bodies from the crosses and the fact that
Joseph of Arimathæa was able before sunset (when the
Passover was about to begin) to purchase the fine linen for
the burial.[3] It is also to be observed that there is no
mention of the Paschal Lamb in the Synoptic narrative of the
Last Supper. The time for it was the evening meal of the
following day. Here, again, we have in the Fourth Gospel
an account written with full knowledge of the Synoptic
tradition, but in complete independence of it.

Another marked feature of the Fourth Gospel is the
omission of incidents which form vital elements of the
Synoptic tradition. Events are not merely dealt with on
an independent footing. Some are silently dropped out.
The *Ministerial* call and ordination of the Twelve [4] form

---

[1] Jo. xiii. 1. That is, " On the day before the Feast of Passover,
Nisan 13th ; the Passover Lamb was eaten on Nisan 14th, after sunset":
Heitmüller in *D. Schriften des N.T.*, ii., p. 818 ; cf. Bacon, *The Fourth
Gospel*, pp. 415 f. ; Sanday, *Authorship of the Fourth Gospel*, p. 201 f. ;
H. J. Holtzmann, *in loc.*, p. 232 ; O. Procksch, *Petrus und Johannes*,
p. 217.

[2] Mk. xiv. 2 ; Matt. xxvi. 5.

[3] Mk. xv. 42, 46.

[4] Mk. iii. 13 f., and parallels.

an epoch in Gospel history. They are entirely passed over by the Fourth Evangelist. Moreover, he makes no mention of the earlier call to discipleship that was given by the Sea of Galilee.[1] It sufficed for his purpose that the two incidents stood in the Synoptic narrative.

His own story [2] of the first contact of the leading men among the future Apostles with their Master explains the Synoptic narrative of the call to discipleship by the lake and its sequel, the solemn ordination on the mountain slope. He had nothing to alter in that recital. There was no need to refer to it.[3]

A more remarkable omission, and one which has caused perplexity to generations of readers of the Fourth Gospel, is its silence as to the institution of the Eucharist. Now, it is evident that the writer's mind plays about it, and hovers over the incidents that accompany it. He imparts the assurance that, with full knowledge of the imminence of His death, the heart of the Saviour was filled with love and yearning for His disciples : " He loved them to the end." If in the Synoptic narrative of what passed, we get the action, in the Fourth Gospel we learn the mind of the Lord Jesus, as He was entering on His Passion.

The Supper is referred to, while nothing is said of the new feast of love of which it was the occasion, and which would henceforth be inseparably connected with it in the mind of every Christian man until the end of time. But even the reference to the Supper is little more than a note of the order of events : " And while Supper was going on " [4] ; knowledge of the treachery of Judas having impressed the Saviour with the certainty that the hour of Redemption

---

[1] Mk. i. 16 f., and parallels.

[2] Jo. i. 37 f.

[3] He was not writing a life of Christ. His purpose was to deal with certain facts and episodes in His ministry, and so to treat of His Person and character as to confirm the faith of believers : Jo. xix. 35 ; xx. 31. Besides, in Jo. vi. 67, " Then said Jesus unto the twelve, Will ye also go away ? " we have what amounts to a confirmation of the Synoptic narrative. Those to whom He so spake had already been called to discipleship.

[4] Jo. xiii. 2, καὶ δείπνου γινομένου. He alludes to the Supper as well known to all who were acquainted with the Synoptic account.

I

had come, " He riseth from Supper " and performs that act of humble, loving ministry to others, which stands as the perpetual model of Christian service and devotion—the washing of His disciples' feet, the wiping of them " with the towel wherewith He was girded." [1]

It was enough for the Fourth Evangelist to have reported the teaching at Capernaum, in which our Lord, a year before, had laid down the meaning and necessity of that union with Himself of which the Sacrament was to be the chief effectual sign and means. It is characteristic of the writer to devote his care and interest to the inner meaning of what was being done. The recorder of the Sermon of the Eucharist had no need to repeat the fourfold (Synoptic and Pauline) description of its institution. The knowledge which he shows of its setting and circumstances is an assurance of his agreement with the Synoptic narrative ; or he must have surely spoken. When he was writing his Gospel, the Eucharist was being celebrated throughout the Church. If it was an unwarranted deduction from what passed at the Last Supper, he must have revealed the fact. His silence on so vital a point as a Sacrament of perpetual obligation, instituted as it was in a group of circumstances of which he shows complete knowledge, confirms the truth of the earlier narratives.[2]

Another omission of the Fourth Evangelist, on which great stress has been laid, is an account of the Agony in Gethsemane. As with his omission of the Baptism and the Temptation, the reason freely assigned is the unwillingness of the writer to record an incident in the Saviour's life that appears to negative the exalted conception of His Person, which he desires throughout the Gospel to put forward.[3]

There would be some point in this objection if the Evangelist had consistently excluded from his narrative

---

[1] Cf. Mk. x. 45, ὁ υἱὸς τοῦ ἀνθρώπου οὐκ ἦλθε διακονηθῆναι, ἀλλὰ διακονῆσαι.
[2] Cf. Chapman, *John the Presbyter*, p. 73.
[3] *V.* E. F. Scott, *The Fourth Gospel*, p. 44. Yet the express statement of Jo. xii. 27, " Now is My soul troubled," with its disclosure of struggle and tension, is entirely in harmony with the Synoptic story of Gethsemane.

all scenes and incidents which might be so interpreted. But the true state of the case is altogether the other way. If the Fourth Gospel is the supreme revelation of the Divinity, it no less truly reveals the complete humanity of our Lord. It is as far as can be from any Docetic taint. If Gnostics were the first, outside the community of Ephesus, to seize upon the Gospel and exploit those elements of its teaching which seemed to favour their own views,[1] they closed their eyes to much that was opposed to them. An Evangelist who carefully records bodily weariness, acute disappointment, heartfelt grief, a wounded spirit, extreme thirst, as endured by Christ in the days of His flesh, is not to be charged with so idealising his Subject, as to lose all touch with reality.[2] He had no mind to repeat what, for all practical purposes, had been fully related in the Gospels that lay before him. He has distinctly stated his object in writing. Is he to be blamed for keeping to it and for bringing out of the fullness of his store of knowledge what would best serve his purpose ? [3]

One of the chief indictments brought against the Fourth Gospel is the lack of development in its story of the disciples' religious experience. If we except one or two early confessions of Christ in St. Matthew,[4] there is no generally attested Synoptic expression of faith until we come to that of St. Peter at Cæsarea Philippi. But in the Fourth Gospel we at once, in the first chapter, have confessions of a far-reaching character from the Baptist and from Nathanael. Christ is hailed as Son of God and Messiah.[5] Is this repre-

---

[1] Both Basileides and Valentinus were teaching during the reign of Hadrian, A.D. 117–138. For the former, v. above, p. 44. For Valentinus and his use of the Prologue of the Gospel, v. the article of Lipsius in *Murray's Dict. of Christian Biogr.*, " Valentinus."

[2] And yet Heitmüller, in face of this evidence, can say, " Everything that could be interpreted as weakness on the part of Jesus is carefully avoided. On the contrary, whatever reveals the supernatural is diligently produced and heightened." In J. Weiss' *D. Schriften des N.T.*, ii., p. 705.

[3] Cf. Inge, in *Dict. of Christ and Gosp.*, i., p. 887, " There can be no question that these omissions are deliberate, and not the result of ignorance."

[4] Matt. ix. 27 ; xiv. 33.

[5] " Jesus is here the same, unchanged from the beginning to the end " : Schmiedel, *Das vierte Evangelium*, p. 27.

sentation historical ?   Does the slowly evolved recognition
of His Divine claims which we find in the Synoptic narrative
exclude the possibility of such early confessions as those
reported by St. John ?

The earlier Gospels themselves supply us with an answer.
They show the existence of a feeling of Messianic expectation
possessed by individuals, which might at any favourable
opportunity ripen into such an open profession of faith as
St. John records.

Long before, when men were waiting for the consolation
of Israel, Zacharias and Simeon and Anna gave their
testimony and confessed their faith.   It takes little imagination to realise how this hope, fanned into fresh fervour by
the preaching of the Baptist, would again assert itself at
the Jordan, when Christ in Person appeared among the
people.   St. Luke tells us how " all men mused in their
hearts of John whether he were the Christ or not." [1]   The
thought of the Messiah was in the air.   What wonder if
so soon after His first appearance in public life, the greatest
of the prophets " looking upon Jesus as He walked," was
moved in ecstasy to say, " Behold the Lamb of God," or
if Nathanael, touched by a conviction that here was One
Who could read the heart, Who " seeth not as man seeth,"
concluded that he was standing face to face with " the Son
of God, the King of Israel." [2]

Evolution is a good working theory, whether we are
tracing a physical or an historical process ; but it offers no
complete key to the phenomena of life.   The critic who
starts his examination of the Gospel record with the fixed
idea that he will find a general conformity to this theory,
and that he must reject everything that is not in line with
it, will find that he is wholly in the wrong.   There are
diversities of character, of gifts, of opportunities, of which
we have to take account.   Historical science knows nothing
of an undeviating course of orderly development in the
experiences of life [3] ; and the sooner this fact is realised the

---

[1] Lk. iii. 15.   [2] Jo. i. 29, 49.
[3] The Johannine account of the Baptist's conviction and confession,
i. 29, 36, 34, receives support from Mk. i. 11 ; Matt. iii. 17.   His intuition

better it will be for the critical study of the New Testament records. The sane and proper course is not to start an investigation on the assumption of a theory, which may or may not hold good in the cases as they arise ; but rather to take the facts as they come, and on them to frame our representation of what actually occurred.

It is true that the general idea of a gradual recognition of our Lord's claims is to be gained from the Synoptic Gospels, and that it seems to receive support from the theory of development. But, after all, the Synoptic record is not a complete account of what occurred, and it is unscientific to have recourse to a theory which is incapable of rigid application, in order to counteract the effect of evidence supplied by other sources.

Moreover, the phenomena of human conduct do not admit of the rigorous application of a theory of development which can be legitimately employed in other fields of scientific inquiry. All men do not think and act alike. Allowance must be made for the possession of exceptional gifts of insight and of prescience. No argument, therefore, against the historical value of our Gospel can be drawn from the fact that it records incidents which appear to break the course of that gradual awaking to knowledge of Christ's Person which the Synoptic writers are thought to prove.

Until the Fourth Gospel was given to the Church, and during the period in which our three earlier Gospels were winning their way to full recognition—roughly speaking between A.D. 70 and 100—men's minds must have been sore perplexed when they tried to find out what happened in the three first years of Christianity. We can only enter into their difficulties by placing ourselves in their position, ignoring so far as possible the later Gospel, and fixing our

---

as a prophet was met and confirmed by what he heard and saw. *On Synoptic grounds* we cannot withhold assent to a condition of mind which might well find expression in the words recorded in the Fourth Gospel.

I find that F. Heiler takes a similar view as to the failure of strictly scientific methods in dealing with questions of metaphysics or of value-judgments. He says, " The attempts to solve the problems will always be of a more or less subjective character and can never establish a claim to general validity." *Das Gebet*, 1920, p. 25.

attention wholly upon the Synoptic narrative. Taking the
Marcan groundwork as our text, we are surprised that,
without any previous explanation or preparation, Jesus,
coming into Galilee and passing by its inland sea, calls to
some fishermen as they are at their work, with the astonishing result that one and all, they abandon their occupation
and begin a wandering life as His disciples. Men do not
act thus without a reason and, so far as the Synoptic
narrative goes, none is to be had. Only if the information
supplied by the Fourth Evangelist[1] is forthcoming do we get
any light upon the problem.

If the main course of the Synoptic narrative is considered, the short period taken up by the Public Ministry
seems quite inadequate for the many momentous issues
which are placed within it. How could the Person and
the claims of the long-expected Messiah be so presented to
the people of Judæa and Galilee as to afford a fair opportunity for reception or rejection in so brief a time? Was
the point to which all the preparation was directed to be
treated with indifference? Was our Lord's presentation
of Himself before people and rulers to be deprived of all
its force by lack of time? The Fourth Gospel alone
supplies the answer in definite terms, while the Synoptic
narrative indirectly corroborates it. St. John's ground plan
finds room for three Passovers, and comprises a space of
two to three years.[2] So far from containing anything to
nullify this position, the earlier Gospels show indications
that their general scheme requires expansion, if it is to
provide the necessary framework for all that they imply.[3]

But a greater difficulty awaits those who depend
exclusively on the main Synoptic account of the local

---

[1] Jo. i.

[2] Jo. ii. 13, the first visit of the Ministry; vi. 4; xi. 55; *v.* Turner in
Hastings' *D.B.*, i., p. 406 f.; Wendt, *D. Lehre Jesu*, p. 440, "That Jesus
was more often in Jerusalem is, in spite of Mark, whose historic sketch is
reproduced by Matthew and Luke, testified by many signs in the Synoptic
tradition." Cf. A. C. Headlam, *The Life and Teaching of Jesus the Christ*,
1923, p. 319; J. Weiss, *D. Aufgaben der N.Tn. Wissenschaft*, p. 44.

[3] Lk. iv. 1, 14, 43 f. All the Synoptists speak of a Harvest in the
midst of the Galilean ministry: Mk. ii. 23 and parallels; *v.* Zahn, *Einleitung*, ii., p. 449.

character of the Public Ministry.   Jerusalem, the city of the great King, the centre of the religious life of the people, the seat of the hierarchy and of the worship, David's city, would, if any spot on earth, claim an early visit from the Son of David, the hope of all the race.   But, if we follow the Synoptic narrative, we read of no such visit until a few days before the end.   Within a week, Christ is welcomed, rejected, judged, condemned, crucified.   Everywhere but in Jerusalem He has taught and healed and presented Himself to the hearts and minds of men.   Not there, where lay all the materials for making the decisive choice, where a whole people, by the voice of their leaders, could declare their will, had they a chance of facing the issues of life and death, in the acceptance or rejection of their Messiah ; except during the few troubled hours with which so much of the Synoptic story is occupied.   We feel instinctively that this cannot be the whole story ; and though nothing definite is said, we conclude that, if the great lament over Jerusalem receives its fair interpretation, more than one visit to the city is plainly indicated.[1]

But directly we turn to the Fourth Gospel we get the state of things that we should have expected.   Through the extended period of the Ministry, the visits to the Holy City are frequent.   He who " came not to destroy the Law but to fulfil it " naturally takes His part in the Feasts that commemorate historic moments in the life of His people.   Being there, He can present Himself to them.   With what results the earlier Gospels themselves inform us.   He is visited even in Galilee by Scribes and Pharisees who came down from Jerusalem [2] ; while St. Luke tells us that early in

---

[1] Matt. xxiii. 37 ; Lk. xiii. 34 ; from " Q ".   Besides, the Synoptic Gospels tell of friends and adherents whom He possessed in the city and its neighbourhood, which nevertheless they fail to tell us that He visited before the last days : v. H. S. Holland, *Philosophy and the Fourth Gospel*, p. 131 ; cf. Mk. xi. 3 ; xiv. 13 ; Lk. xix. 30.   There is also the moral aspect of the question to be considered.   If the Synoptic narrative of Christ's presence in Jerusalem were *complete*, how could we reconcile the doom of the city with our conception of the Divine justice and equity ?

[2] Mk. vii. 1 ; Matt. xv. 1 ; cf. Mk. iii. 7, 8, 22 ; Lk. v. 17.   How came the owner of the colt to send it at once for Christ's use, when He demanded it ?   Christ had made the man's acquaintance during a former visit. Mk. xi. 3.

His Ministry, He was preaching in the Synagogues of
Judæa.[1]

A more grave phenomenon to be encountered in comparing
Synoptic with Johannine material is that of Synoptic
omissions. Of these, by far the most important is the
raising of Lazarus. Quite apart from the large demands
that the story makes upon our faith, and from the clear
evidence which it affords of a didactic and edifying purpose,
its entire omission from the Synoptic scheme is thought
to cast great doubt upon its actual occurrence ; all the more
so from the fact that the Evangelist himself appears to
regard it as the final and determining factor which decided
the Jewish authorities to put our Lord to death. And if
he was justified in this view, how does it come to pass that
not a trace of the miracle has found its way into the Synoptic
records ?

But, is it true that St. John attributes the plot of the
authorities to the raising of Lazarus, and to nothing else ?
It was certainly a chief factor, as we gather from xi. 47, 53.
But the Evangelist himself records previous acts of hostility
on the part of " the Jews " that led to our Lord's withdrawal
from Judæa.[2] The miracle was far from being the sole
cause of hostility. The cleansing of the Temple and the
Parable of the Vineyard are plainly declared to have contributed to it, as the time drew towards the end.[3] It was
natural for the Evangelist, who related the raising of
Lazarus and was aware of the perturbation which it caused
among the authorities, to place great emphasis on its

---

[1] Lk. iv. 44 ; for Γαλιλαίας read ʼΙουδαίας, used possibly in the more
limited sense ; but of Palestine as a whole, according to Loisy, Le Quatr.
Evangile, p. 39 ; Plummer, ad loc. ; Clemen, D. Entstehung des Johan.
Evangeliums, p. 62 ; Zahn, Einleit., ii., pp. 379, 395, 449. Lk. i. 5 ; xxiii.
5, can be quoted for this wider meaning.

Heitmüller, in accordance with his fixed principle of comparison
between the two strains of evidence, will not acknowledge the superiority
of St. John as to either the scene or the duration of the Ministry. D.
Schriften des N.T., ii., p. 704.

Apart from Synoptic indications of earlier visits to Jerusalem, the way
in which St. Luke shows that, after the Ascension, the Apostles appear
to be quite at home in the city and to mix naturally in its life, points in
the same direction. Cf. Acts i. 13 ; ii. 46 ; iii. 1 ; v. 42.

[2] Jo. x. 39 f. ; cf. viii. 59, not to speak of still earlier cases.

[3] Mk. xi. 18 ; Mt. xxi. 45, 46 ; Lk. xix. 47.

influence upon the course of events. But that influence, as we see both from the Synoptics and from St. John, was not of such a character as to oblige the former to include the miracle in their narrative at the cost of breaking its order and symmetry.

We should probably all agree to reject such explanations of this silence as the fear of endangering the security of Lazarus and of his sisters. Such a consideration would have passed away when the Gospels took their present shape. A more plausible reason is the fact—strange as it appears—that the Synoptic history is almost entirely [1] confined to the Galilean ministry. Only during the last few days of the Saviour's life does it record what passed in Judæa. As this is the actual state of the case, and as we have to take into account the writers' scheme, whether we like it or not, it is unreasonable to require that a certain event, which falls outside the scheme, should be included in it on pain of being rejected as unhistorical ; and this for the purpose of satisfying *our* conception of what the scheme should contain.

But there is another aspect of this Synoptic omission to be considered. If the earlier Gospels do not recount this miracle, they recount other raisings from the dead ; and it can be argued that the distinction which the modern man is apt to draw between the miracles which they contain and this which they omit, is one that in all probability would not have presented itself with equal force to the writers' minds. In each kind of raising to life again—Jairus' daughter upon the bed on which she had just breathed her last, the widow's son as he was being carried to the grave, Lazarus already for four days in his tomb—the point and kernel of the act of power was the same—the restoration of life, the recall of the departed spirit. *There* lay the miracle. In the main act itself—not in its details—was the sign of the power of the Lord of Life and Death. The

---

[1] As Westcott says, the common plan of the Synoptic Gospels " excluded all working at Jerusalem till the triumphal entry." *Gospel of St. John*, chap. xi., prefatory note.

earlier Evangelists, who tell of what, to our view, may seem the lesser miracles, had not the intellectual inducement, that appeals to some of us, to speak of Lazarus. When, too, we bear in mind that that episode falls outside the plan on which they worked, the omission should present less difficulty. Be this as it may, it should not be allowed to prejudice the historical character of the miracle as recorded.

The historical character: for such we believe it to possess. It is true that it embodies a certain amount of symbolism, and that this is placed by the writer in the lips of Christ Himself. But there is nothing in the dramatic and figurative language so assigned to break the historical sequence of the narrative; and it is characteristic of St. John to seize and use to the utmost for the purpose of his Gospel anything of this nature that recurs to his mind. Yet the narrative is so involved in fact and incident, it touches actual happenings at so many points, that the event, as a whole, refuses to be dissolved into symbol.

Specially unfortunate is the attempt to derive it from the parable of Dives and Lazarus, as though the Evangelist reflecting on Christ's warning that, if men " hear not Moses and the Prophets, neither will they be persuaded if one rose from the dead," had marked its fulfilment in the Jewish attitude towards His own Resurrection. Then, as a consequence of his reflection, he proceeds (so it is alleged) to construct for the edification of the Church a return of Lazarus from Paradise, with its result of hostility on the part of the Jews, and its additional proof of the Saviour's prophecy.

Now, in the first place, such a project would at once cast the gravest doubts upon those claims to write true history which the Evangelist so solemnly advances, and our hesitation would be increased by the manifest desire to link teaching on to what purports to be actual fact. So many separate acts take place from the start from beyond the Jordan onwards. So many different persons are concerned, and are conversed with. Emotions of tenderness, of grief, of sympathy are ascribed to our Lord in a manner that would be wholly presumptuous and even profane if they had no existence in fact.

At one point, it is true that our Lord Himself employs figurative language. Face to face with the realities of life and death, He instinctively sees them against the background of the eternal verities. He can but think of life and death from the spiritual standpoint. As he speaks to Martha about her brother, and remembers the object with which He came into the world, the death of Lazarus and the awakening which was already in His mind become a symbol of that call to newness of life which He felt to be the most insistent that sinful man can ever hear. But this turning of the actual to spiritual profit, this lifting of the ordinary experience of man in the death of the body into the region of the Eternal issues, is all of a piece with Christ's usual practice [1] ; and He at once shows, by proceeding in His course of action, that He is not to be diverted from His purpose to restore the dead to life. He is there for a certain definite object—" I go that I may awake him out of sleep " —and He carries it out. His sense of the deeper meanings of life and death is no restraint upon His will to restore happiness to a desolated home.

But the theory of an imaginative construction of the Evangelist's, whether designed by himself or founded on the striking forecast of the Lucan parable, is negatived by the evidence of friends and foes alike to the fact of the actual occurrence of the miracle. " This thing was not done in a corner." In speaking of it in his Gospel, the Evangelist was challenging the memory of many who, from their own knowledge or from family tradition, were in a position to pass judgment on his narrative. Would he have saddled his Gospel with a recital that, if untrue to fact, could be at once refuted by friendly and hostile readers alike ? As he tells us, " many of the Jews which came to Mary, and had seen the things which Jesus did, believed on Him "; and afterwards, at Bethany, " much

[1] Cf. Mk. ii. 3 f.; x. 51 f.; Jo. ix. 1 f.; vi. 5–15, 27.

people of the Jews . . . came not for Jesus' sake only, but that they might see Lazarus also, whom He had raised from the dead " ; and at the public entry to Jerusalem on the following day, " for this cause the people also met Him, for that they heard that He had done this miracle." [1] So much for the witness of friendly, or at least not unfriendly, people.

But still stronger is the evidence of foes.   The Evangelist, as we have seen, lays great stress on the effect of the miracle upon the minds of the Jewish authorities.   When news of it is brought to them, they at once call the Sanhedrin together, at which, be it noticed, they admit that " this Man doeth many miracles." [2]   They express the fear that, as the result of this exhibition of supernatural power, He will win over the allegiance of the people to such an extent that the Romans will strip them of whatever sovereignty and freedom they still possessed.   Not only does knowledge of the miracle produce this state of tension and alarm among the members of the council, but it hardens their long-growing animosity to the point of action.   The Evangelist marks the day as a turning point in the way of the Cross.   Hatred slumbering and uncertain how to act now sets to work to scheme and plan.   " From that day forth they took council together for to put Him to death." [3]

The endeavour to remove the raising of Lazarus from the plane of history to that of figure and symbol appears, therefore, to have no success.   The roots of the story go down too deep and are too greatly ramified.   To tear them up is to lacerate the Gospel, and that, too, at a point in its narrative at which its solemnity is increasingly manifest and at which its claim to truth is about to be pressed most urgently.[4]

In his narrative of the last days at Jerusalem, of the

[1] Jo. xi. 45 ; xii. 9, 18.   According to St. Matthew, there was a great crowd, Matt. xxi. 8.   Why ? St. Jo. xii. 18, explains.
[2] Jo. xi. 47.   [3] Jo. xi. 53.
[4] " For historical criticism the Johannine narrative remains, unexplained, and inexplicable if we decline to admit its fidelity to fact." B. Weiss, *Leben Jesu*, ii., p. 396 ; cf. *ib.*, p. 394 ; Sanday, *Criticism of the Fourth Gospel*, p. 170 ; B. Weiss, *ad* Jo. xi. 43.

Cross and the Burial, the Fourth Evangelist shows acquaintance with the Synoptic records together with many indications of distinct information. There is close agreement
in matters of fact.[1] There is also a large addition of
material which is not to be found in the earlier Gospels.[2]
The writer has seen and heard much of which the other
writers were unaware, or which they did not see fit to relate.
At the same time, he omits certain details of deep interest
and value ; either because he regards their repetition as
unnecessary, or because they did not come within his
immediate purview.[3] There is little or no trace of defective
knowledge. Where we can detect so many points of contact
with the earlier Gospels, we are justified in attributing
omissions to deliberate intention rather than to ignorance
of the true course of events.

The Resurrection narrative of St. John presents features
peculiar to itself. Here, too, there is close resemblance to

---

[1] With Jo. xii. 1-9, cf. Mk. xiv. 3-10 ; Matt. xxvi. 6-14. With
Jo. xii. 12-16, cf. Mk. xi. 1-12 ; Matt. xxi. 1-10 ; Lk. xix. 29-39. With
Jo. xiii. 21-31, cf. Mk. xiv. 18-22 ; Matt. xxvi. 21-26 ; Lk. xxii. 21-24.
With Jo. xviii. 2, πολλάκις συνήχθη ὁ Ἰησοῦς ἐκεῖ, cf. Lk. xxii. 39, ἐπορεύθη
κατὰ τὸ ἔθος. With Jo. xviii. 3-12, cf. Mk. xiv. 43-48 ; Matt. xxvi.
47-55 ; Lk. xxii. 47-52. With Mk. xiv. 58 ; xv. 29 ; Matt. xxvi. 61, cf.
Jo. ii. 19.

[2] He claims to speak with special knowledge of the motives and action
of Judas, xii. 4-8 ; xiii. 26 f. The " sacrament " of the washing of the
disciples' feet, as it has been called, is found only in Jo. xiii. 2-18. The
discourse after Supper in the Upper Room and on the way to the Garden
stands alone, Jo. xiv.–xviii. At the betrayal, he gives his own account
of what occurred as it comes vividly to memory : the flashing of the
lanterns, the majestic answer of the Saviour with its effect on the officers
of the priests, the name of the servant wounded by Peter, xviii. 3 f. He
notes that Christ was first brought before Annas, who sent Him to the
acting High Priest Caiaphas. " Another disciple " (himself) brings
Peter into the palace. He has special knowledge of the interview between
Pilate and Christ, xviii. 33-39 ; xix. 4-6, 8-16. He notes the three
languages of the title on the Cross (cf. Lk. xxiii. 38 only), the impatient
answer of Pilate to the expostulations of the priests, the seamless coat,
xix. 23-25. His own presence at the Cross with the Mother of the Lord,
and the parting charge, are recounted by himself alone. Again, he shows
himself to be minutely informed as to what took place at the Cross, in the
last moments ; the cry " It is finished " ; the piercing of the Saviour's
side, with its result, so solemnly attested, xix. 30-36. While in accord
with the earlier Gospels in his story of the burial, he adds the deeply
interesting fact that Nicodemus took part in it, specifying the amount of
the spices which he brought, adding that the burial was carried out
according to Jewish (i.e. not in the Egyptian) manner, xix. 38 f. ; v.
H. Holtzmann, ad loc.

[3] V. p. 118. He omits certain of the Last Words from the Cross.

the Synoptic account in the main facts of the story. All the Gospels speak of the visit to the sepulchre in the early morning of the first day of the week and imply that it was empty. All relate appearances of the risen Christ to disciples. There is divergence in the manner and circumstances of the appearances. St. John shows direct and first-hand knowledge. Certain details are fixed in his memory. The experiences of Mary Magdalene are given very fully. She is the only woman among those who went to the grave whom he cares to mention. It is she who brings the news of the empty grave to St. Peter and " the disciple whom Jesus loved." They at once act upon her tidings, and the incident is told with the fulness and minuteness of detail which point to a recital of personal experiences. St. Matthew and St. Mark,[1] followed by the " Gospel of Peter," [2] lead us to infer that the meeting place of the risen Lord with the disciples was Galilee. Yet both St. Matthew and the Marcan appendix narrate an appearance to the women, or to Mary Magdalene, on the day of the Resurrection, and at Jerusalem ; while both St. Luke and St. John speak of appearances in Jerusalem to the disciples, St. John also coinciding with St. Matthew in recounting an appearance to Mary Magdalene on the same day.[3] Thus, it will be seen that the balance of the evidence inclines to the narrative of St. John. Without excluding appearances in Galilee, to which St. Matthew and St. Mark point,[4] and which St. Matthew and St. John record,[5] we are justified in regarding appearances at Jerusalem as historically certain. The scenes of the appearances are not mutually exclusive. There was time for each.[6]

---

[1] Matt. xxviii. 7, 10, 16 ; Mk. xvi. 7.

[2] vv. 59, 60, Preuschen, *Antilegomena*, p. 20.

[3] *V*. Loofs, *D. Auferstehungsberichte u. ihr Wert.* pp. 26, 32, 36.

[4] Matt. xxviii. 7 ; Mk. xvi. 7.

[5] Matt. xxviii. 9, 10 ; Jo. xxi. (the Appendix).

[6] No argument against this view can be drawn from Lk. xxiv. 50. If the Ascension is referred to, there is no note of time to make it synchronous with the Resurrection. Besides, both St. Luke elsewhere (Acts i. 3, 9) and St. Paul (Acts xiii. 31) speak of a lengthened interval (" 40 days " ; " He was seen many days of them ") between the two events. No evidence to the contrary can be drawn from the Epistle of Barnabas, xv. 9, as Schmiedel, *Encycl. Bibl.*, cols. 4059 f., and Harnack,

After considering these instances of conflicting or, at least, of differing representation between the two main Gospel narratives, the Synoptics and St. John, we may try to answer the question with which we started : What was the attitude of the Fourth Evangelist towards the three earlier works which lay before him ?

We have seen that it was not one of servitude. In no case does he appear to be bound by their authority. This position has important consequences. He feels free to criticise ; although the results of his criticism are never paraded. He modifies or corrects by silent substitution. Whatever theory of verbal infallibility came to be adopted in certain quarters in after years, it gets no sanction from the action of the Fourth Evangelist. But he never refers to the need of correction or to the fact that he is supplying it. Is this negative attitude due to respect or indifference ? We think that neither alternative is involved. He was not deterred from amending the earlier writers by any exaggerated feeling of deference ; yet he nowhere betrays any sign that he is unmindful of their general claims to attention. The answer lies rather in the position and character of the Evangelist himself, and in the occasion and circumstances in which he wrote. He could simply tell his tale as one whose knowledge is first-hand. Besides, he was writing, not for critics in the outside world, but for a close corporation of converts and adherents who knew that he had moved in the scenes which he described and had heard the sacred voice whose echoes are given back from his pages. He did not need to explain differences, or to make those reservations which would be required of one who stood in a different relation to the substance of his narrative. On the part of the community, their certainty of the truth of the main strain of his narrative outweighed any difficulties

---

Dogmengeschichte, i., p. 146, suggest. There the writer is giving the reason for the observance of the eighth day (1st day of the week). It is because Christ both rose and ascended (he seems to place the Ascension on a Sunday) on the " eighth day " ; but, *not on the same eighth day*, διὸ καὶ ἄγομεν τὴν ἡμέραν τὴν ὀγδόην εἰς εὐφροσύνην, ἐν ᾗ καὶ ὁ Ἰησοῦς ἀνέστη ἐκ νεκρῶν καὶ φανερωθεὶς ἀνέβη εἰς οὐρανούς.

which seemed to point to the contrary; while the wonderful spiritual power of the book compelled its acceptance.

But difficulties remain. There are problems which are still unsolved. The old methods of harmonising what is clearly incompatible are out of date. They do not satisfy. Rather than twist into apparent agreement things which decline to correspond, it is better to note the differences and to leave the task of reconciliation to the future, when further study and, perhaps, discovery, may bring the discordant elements together.[1]

But it is a meditation rather than a set narrative, an old man's reproduction of an ever-living and unforgotten past, the record of a personal experience. It is Jesus the Lord, not as He appeared to the world or even to the main body of His disciples at the moment; but as He was revealed to a devout and intimate follower through the power of the Holy Spirit.[2] The Fourth Gospel is the Gospel of " Christ manifested in remembrance " in accordance with His own promise as the writer recalls it. It is this character —the spiritualising of historic fact without impairing its actuality—that has endeared the Fourth Gospel to the people of God through all the Christian ages. The value of the Synoptic narrative lies in the presentation of Christ as He lived among men in the days of His flesh, and in that comparative absence of theological interpretation which is one of its chief characteristics. The value of St. John lies not only in the historic truth to which its writer makes solemn claim, but in the inspired interpretation which he places upon his narrative. It shows us Christ

---

[1] The two following paragraphs have appeared in rather different form in an earlier book by the present writer.

[2] " He is writing and selecting in the light of his later experiences." H. S. Holland, *Phil. and the Fourth Gospel*, p. 201 ; cf. J. Armitage Robinson, *Study of the Gospels*, p. 149, " The old disciple needs no documents, to compile, as others might compile, a laboured history. The whole is present in his memory, shaped by years of reflection, illuminated by the experience of a lifetime. He knows the Christ far better now than he knew Him in Galilee or Jerusalem half a century before. He knew, Who and what He is, as he hardly guessed then." *V.* Inge, *Personal Idealism*, p. 61, " St. John allows the experience of the Christian Church to throw light upon the Gospel history instead of making the historical records bear the whole weight of the Church's faith."

the Lord as revealed by the Holy Spirit—the same Christ, but, as when He stood on the Mount, transfigured.

Those who, in the pursuit of a reverent criticism, have most deeply investigated the problems that arise in comparing the two great streams of Gospel narrative, admit the surpassing value of the one which completes the fourfold presentation of Christ, Son of Man, Son of God.   They own that here we have the fullest and truest portrait of our Redeemer.[1] Ὁ ἐπιστήθιος, " the man who lay upon (the Saviour's) breast," [2] has looked most deeply into the truth of His Divine-human being.   He knew Christ as no one else had known Him ; and out of the fullness of his store of memories, like a wise householder, he has brought forth things new and old : old in their actual setting in the long, historic past, new in the fresh light reflected on them by the Spirit Who inspired him.

[1] " Its greatness, its supreme and unique position in the literature of the world depends on its truth."   Ramsay, *The First Christian Century*, p. 89.

[2] Cf. Origen, *In Joan*, Tom. i., p. 438 c ; 6 c. (Ed. Bened. vol. iv.).

K

CHAPTER X

The Discourses of Christ

WE have seen that, apart from the Fourth Gospel, the Synoptic record of the leading events and episodes of our Lord's ministry present an insoluble problem.

Occurrences take place for which there is no adequate ground. Momentous issues appear, and they lack explanation. A supplementary Gospel is clearly needed, if the course of the ministry is to be unrolled before the Church. We cannot doubt that a sense of this requirement was a moving cause of the production of St. John. Quietly and decisively, with the sure touch of one who knows, the writer has filled up many of the blanks and reconciled many of what would otherwise appear as inconsistencies left by the threefold narrative.

Nor are we left in doubt as to the measure of his success. Problems there are still, and they are likely to remain. But it is possible to obtain—what was beyond men's reach before—a clear account, not only of the course of the ministry, but of the causes which brought it to an end. If any success has attended the various efforts that have been made to write a Life of Christ, it has been largely due to the work of the Fourth Evangelist. What is true of the narrative portions of the ministry is hardly borne out when we turn to the record of our Lord's speeches and sayings. So far from confirming and illuminating the Synoptic report, the discourses of the Fourth Gospel are thought by many to lack the character of genuine and authentic utterances.

There is good ground for believing that, in the Synoptic ecords of His sayings, we have *practically* [1] the *ipsissima erba* of our Lord. This is particularly the case with ayings preserved by " Q " and, still more certainly, with hose which are found in St. Mark as well as in " Q." For hey come to us on the word of two Apostolic hearers, one f whom, St. Peter, had been admitted to close intimacy vith his Master.

The other was St. Matthew, who, as Papias tells us, " made a collection of the sayings of Christ in the Hebrew ongue." [2] That this book was compiled by the Apostle lay by day as the words were spoken is rendered highly probable by the fact that, before his call to discipleship, he ad been in the habit, as a collector of taxes, of punctiliously ecording the transactions of the day. This habit he would ot lose on his change of career ; but it takes a different orm. He has another purpose in life. He now records he sayings of his Master almost as they come from His lips. Ie felt with the Psalmist, " The law of Thy mouth is better o me than thousands of gold and silver." [3] He had left ll to follow Him.[4]

But, however this may be, St. Matthew's collection of hrist's sayings is now thought to have been formed, if not uring his lifetime, at most a few years later. It is generally dentified with the material common to the First and Third ospels—largely consisting of sayings—which is not found 1 St. Mark, and to which the term Quelle (Q) is assigned.[5]

We may therefore feel assured that in the reports of ur Lord's sayings for which the earlier Gospels are respon- ible, while making all allowance for verbal changes due to ranslation from the Aramaic in which they were spoken, nd for certain glosses and interpolations that have crept

[1] *V.* Wellhausen, *Einleit. in d. drei ersten Evang.*, p. 42 ; J. Weiss, *esus von Nazareth*, p. 157 ; C. F. Nolloth, *The Historic Personality of hrist*, 1911, p. 29.
[2] In Euseb., *H.E.*, iii. 39.
[3] Ps. cxix. 72.
[4] Lk. v. 28.
[5] On the early composition of " Q," *v.* the present writer's *The Rise the Christian Religion*, 1917, p. 23, n. 1.

into the text, we have the equivalent of His sayings whic
are recorded in them.[1]

But it is evident that the first three Gospels contain bu
a small part of His teaching ; so small that we may we
wonder, when we think Who was the speaker and wha
issues hang upon His words.[2] To one at least of H
adherents this thought presented itself and, late in life an
long after the words were spoken, he set to work to wri
down what had often been the subject of his own ora
teaching—sayings and discourses, either unknown to th
earlier writers, or if heard by the first-hand authoriti
which they employed, little noticed and understood.

So that at once we get material for comparison.
certain rivalry seems to be set up. These dialogues an
allegories, these " metaphysical " discourses, so unlike tho
of the earlier Gospels in form and substance, how do the
stand when brought side by side with them ? Are thes
authentic sayings of the Teacher Whose voice we hear i
the Sermon on the Mount and in those parables and bri
sayings which are their own best proof that they proceede
from Him and from no one else ?

We can at once reply that, if the Synoptic account o
what our Lord said in the course of His Ministry must b
taken as the criterion to which all other accounts must b
referred when we come to test their genuineness, there woul
be great difficulty in receiving the Johannine speeches an
sayings as His words.

But do the Synoptic Gospels so set the norm for a
reporting of Christ's sayings,[3] that every departure fro
it is to be ruled out as untrustworthy ? [4] We think no

---

[1] V. Salmon, The Human Element in the Gospels, p. 274, " The mo
I study the Gospels, the more convinced I am that we have in the
contemporaneous history . . . stories told of Jesus . . . which had be
put into writing while He was yet alive." E. Meyer takes a simil
view, Ursprung und Anfänge des Christentums, i. 1921, p. 236.

[2] " Paul's doctrine of Christ, unless invented, pre-supposes a larg
amount of dogmatic material in Christ's sayings than the Synopti
contain." Lücke, Comment. über Evang. Joh., i., p. 127.

[3] Cf. Lücke, op. cit., ii., p. 96 ; i., p. 121 f.

[4] This appears to be Dr. Rashdall's view : " If we accept the Synopt
discourses as substantially authentic . . . it is impossible to regard t
Johannine discourses as equally accurate reports." Mod. Churchma
Sept. 1921, p. 279, n. 2.

or the following reasons. Taken in the mass, they form a
very slight volume presenting mere samples of teaching
hat appears to have been given daily for a period of more
han two years. They largely consist of parables spoken
to people who, on the whole, remained outside the circle of
actual disciples and adherents. There was little esoteric
teaching in these more or less popular discourses. Afterwards, when alone with the Twelve, our Lord would disclose
the inner meaning of what He had been saying, if He were
asked to do so.[1] But in many cases the meaning lay upon
the surface.[2] Only here and there we come upon a saying
that needed interpretation. This is generally true of the
whole range of the Synoptic teaching.

Now it might be anticipated that One, Who came to
reveal the Father and in Whose Person, *apart from His
teaching*, lay deep mysteries of Being, which suddenly
flashed into sight and were as suddenly withdrawn from it,
would on occasion and to chosen and receptive minds,
speak of the hidden things ; that there would be times
when He would invite thought on the nature and mode of
the Revelation He had come to bring ; when He would
care to direct attention to Himself. We are prepared to
expect such departures from the ordinary course of His
teaching by indications afforded by the Synoptic writers
themselves. It is not only in the Fourth Gospel that our
Lord calls upon men to reflect upon His Person and His
claims, or asserts an authority and power which belong to
the province of God.[3]

If, then, in the Fourth Gospel, greater stress is laid upon
this element of His teaching than elsewhere, its authentic
character is by no means imperilled. On the contrary, the
later date of its composition, combined with the natural
effect of meditation on the deeper sayings, would lead us to

[1] Cf. Mt. xiii. 36 ; Mk. iv. 10, 34 ; Lk. viii. 9.
[2] Mt. xiii. 51.
[3] *V.* Mt. xvi. 13 f. and parallels ; Mt. xi. 27 f. ; Lk. x. 22 ; Mt. v.
21 f., 27 f., 33 f. ; Mk. ii. 5 f. But according to Foakes Jackson, " the
Synoptic Jesus preached God and the Kingdom, not as we believe Himself." *Mod. Churchman*, Sept. 1921, p. 234.

expect such emphasis and even to doubt a record which bore no sign of it.

But it is easy to show that it would be in the highest degree unreasonable to expect similarity in reports of sayings which were uttered on different occasions and in various circumstances, because they were spoken by the same person.[1] It is even objected that so many of our Lord's discourses in St. John take the form of dialogue, or of argument with groups of people, modes of conversation which are not indeed wanting, but are less frequent in the other Gospels.[2] On what principle of literary criticism can this objection be justified? If an ordinary writer or speaker, possessed of some imagination and adaptability, varies his method and style to suit the occasion, is it probable that an unique Personality like our Lord would speak in the same style and manner on all occasions, on all subjects, to all people?

Yet this is what seems to be demanded by a certain group of critics.[3] Because Christ spoke in parables in the greater portion of the sayings handed down by the Synoptic writers, He must needs speak thus, if any further report of His utterences can be received as genuine; and if the substance of His teaching, as we have it in the earlier Gospels, dealt preponderantly with the moral and spiritual realities which are summed up in " the Kingdom of God," no additional Gospel writing which had other ends in view can make good its claim to authority. The burden of the Synoptic sayings is " The Kingdom of God." That of the Fourth Gospel is the King Himself; and the change, so they say, is fatal to its authenticity.[4]

---

[1] V. Lücke, *Comment. über Evang. Joh.*, i., p. 124 ; Swete, *The Last Discourse and Prayer of our Lord*, p. viii.

[2] Mk. viii. 32 f.; vii. 24 f.; ix. 17 f.; x. 17 f.; xi. 27 f.; xii. 18 f.

[3] V. Loisy, *Le Quatr. Evangile*, pp. 75, 89.

[4] Thus Scholten says, " The Synoptic Jesus sets in the foreground of His preaching not Himself but the subject for which He lives, and herein consists His moral grandeur. With the Fourth Evangelist, Jesus Himself is and must be, according to the author's conception of doctrine, the main burden of His preaching . . . he not only preaches about Christ, but as his chosen dramatic style demanded, places the preaching of Christ in Jesus' own mouth." *D. Evang. nach Joh.*, p. 237. V. Jülicher,

This demand might have some justification if St. John were contemporary with the Synoptic Gospels. The dissonance, if such there be, would need much explanation, and it would seem heightened by the evident concurrence of the three with one another. But St. John appeared, perhaps, a generation after the latest of them. The writer had read and to some extent made use of them.[1]

If he differed in his conception of what a Gospel should contain, he did so with his eyes open and with clear intention.[2]

To bear this in mind would obviate many of the objections which have been raised and repeated, with parrot-like fidelity, to the disadvantage of the Fourth Gospel. Is it a valid ground of complaint that the writer felt free to

Einleitung in d. N.T., p. 421 (*E.T.*), " A Jesus Who preached alternately in the manner of the Sermon on the Mount and of Jo. xiv.–xvii. is a psychological impossibility." In reply to Scholten, it is to be noted that the Johannine Christ, like the Synoptic, does speak of the Kingdom of God, iii. 3, 5. As to Jülicher's statement, our knowledge of the psychology of Christ's teaching does not justify so dogmatic a pronouncement.

R. Otto, after saying that the utterances of Christ are neither adequate nor adapted to the construction of a theory of the " Self-consciousness of Jesus," remarks that " Jesus makes the ' Kingdom,' its blessedness and its righteousness, not Himself, the content of His preaching and of His sayings. . . . What we meet with in allusions to Himself (Selbstaussagen) is occasional and fragmentary." This is so far true, that the definite assertion of His Person and claims did not constitute the main subject of His teaching. But for all that, as we have seen, He was fully convinced of the fact that the right relation to Himself is the chief concern of man as he passes through life. Otto is here insisting that belief in authority may be aroused by self-assertion, but not that peculiar experience, that spontaneous insight and cognition of the Holy, which we find in the confession, " we know that this is indeed the Christ " (Jo. iv. 42). *Das Heilige*, 1922, p. 184 f. ; cf. p. 189.

[1] This is proved by both internal and external evidence. Cf. Jo. iii. 24, with Mk. i. 14 ; Mt. iv. 12. *V.* Clem. Alex. in Euseb., *H.E.*, vi. 14 ; Zahn, *Einleitung in d. N.T.*, ii., p. 507 f. *V.* above, p. 111, n. 3.

[2] But with all the difference of representation, it is true that " the ideas (of the Fourth Gospel) are the ideas which animate the sayings in the Synoptic Gospels." Burkitt, *The Gospel History and its Transmission*, p. 237. " To the religious consciousness of Christendom there has never been any hesitation in recognising the profound agreement between the Synoptic and the Johannine presentations of Jesus Christ." Inge in *Dict. of Christ and the Gospels*, i., p. 889. " In the present day, the connection (of the Synoptic Gospels) with Johannine thought has been increasingly recognised." Procksch, *Petrus und Johannes*, p. 2. H. Holtzmann gives the following instances of Synoptic sayings found in St. John : ii. 19 ; iv. 44 ; v. 8 ; vi. 20 ; xii. 7, 8, 25, 27 ; xiii. 16, 20, 21, 38 ; xiv. 31 ; xv. 20 ; xvi. 32 ; xviii. 11, 20, 37, 39. *Einleitung in d. N.T.*, p. 430.

report what specially struck him when the words were spoken and what, after years of reflection, seemed to need the telling ?

At such a point in our discussion as this, it seems legitimate to take into consideration the practically universal belief of the second century that the writer had seen the Divine Speaker and listened to His words.

We may now turn to what appear to be positive indications of the genuineness of the Johannine discourses, when brought into comparison with the Synoptic sayings.

The writer reports discourses which explain events and occasions that would otherwise lack support and background. The universal insistence in the early Church upon the necessity of the two sacraments of Baptism and the Eucharist finds its justification in the will of Christ as set forth in the three earlier Gospels and by St. Paul. But until the Fourth Gospel was given to the world, men had no authoritative *written* account of the deep spiritual reasons that lay at the ground of His action. If no such document had ever existed ; if we did not possess St. John iii. and vi., the Church would be confronted with a great difficulty. We know that from the first the two great sacraments of Baptism and the Eucharist have been regarded as of perpetual and universal obligation. But apart from these chapters of the Fourth Gospel, there is no authoritative teaching of our Lord upon their meaning. Yet the practice of the Sacraments has always been referred to His initiative. We cannot doubt that if He inaugurated them, He would be careful to give some explanation of them. This consideration points to the authentic character of the discourses in question.

The command to baptize all nations [1] receives the explanation of its meaning and urgency in the discourse with Nicodemus. The true significance of the Eucharist only became manifest when the discourse in the Synagogue at Capernaum was published. In each case, the Sacrament is shown to be rooted in the fundamental relations of God

[1] Mt. xxviii. 19 ; cf. Lk. xxiv. 47.

and man, and to be the application of the principle of the Incarnation to the spiritual needs of the individual.

Now, although we cannot say that the appropriateness of these two discourses would of itself confirm the fact of their origin, it goes far to lessen the weight of many of the objections which are brought against them. From the very first, the two great sacramental rites with which the Church started on her course took their sanction from what was believed to be her Lord's own will and pleasure. But there was little knowledge of the reasons that underlay the rites among the rank and file of disciples. It took time to adjust thought to the true nature of the Lord's Person, and to understand sufficiently for the needs of practical life the necessity for gaining and maintaining spiritual union with Him.[1] The writer of the Fourth Gospel lived through this period, and with a mind open to the necessities of the time he brought out from the stores of his memory the substance of His Master's teaching on the subject.

When we think of the place which is occupied by the two great Sacraments of our Redemption in the life and religion of Christian people, a place justified by the fact of Christ's own appointment of them, we are not surprised that, on the showing of the latest Gospel, He took occasion to reveal the principles on which they rest, and the deeplying necessity of their observance for all who would profit by His saving work. The absence of any such teaching from the Gospel records would constitute a difficulty hard to overcome. Its presence is eminently natural.

This impression is strengthened when we study the two discourses and observe their historical setting. They each bear upon the surface the marks of their Divine origin. Who but Christ Himself could have conceived and uttered teaching of such spiritual depth and unchanging truth, going down into the inner mysteries of man's relation to God and of eternal life? A view which regards these profound discourses as the composition of an inventive

---

[1] This is evident from the effect of His teaching on disciples as reported, Jo. vi. 60 f.

scribe of the second century is self-condemned. As a mere literary question, apart from the religious issues involved, the thing is impossible. Not only was the period incapable of producing the mind required for such an effort, if we may judge from the literature that has come down to us, but the discourses themselves show that they could only have proceeded at the time stated and from the Speaker to Whom they are referred.

And this judgment is upheld by their historical setting and by the circumstances attending their utterance.[1] In each case there was an audience, and we can learn the effect upon them of the spoken words. Nicodemus vanishes from the foreground and we are told of the state of mind in which he parted from our Lord. But we meet with him again, and his conduct goes to confirm the supposition that his interview with Christ had made a deep impression upon him. He, who had shrunk from approach to Christ except under cover of darkness, now stands up boldly, as a member of the Sanhedrin, to plead for justice and a fair hearing for Him. And when the last offices of love and care for the Saviour, for Whom he had vainly pleaded, are to be carried out, he comes forward without fear to take his share in the sacred task. The once timid[2] seeker after Truth is the open confessor of the Truth which he had found.

There is a similar kind of confirmation to be found in the historical circumstances attending the other discourse. It is the one *public* utterance of our Lord's Galilean ministry reported in the Fourth Gospel. There is no attempt on the part of the Evangelist to enhance its effect upon the crowd. On the contrary, he faithfully informs us that it was ill-received. Murmurs interrupted its delivery, when the expectation of bodily advantage was found to be vain, and the speaker led their thoughts into regions that were too high for them. As He proceeded to unveil the secret of true spiritual life and its sustenance, and to concentrate

---

[1] We are prepared for the visit of Nicodemus to Christ by the statement in the previous chapter (ii. 23) that "when He was in Jerusalem at the feast, many believed in His Name."

[2] Jo. iii. 2.

their attention upon His own Person, the revulsion of feeling increased, and we are plainly told that so great was the offence given, that even of His own disciples and adherents " many went back and walked no more with Him."

So far is the whole recital from being—what so many attribute to the Fourth Gospel—an unhistorical attempt to deify the human Prophet of Nazareth, that it is perhaps the most signal instance in the Gospels of the bare and faithful admission of the failure and disillusionment that so often attended our Lord's efforts for the salvation of men.

Thus, in both of these reports of discourses and of their surroundings, the Evangelist unconsciously supplies answers to doubts and objections as to their authentic character.[1]

The discourse with the woman of Samaria contains much of that element of the unexpected which is so characteristic of the Fourth Gospel. The place, a Samaritan village, the strange scene of an interview between One Who came to fulfil the Law and one who, according to every exponent of that Law, had no part or lot in Israel ; still more, the character and poor intelligence of the woman contrasted with the depth and elevation of the Saviour's language—all these incongruities startle and surprise us, when we try to enter into the story with fresh minds, unbiassed by the influences of old and familiar association.

The earlier Gospels are not without interviews which bear a certain resemblance to this. The Syro-Phenician woman, the one grateful Samaritan among the ten lepers that were healed, Mary Magdalene, Simon the leper, were all recipients of our Lord's gracious dealing. The story in itself, therefore, is not to be rejected *prima facie* on the ground of a too daring improbability. It was not entirely exceptional for Him to bestow His favours of teaching or consideration in unlikely quarters.[2]

---

[1] Harmony with Synoptic accounts should be noticed. With Jo. vi. 68, cf. Mt. xiv. 33 ; xvi. 16. " As in the Synoptics, Peter is the great Confessor." Zahn, *Einleitung*, ii. p. 566. *V.* further, p. 161 f.

[2] " In no place in his book does John show so clearly as in the account of the sojourn with the Samaritans that, while attending his Master, he has beheld with his own eyes the scene of his narrative." Zahn in *Neue Kirchl. Zeitschrift*, March, 1908, p. 207.

At the same time, we cannot fail to be struck with the wide range of subject, the lofty and spiritual character of the treatment, the wealth of new revelation, which make the discourse unparalleled among those that have come down to us. Without the reserve habitually practised by Him, our Lord proclaims Himself as the Giver of the Water of Life, and tells of its effect on its recipients. From that topic He passes on to foretell the universality of true religion, set free from its present barriers of place and custom. From the thought of religion He rises to a revelation of its supreme Object, and discloses the great fact that God is Spirit and, being such, requires from all who seek Him worship that corresponds to His own Nature.

Then, to crown this unveiling of the great realities that underlie the true relation of God and man, our Lord discloses that the Revealer Himself—the Christ Whom the Samaritan expected—stood before her in person : " I that speak unto thee am He."

It is perhaps true to say that the whole discourse, unique and, so far, isolated, as it stands in the Gospel records, is its own best proof that it embodies actual speech of Christ. Its daring excludes the thought of fabrication. The contrasts and anomalies presented by the historical setting and circumstances demand its reception. Its paradox in occasion and choice of subject proclaims its truth.

When we have said this, we may go on to find authentication in other sayings of our Lord in the same Gospel. There is analogy in vi. 27, 35 ; vii. 37-40, to the portion which deals with the " living water." There is the same forecast of the universal character of the true religion in the discourse suggested to our Lord by the request of the Greeks to see Him : " I, if I be lifted up from the earth, will draw all men unto Me."

Thus, for all its unique and striking character, the discourse is no errant block in the Johannine formation. It has its points of contact both in thought and setting and, as we have seen, is not without support in Synoptic incidents.[1]

[1] Cf. p. 140, n. 2.

The discourse contained in chapters xiv.–xviii. is remarkable not so much by reason of its length ; that is paralleled by the Sermon on the Mount and the eschatological discourse in St. Matthew xxiv. 4–xxvi. Rather, it is the mingled strain of counsel and comfort for the disciples and of personal communion with the Father, which marks it out in form and character from other discourses ; while the developed stage of our Lord's own Messianic consciousness that it presents raises questions of Christology which need investigation.

But, it is first to be remarked that some such farewell discourse as this is eminently natural. The occasion required it. The meagre account of Christ's language during the last meeting with His disciples before the end came, which is supplied in the Synoptic narrative, leaves us quite certain that it covers a very small part of what actually passed. Putting St. John for the moment out of consideration, we should feel that our Lord, at such a time, *must* have said much more than we are told. With the end of His ministry before Him, with His passion and death full in view, there were certain things which needed to be said—words of consolation and encouragement, of hope and warning. For, *He was not surprised into His fate.* " He knew what was in man," and the knowledge was a revelation of what would befall Him. Everything points to the certainty that He would have much to say before He left His disciples. Why so little has found a place in the Synoptic report it is hard to tell. But one or two considerations should be borne in mind. The First and Third Evangelists are dependent for the closing period on St. Mark. Their common source (" Q ") appears to have ended, although they each record incidents emanating from their own special sources.[1] But their generally close adhesion to St. Mark shows that they regard that Gospel writing as their chief authority. Behind it was the witness of St. Peter. Now, very early in that momentous evening, the Apostle received the warning of his coming denial of his

[1] *E.g.* Lk. xxii. 24–30 ; xxiii. 26–33 ; Mt. xxvii. 51–54.

Master [1]—a warning speedily realised. Is it not probable that the circumstances of this moral breakdown would colour all his subsequent reflection on the events of the evening? His contrition, his passionate sorrow for his defection would make him ill at ease in all his references to what occurred, as he looked back upon it during his Apostolic ministry; while it is not to be forgotten that the agitation which must have followed upon our Lord's warning would have greatly impeded his attentive reception of any lengthy utterances on the same occasion.

These considerations, if not fully accounting for the Synoptic omissions, may help to remove certain of the difficulties which attend them. But there is the Fourth Gospel. Here we have at any rate a recital which appears germane to the circumstances. It is in harmony with the historical situation. There is, indeed, much which lacks a parallel in form and style with the Synoptic version of our Lord's sayings; but nothing that in substance conflicts with what we have good reason for regarding as the true expression of His mind, as reported either by the first three Evangelists or by St. John himself elsewhere. Moreover, the occasion was one which made a special appeal to a disciple so near to the Master's heart. As he noted the absence of any adequate record of the sayings of that last evening in the three Gospels which were familiar to him, it is not surprising that he was moved by every impulse of love and gratitude to supply the blank and to bequeath to his disciples and the Church at large a faithful memorial of his Master's words.[2]

But can we assure ourselves that we have in these chapters an accurate report of what was said? It has been alleged that their historical character is placed in doubt

[1] Matthew, following Mark, places the warning after the departure from the Upper Room. Luke, with whom John concurs, assigns it to the time previous to the departure for the Garden. Practically it is a case of the agreement of two sources against one—Matthew–Mark.

[2] Cf. the analogy presented by Plato's account in the *Phædo* of the sayings of Socrates as he waited for the cup of hemlock. W. Pater remarks: " The Phædo of Plato has impressed most readers as a veritable record of those last discourses of Socrates." *Plato and Platonism*, p. 94. V. W. D. Ross, *Aristotle's Metaphysics*, 1924, i. p. xliv.

by their lack of harmony with the Synoptic story of the Agony in Gethsemane ; [1] or again, by their substitution of the sending of the Comforter for the Synoptic promise of the παρουσία.[2] Exception is also taken to the misunderstandings and questionings of disciples, which intervene at different points.[3]

The first of these three objections raises the whole question of the supposed contradiction between the Johannine Christology and that of the earliest stratum of the Synoptic account. The contrast has been sharply defined in the terse saying, "Here (in the Synoptics) the Man ; there (John) the God." [4] And the conclusion has been drawn, that if the human portrait is confessedly the true one, the Divine picture is a later retouching of the original. They cannot both, it is said, be true to fact and, as we must choose between them, we should have no hesitation in making our choice.

Now, a problem of this kind cannot be made the subject of alternatives in such a way that the truth of one necessarily excludes the other. It is easy to show that the subject-matter itself is not one that can be so apportioned between mutually exclusive terms as to bear the separation which the *entweder-oder* of a ruthless alternative requires. For in each current of Gospel tradition, elements both human and Divine are clearly to be detected. It is contrary to the evidence to maintain that the divinity of Jesus is so prominent in the Fourth Gospel as to leave no place for the delineation of the man. Where, as in that Gospel, can we find so complete a picture of one who was in all

---

[1] *V.* Clemen, *D. Entstehung des Joh. Evang.*, p. 254. He sees in Lk. xxii. 40 f. a weakening of the description of Christ's mental suffering, which the first two Evangelists give, in deference to the later Christology, a weakening carried to the point of entire suppression by St. John. But St. Luke is, if anything, more insistent than the other Synoptists in the portrayal of the Agony, and if St. John omits it altogether, there was no need to repeat what had already been thrice told circumstantially.

[2] Wellhausen, *D. Evang. Joh.*, p. 62, " Instead of the prophecy of the Parousia in the Synoptics, stands here (Jo. xiv.), also in prophetic style, a discourse in which the Parousia is replaced by something else."

[3] Jo. xiv. 5, 8, 22. *V.* Clemen, *ib.*, p. 255.

[4] Wernle, *D. Quellen des Lebens Jesu*, p. 25.

points subject to trial and weakness ? [1] Where, so fully as in the Synoptic narrative, is to be traced the transcendence of Him Who has declared that the criterion of judgment at the last day will be according as men have done, or foreborne to do, acts of love and pity in His Name, as they passed through their earthly life ? [2] Or, again, is any Johannine passage more charged with the atmosphere of deity than that in which the Saviour bids all the weary of this world come to Him and, coming, find rest unto their souls ? [3]

The Fourth Gospel is not to be discredited in that rough-and-ready way. The Divine-human character of Christ shines out in each component part of the fourfold tradition. It is, of course, true that the humanity of our Lord was evident to His disciples before it began to dawn upon their minds that He was more than man ; but that they had received the truth of His divinity before a line of our Gospels was written is clear not only from the contents of those Gospels,[4] but from what we learn of primitive belief in the Book of Acts [5] and in the Epistles of St. Paul.[6]

At the same time, in tracing the development of thought as directed upon the Person of our Lord, we have to bear

[1] Cf. Jo. iv. 6 ; xii. 27 ; xix. 28.
[2] Mt. xxv. 31 f.
[3] Mt. xi. 28 f.
[4] *E.g.* Mt. xi. 27 ; Lk. x. 22, from the oldest Gospel source, " Q." The knowledge of the Father and the Son is mutual, and is regarded as equivalent. It is in each case divine. " It stands in necessary connection with their Fatherhood and Sonship " : Wendt, *D. Lehre Jesu,* ii., p. 126 (*E.T.*) ; cf. Mk. xiii. 32. The relation of the Son to the Father is admittedly unique and metaphysical. Cf. O. Pfleiderer, *D. Entstehung des Christentums,* p. 202 (who, however, on *à priori* grounds, regards the idea as historically unthinkable) ; Loisy, *L'Evangile et l'Eglise,* p. 78. Cf. the remarkable avowals of H. J. Holtzmann, *Lehrbuch der N.T. Theologie,* i., p. 295 ; Bousset, *Gottesglaube,* 1908, p. 62.
[5] Christ's Lordship, as revealed to men through His Resurrection, is the dominant feature of the Christology of the early chapters of Acts. Thus, from the first days of the Christian Church (Acts ii. 36), the full truth of His Divinity formed part of the Apostolic teaching (Acts x. 36, 42). A. Meyer misreads the evidence when he says, " for the original, Jewish community, Jesus was still a human Messiah." *Was uns Jesus Heute ist.,* 1907, p. 18.
[6] The critics are right who say that St. Paul deifies Christ. His writings show this clearly. Cf. Col. i. 15 ; ii. 9 ; 2 Cor. iv. 4. They are wrong in saying, as A. Meyer does, that he is the first to do so. *Wer hat das Christentum begründet,* p. 95 ; *v.* Lightfoot on Phil. ii. 5.

in mind that men would naturally apprehend His Divine nature at a later period.   First would come, by association and intercourse, the impression that here was a man of exceptional character and gifts, possibly of the prophetic order, and as they heard and watched Him, comparing the humility and graciousness of His bearing with the greatness of His claims upon their reverence and obedience, a higher conception of His Person began to form within their minds. We can detect what was going on by the chance utterances of the people as well as by sayings of disciples.

And if disciples generally were slow to grasp the full truth, Christ Himself practised a corresponding reserve in imparting it.   Hence those moments of silence when we should have expected speech ; the command " to tell no man " after some act of power ; the refusal to work signs and miracles at the bidding of men who seemed likely to commit themselves to His cause.

But, at the period to which the farewell discourses belong, the time for reserve had passed.   He was to leave His disciples.   It seems natural that, if any account of His last sayings were preserved, it should contain some such statements of His character and Personality as are to be found in these chapters.   If they offend the critical sense, it is because they run counter to the low, depreciatory view of Christ which criticism of a certain kind claims to have established.   Certainly, it is not possible to accept the teaching of these chapters and, at the same time, to withhold from our Lord the ascription of Divinity.[1]   But, no less certainly, is the revelation met and justified by what we gather from Synoptic sources.[2]

[1] Cf. Jo. xiii. 31, 32 ; xiv. 9, 23 ; xv. 26 ; xvi. 3, 7, 15 ; xvii. 3, 5, 6.
[2] V. p. 220. Clemen thinks that Jo. xiv. 1b, " Ye believe in God, believe also in Me," has been placed in Christ's mouth at a late period, such a plea for surrender to Himself belonging to a developed Christology. Passages like Jo. xv. 8, he regards as " specifically Johannine ideas." He has been answered point by point by Stettinger, *Geschichtlichkeit der Johan. Abschiedsreden.*, 1919, p. 69.   But Clemen's criticism is too subjective to receive any general adhesion.   A saying is not to be rejected because it has no parallel in Synoptic narratives of quite different circumstances and occasions, or because it seems at first sight to run counter to sayings which occur in another context.   The chief test of genuineness is its compatibility with the general representation of our Lord conveyed

Now, is this high strain of His self-consciousness, as it appears again and again in the farewell discourse, contradicted by the Synoptic narrative of the Agony in the Garden ? And is a sense of this incompatibility the reason for the omission of that episode by the Fourth Evangelist ? We cannot think so. It is mere Docetism to regard the Divine nature of the Son of God as so predominant in the complex of His Incarnate life as to exclude the possibility of such an experience as that of Gethsemane. He was truly human—sin only excepted ; and the perfection of His manhood only made Him all the more susceptible to the onslaught of those griefs and fears, and to that repugnance to whatever mars and hurts the integrity of human nature, which were inseparable from those dread moments in the Garden. To shrink from the extremity of suffering was only natural to human nature. To refuse to bear it would be to go back from that resolution of which the Psalmist spoke—" I delight to do Thy will, O my God " ; [1] it would be to forgo the Redemption of man, so dear to His Father's heart and to His own. There is no incompatibility between the story of Gethsemane and the farewell discourse. If St. John saw fit to give no account of the former, it was because it had been narrated in the Gospels that lay before him ; not because he saw in it something that conflicted with the truth of the Saviour's Personality. This is evident on his own showing. For not only does he confirm by his silence the Synoptic record of Gethsemane, but he narrates an incident which reveals a condition of mind on the part of Christ strikingly analogous to His experience in the Garden. The visit of the Greeks disclosed to the Saviour's mind a vision of the future. The glory of the Gospel unrolls itself before Him for the moment ; but on the

by the other Gospels. If it goes beyond that conception, so far as to *negative* its meaning, then the saying stands self-condemned. Not otherwise. Clemen constructs for himself a Christological framework and rejects whatever declines to adapt itself to it, *Entstehung des Johan. Evangeliums*, pp. 255, 260. But he warns us against his own practice, *ib.*, p. 31. He will not even allow to Christ a glimpse into the future missionary activity of His disciples (Jo. xvii. 20), *ib.*, p. 268. Yet, apart from Mt. xxviii. 19, cf. Jo. xii. 24.

[1] Ps. xl. 8.

condition of sacrifice, which He clearly apprehends. The effect is remarkable. There is a most human transition from a state of ecstasy to one of the deepest depression, recalling both in substance and in form St. Mark's story of the Garden.[1] The Evangelist who has scaled the loftiest heights of our Lord's self-revelation shows that he finds no incongruity in relating His moments of fear and shrinking, as He thinks of the prospect before Him.[2]

Another difficulty arises from what is sometimes regarded as the substitution of the gift of the Holy Spirit for the παρουσία in the farewell discourse, or as it has been put, "the return of Christ is mixed up with the coming of the Spirit." [3] Here, again, there is thought to be conflict with the Synoptic teaching on the subject. The visible return of Christ appears to be set aside and its place to be taken by the coming, at Pentecost and onwards in the course of the ages, of the Holy Spirit.[4] And along with this view, it is held that the Fourth Gospel passes over that conception of a General Judgment at the last day, which occupies so prominent a place in the Synoptic teaching. It substitutes for it the act of acceptance or rejection of the preaching of Christ as the ground and criterion of judgment.[5]

---

[1] Jo. xii. 27. With σῶσόν με ἐκ τῆς ὥρας ταύτης, cf. Mk. xiv. 35, προσηύχετο . . . παρέλθῃ ἀπ' αὐτοῦ ἡ ὥρα. And yet Clemen (p. 254) can say that it tells against the farewell discourses that they fit in too little with the agony of prayer in Gethsemane as the Synoptists recount it. To the Fourth Evangelist, the two moods, if seemingly conflicting, present no difficulty.

V. F. Heiler, *Das Gebet*, p. 385, "The Fourth Gospel offers a notable variant to the prayer of Jesus in Gethsemane, which at the same time contains a reconciliation with the thought of suffering, perhaps an independent, genuine prayer from the lips of Jesus, but apparently only an accurate Johannine paraphrase of the prayer on the Mount of Olives. Jesus clearly recognises the unavoidableness of His sacrifice (xii. 24). The thought of death stirs in Him a healthy, genuinely human dread, which He expresses in the prayer, *v.* 27. Then He entirely forgets all fear and self-regarding desire ; He sees only the one high object to be served by His death, the setting up of God's Kingdom ; therefore He says, ' Father, glorify Thy Name.' "

[2] After raising this difficulty, Clemen admits that the farewell discourse "perhaps contains genuine thoughts of Jesus, only brought into this shape at a later period and transferred to this occasion." *Ib.*, p. 255.

[3] H. Holtzmann, *Evang. des Johan.*, p. 248.

[4] Thus P. Corssen, " This Gospel goes far beyond the Pauline Gospel in freedom. It denies not only the παρουσία but the judgment bound up with it (xvi. 8–10)." *Zeitschr. für d. N.T. Wissensch.*, 1907, p. 130.

[5] Jo. xii. 47, 48.

Before dealing with these two questions, we should bear in mind the position of advantage occupied by the writer of the Fourth Gospel. He had witnessed the passing away of the hope of an immediate visible return of Christ which had undoubtedly been cherished in the primitive Church ; a process which could be traced in the Epistles of St. Paul, if read in their historical order. The readjustment of thought required to meet this significant change of outlook was considerable. Some idea of its gravity can be formed by consideration of the startling theories put forward in our time by the new eschatological school.[1] Instead of a speedy return of Christ to wind up the age within the lifetime of His first disciples, as required by the eschatological theory, we are confronted in the Fourth Gospel with a coming of Christ following, indeed, closely upon His leaving the world to go to the Father, but a coming effected by the Holy Spirit.

What is more, the Evangelist produces from the store of his memory of Christ's teaching the authority for such a change of view ; and this, at the very time when such conclusive authority was needed to confirm the Church in her altered outlook and to assure men that, under the dispensation of the Spirit, the promised return of the Master was being fulfilled in a way at first undreamed of. Christ so present, as no longer to be seen and handled, but in the power and in the gifts of the Spirit—this was the new fulfilment of the old promise of a return, partial indeed, *for it does not cover all the ground*, yet very real and full of hope for a future yet to be revealed.

A partial fulfilment, for it is a mistake to imagine that,

---

[1] J. Weiss, in his *D. Predigt Jesu vom Reiche Gottes*, and A. Schweitzer in *Von Reimarus zu Wrede*. But, it is a question whether an undue emphasis has not been placed upon the Apostolic witness to an early fulfilment of the παρουσία. St. Paul, in 1 Thess. iv. and Rom. xiii. 12, seems to imply a speedy Advent. But elsewhere, when speaking of the conversion of the Jewish people, following upon that of the Gentiles (Rom. xi. 25, 26), it is clear that a large space of time is required before the final Coming. The result of this contrast is that we are not justified in assuming that the Apostle expected a return of Christ during his own lifetime. " Il faut reconnaitre que les passages eschatologiques les plus détaillés s'opposent à toute certitude, et même à toute probabilité, d'une Parousie prochaine." Allo, *S. Jean l'Apoc.*, p. cxxii.

in this new report of Christ's actual teaching, for which
we have to thank the Fourth Evangelist, there is any
intention on his part to supersede the Synoptic teaching,
which holds out the prospect of a visible return for Judgment at the end of the age. His language is as clear and
definite as possible. In v. 22 ff. our Lord proclaims the
certainty of a twofold resurrection : that from sin, which
was taking effect at the time He was speaking,[1] and a
resurrection in the future [2] for life or for death. With this
clear pronouncement, which is wholly in line with our Lord's
Synoptic teaching on the subject, we can compare the
saying that His spoken Word will, apart from any need for
Himself to sit in Judgment, suffice to condemn or to acquit
" *in the last day.*" [3] But in both passages there is assurance
of a final judgment pronounced by the Judge Himself, or
made known automatically by the attitude of men to His
Word.

How, then, are we to interpret the change of view
which to some minds constitutes so great a difficulty when
the Synoptic presentation of the παρουσία is compared with
that of the Fourth Gospel ?

In the first place, the sayings which convey the promise
of the Comforter, and imply that in His coming the return
of Christ is already made effectual, give the impression
of having been, in substance and perhaps in form, actual
words of His, recalled for present needs by the disciple
who reports them. They were evidently first upon His
lips. They are not the consciousness of the Church expressing itself in sayings attributed by literary artifice to Christ.

---

[1] *v.* 25, ἔρχεται ὥρα καὶ νῦν ἐστιν.

[2] *v.* 28 f., ἔρχεται ὥρα *not* followed by καὶ νῦν ἐστιν, as in the other
case. Charles considers that *vv.* 28, 29, are questionable because opposed
(as to resurrection of the wicked) to St. John's teaching as a whole :
Eschatology, p. 371. But, as Moffatt says, the passage " cannot be elimi-
nated as a later interpolation." *Introd. to Liter. of N.T.,* p. 537 ; cf.
1 Jo. ii. 28 ; iv. 17.

[3] Jo. xii. 47, 48. This passage in no way contradicts St. John's
teaching elsewhere. He, the Incarnate Word, will still be the Judge ;
but the decisions will have already been effected by men's own attitude
to His Gospel—His spoken Word—their acceptance or rejection of it.
As in a court of Law, it is the criminal's own act—not the Judge—that
condemns him, and yet the Judge is there presiding and confirming the

This appears certain, not only from the character of the sayings, with their deep note of spiritual force and reality, but from the verdict of Christian experience in every succeeding age, which bears witness to the truth of Christ's spiritual presence in the Church at large and in the soul of the individual believer. Christ has come again in the power of His Spirit. The first miracles of the Pentecostal Church were wrought " in His Name," [1] and it has been the unvarying belief ever since that the miracles of grace which have accompanied the preaching of the Gospel have been due to the same cause. Experience of its fulfilment must have helped the Fourth Evangelist to recall and to fix in writing our Lord's own teaching on the subject.

And, secondly, if the language itself bears every mark of genuine utterances of Christ, it is not without support in Synoptic reports of His teaching.[2] It is to St. Matthew that we owe the great charter of public worship—the assurance " Where two or three are gathered together in My Name, there am I in the midst of them," a prophecy of a real, spiritual presence, good for all time; a promise confirmed by the closing words of the same Gospel, " Lo, I am with you alway, even unto the end of the world." [3]

The agreement of this teaching with that of the farewell discourse is patent. The Synoptic " Lo, I am with you alway," on the eve of the departure, is entirely consonant with the Johannine " I will not leave you comfortless; I will come to you " ; and the agreement is strengthened by the probability that the lost ending of St. Mark contained a promise similar to that of St. Matthew, while the present ending tells us that, after the Ascension, the disciples " went forth and preached everywhere, the Lord working

action of the Law; so at the last Judgment, when all things will be naked and open to Him with Whom we have to do, His Word accepted or rejected will have acquitted or condemned. His presence will ratify what has passed.

[1] Acts iii. 6; iv. 10 f., 30; cf. 1 Cor. v. 4.

[2] Cf. Mk. xiii. 11, " We have here the germ of the doctrine of the ' other Paraclete ' which is developed in the Fourth Gospel." Swete, *The Holy Spirit in the N.T.*, p. 122.

[3] Mt. xviii. 20; xxviii. 20.

with them and confirming the word with signs following." [1]
Nor is a corresponding note lacking in the Third Gospel,
" Behold, I send the promise of My Father upon you,"
reminding us of the discourse in the Upper Room, " when
the Comforter is come, Whom I will send unto you from the
Father " ; [2] for we have to bear in mind that with the
presence of the Spirit there was involved the presence
among men of Christ Himself.[3] The gift of the Spirit,
coming from the Father through the Son, carried with it
the real, if unseen, presence of the Son. Henceforth Christ
worked on earth by the Spirit. In this sense there was a
true παρουσία. So far is the Fourth Gospel from contra-
dicting the Synoptic representation of the Return, that in
reality it falls in line with it, and even makes for the elucida-
tion of the problem of the primitive eschatology. For it
brings into clearer light the fact that the Return of Christ
is a process of varied and complex character, not to be
comprised in any one event however momentous ; fulfilled
in part at Pentecost, in the destruction of the City and the
Temple, and in episodes of the Church's history which
have been critical in their bearing upon the progress of the
Gospel, although little heeded at the time.[4]

And while the Johannine eschatology is in correspondence with the Synoptic in its emphasis on the complexity of the process, it agrees with it in laying stress on

[1] Mk. xvi. 20.

[2] Lk. xxiv. 49 ; Jo. xv. 26.

[3] It is only by such teaching as that of the farewell discourse that
we can interpret the difficult saying of St. Paul, " The Lord is the Spirit,"
2 Cor. iii. 17 ; cf. v. 18, R.V., passages sometimes quoted to prove the
identity of " the Spirit " with the Person of Christ—a meaning impossible
in view of the passages, Synoptic and Johannine, cited above. The
ἄλλον παράκλητον of Jo. xiv. 16, " another besides Himself," is sufficient
proof of distinction ; v. Stettinger, D. Geschichtlichkeit der Johan.
Abschiedsreden Jesu, p. 242. Zahn interprets Jo. xiv. 18 of the final
παρουσία, ad loc. This contradicts the general sense of the passage xiv.
15–29, which, while promising another Comforter than Himself Who is
leaving them, declares His own return (ἔρχομαι) to His bereft disciples.
Cf. Mt. xxviii. 20.

[4] " Ces sortes d'avènements partiels sont comme les prodromes ou un
commencement, de la Parousie qu'ils annoncent. Ils sont englobés dans
la même perspective que la consommation, quoique la date du grand jour
soit laissée volontairement par le Christ dans une ombre impénétrable,
pour que les disciples songent à veiller, et à être tonjours prêts." Allo,
Saint Jean, l'Apocalypse, p. ciii.

the final Return for Judgment. It is impossible, without doing violence to the text, to eliminate from the Gospel the assurance of the Lord's appearing at the close of the age. And it is found in every part of the narrative. The Fourth Gospel is as clear as the rest in proclaiming that final coming. "All judgment" is committed to the Son, as Son of Man.[1] With it is closely bound up the resurrection of the evil as well as the good.[2] By his inclusion of these words among the sayings of Christ, the Fourth Evangelist places the stamp of his approval on the Judgment paragraphs of the Synoptic Gospels. It is the same event in each account. The final $\pi\alpha\rho o\upsilon\sigma i\alpha$ has the attestation of every Gospel source.[3]

So far, then, is the Fourth Evangelist from impugning the Synoptic prospect of the visible return of Christ for Judgment at the end of the age, that he directly reinforces it ; while at the same time he corrects early misinterpretations of Synoptic sayings by his report of the discourse in the Upper Room. We may state the case thus : our Lord undoubtedly spoke to His disciples about His return for Judgment. Rightly or wrongly, the idea arose that this return would be a single act, very soon to come about. As time went on, one event after another, Pentecost, the Fall of Jerusalem, the accession of the Gentiles, while seeming partially to fulfil the promise were found to be inadequate. Then comes the Fourth Evangelist with his recollection of the sayings in the Upper Room, with all the light they throw upon those scattered Synoptic hints to which we have alluded.[4]

There is also a harmony to be observed in the Person

---

[1] Cf. 1 Enoch, 6, 9, 27, "And the sum of judgment was given to the Son of Man."

[2] Jo. v. 28, 29, *v.* above, p. 155, n. 2.

[3] "On peut dire que, pour les Évangiles, tout ce qui suit la vie terrestre de Jésus est une eschatologie." Allo, *Saint Jean, l'Apocalypse*, p. ciii. It would, perhaps, be more true to say "pour le Quatrième Evangile, etc."

[4] *V.* above, p. 148. Cf. Swete, *The Last Discourse and Prayer of Our Lord*, p. x., "Repeated study of these chapters (xiv.–xvii.) confirms my conviction that they approach as near to the words actually spoken by our Lord, as the memory of one who heard them can bring us."

of the Judge Himself, as He is presented in the Synoptics and in St. John. In each case it is the Son of Man Who is the Judge, One Who " was in all points tempted like as we are " ; Whose human heart could still beat in sympathy with those who stand before Him. There is no disparity in the respective accounts.[1] It is true that in Revelation, Judgment—the final winding up of the affairs of men—is, like their beginning, ascribed to God the Father.[2] But in each case, we are told repeatedly that He acts through the Son.[3] The ultimate cause, as the ultimate goal, of human life is ὁ Θεός.[4] But in everything He is so closely associated with the Son that either Person may be said to act. There is no contradiction here, either between the Synoptics and the Fourth Gospel, or between that Gospel and the Apocalypse.

It will probably always remain a problem how far the Johannine sayings of our Lord represent His *ipsissima verba* and to what extent their form is due to the literary art of the Evangelist. While the Aramaic background of the Greek Gospel is becoming more generally recognised, and allowance has to be made for translation of written or oral sources from their Aramaic dress into Greek, there is another phenomenon which also requires to be kept in mind—the fact that many of these sayings reveal their origin quite unmistakably. They *must* have been first upon the lips of the Lord. They are plainly the words of Jesus, and of no one else.[5] The chief effect of their transference to the pages of our Gospel has been due to their

---

[1] *V.* Mt. vii. 22, 23 ; xvi. 27 ; Jo. v. 22.

[2] Rev. xx. 11–15.

[3] Jo. v. 22 ; i. 2 ; Rev. xxii. 13, where attributes of the Father are ascribed to the Son. Cf. Rom. xiv. 10 ; 2 Cor. v. 10. *V.* Charles, *The Revelation of St. John,* ii., p. 192.

[4] Cf. Rom. xi. 36 ; 1 Cor. xv. 28.

[5] " The discourses of Christ have a sweet and melancholy charm, with an indescribable dignity and grandeur." Inge in *Dict. of Christ and the Gospels,* i., p. 889. " That the discourses as a whole are the work of the author of the Gospel is inconceivable . . . we hear the voice of the Master." Swete, *The Last Discourse and Prayer of Our Lord,* p. viii. " The whole work as it stands is evidence of the impression which Jesus had made ; and it may be claimed . . . that the great themes at least, dwelt upon in the discourses which are attributed to Him, proceeded from Himself." Stanton, *The Gospels,* pt. iii., p. 283.

translation, with the possible addition of some slight changes in the form and mould of sentences. *The ideas remain*, and it is they that count and that prove the source from which they come.

It is not merely the originality of the sayings that produces the feeling of certainty that they were spoken by Christ. Some of His most characteristic utterances had been partly, if not altogether, anticipated. What proclaims them as His is their character of unearthliness, their audacity (from a human standpoint), their circumstances and environment. The context often makes all the difference. Who but Himself would thus have spoken *then*? Mere originality does not suffice to stamp a saying as His, nor does the lack of it prove the contrary.

In drawing attention to the following passages, it is to be noted that they are only a selection from what might be produced to illustrate our point. Others will commend themselves to other minds. The evidence is admittedly subjective in a high degree, like the basis of so many judgments in æsthetics, in art, and in literature ; and yet some such judgments can make good claim to validity.

Let us first take two passages from the discourse with the woman of Samaria. The sayings about the gift of " living water," [1] as addressed to a person of her character, would not have been placed in our Lord's mouth by any writer who tried to construct an edifying and approximately correct representation of His life and conversation. So deeply spiritual a subject and one of so far-reaching a significance would seem out of place in these circumstances. We might even say that Christ's own warning would deter the writer from such a course.[2] But the actual speaker was the best judge of what was fitting, and the fact that it was so judged is the best proof that He *was* the Speaker.[3]

To any audience, the disclosure would be remarkable. The gift of the Holy Spirit, *His* gift, to be at once the seal and crown of the accomplishment of His own Messianic

[1] Jo. iv. 10, 14. [2] Mt. vii. 6. [3] *V*. above, p. 145

work, and the eternal and complete refreshment of all who will to profit by it. And this to a poor ignorant Samaritan of a more than doubtful past and present! The words are His Who " seeth not as man seeth," Whose thoughts are not our thoughts.[1] Not the language merely, but its *direction*, proclaims the Speaker.

The same may be said of the declaration of what is nothing less than the charter of all true religion : " God is Spirit." Here, again, it is the choice of His auditor that moves our wonder almost as much as does the content of the saying. This penetrating ray of light into the inner being and nature of God goes, it is true, beyond the reach of any Old Testament revelation.[2] But the recipient of this Divine communication, the circumstances of its utter- ance ; it is these things which seem to place it securely upon the lips of the Incarnate Truth. It is *His* saying, reported by the woman, or overheard by the Evangelist. No other source is conceivable.

The discourse at Capernaum contains much that can only have come from the mouth of Christ Himself. It is wholly improbable that a late writer—even if his literary code permitted such a course—would make our Lord speak of Himself as " the bread of God," or as " the bread which cometh down from heaven," *without the most direct authority*. Still less would the conception of the flesh and blood of Christ as the food and nourishment of man have been thus attributed to Him. Nothing short of His own express statement will account for language the difficulty of which has been felt by thinkers of very different kinds. His hearers are at once perturbed and hotly debate " how can this Man give His flesh to eat ? " So far from softening down the offending phrase, our Lord enforces it with the warn- ing that neglect thus to partake will involve the absence of all life in its true sense,[3] while He goes on to use the strongest possible expression [4] for the manner of their participation.

---

[1] 1 Sam. xvi. 7 ; Is. lv. 8.
[2] Cf. Kautzsch in Hastings, *Dict. of the Bible*, v. p. 679; Bousset, *Jesus*, p. 51.
[3] Jo. vi. 52, 53. [4] ὁ τρώγων, v. 56.

Now, it may be said that this language is Pauline; hence its employment by the writer. As a matter of fact, the borrowing, if such there be, is in the other direction. " I have received of the Lord that which also I delivered unto you," writes St. Paul.[1] If this was the case with regard to the institution of the Eucharist, it is against reason to attribute the formation of a theology of the Sacrament to a writer, who not only was not an original disciple, but was indebted for his knowledge of the subject and of its significance to those disciples who had seen and heard the Lord. Besides, in strength and intensity of expression, the words placed by the Evangelist in Christ's own lips surpass the phraseology of St. Paul.[2] On any sound principles of criticism, it is difficult to avoid the conclusion that such language proclaims itself to be what the Evangelist tells us it is—the utterance of Christ Himself.

Another passage which proves its own provenance is that in which our Lord declares His oneness with His Father.[3] Not only does the remarkable character of the statement, expressive of unity without identity, betray its origin; for no disciple would venture to enter upon such sacred ground on his own initiative; but there is the additional guarantee of the historical situation. The Jews regard the saying as blasphemous: " Thou, being a man, makest Thyself God." Our Lord proceeds to reason with them and to show that there was nothing in His saying which could be so construed. He does not claim to be God, in an exclusive sense, but as the form of His saying shows (" My Father "), He does claim in Sonship to be of the nature of the Father, or, as the neuter gender of His saying indicates, of the same essential being as the Father.

---

[1] 1 Cor. xi. 23; cf. Feine, *Theologie des N.T.*[2], p. 161, " Paul ascertained his historical information about the Supper by a way which opened directly to the Lord and proceeded from Him." *Id., Jesus Christus und Paulus*, p. 228, " The knowledge came to him through the Community from the Lord."

[2] Cf. with the Pauline τὸ σῶμα, 1 Cor. xi. 24, and elsewhere, ἡ σάρξ μου, Jo. vi. 51 etc.; with τὸ ποτήριον . . . ἐν τῷ ἐμῷ αἵματι, 1 Cor. xi. 25, πίνων μου τὸ αἷμα, Jo. vi. 56. For ἡ σάρξ μου, cf. Justin M., *Apol.*, i. 66; Ignat., *ad Rom.*, vii. 3; Athan., *Ad Serap.*, iv. 19; Jer. Taylor, *The Real Presence*, i. § 11.

[3] Jo. x. 30.

In view of the widely received Palestinian origin of the writer, his own references to his fellow-countrymen, when in controversy with our Lord, are regarded by some as unnatural; all the more so if he is to be identified with the Apostle, whose ministry had been, by general agreement, devoted to " the Circumcision." [1] Not only does he constantly allude to them as " the Jews " in a detached kind of way, as though he himself belonged to another race,[2] but he represents them, no doubt quite faithfully, as singularly dull and unimaginative in their methods of controversy. They are always, and very badly, in the wrong.[3] Then, the careful explanation repeatedly given, that the Passover was a Feast of the Jews strikes one as curious.[4]

This procedure of the Evangelist, strange as it appears at first sight, is explained when we think of the lapse of time and of all that the years had witnessed since he was living in Jerusalem. The controversies lay far back in the past. The Temple and its Worship had been overthrown; the people judged and condemned for their part in the rejection of their Messiah. Besides, the author was writing for a group of Christians containing many Gentiles whose knowledge of Jewish worship and customs depended upon hearsay. It was a far cry from Jerusalem to Ephesus; another world in which his Gospel saw the light. And this

[1] Gal. ii. 9.

[2] Jo. ii. 13, 18, 20; xi. 8, 19, 36; xii. 11; xi. 54; xviii. 12; xix. 7. V. C. H. Turner, J.T.S. for 1913, p. 174.

[3] Jo. viii. 22, 33, 39, 48; cf. ix. 18; x. 31 f.

[4] Jo. ii. 13; vi. 4; xi. 55; cf. vii. 2. The same detached manner of speaking is attributed to Christ, xiii. 33. At times His attitude appears to be almost provocative. He seems to invite opposition, viii. 44, 55. " The temper of his (the writer's) own age was unconsciously transferred to the ministry of Jesus, Who certainly could not have adopted the attitude of uncompromising antagonism to ' the Jews ' which we find in this Gospel ": Inge, Dict. of Christ and the Gospels, i., p. 889. But compare our Lord's denunciations of Scribes and Pharisees in the Synoptic Gospels, Mt. xxiii., Lk. xi. Dr. Inge also refers to misunderstandings by the Jews as " a favourite literary device of the Evangelist." ib., p. 894. But the factious opposition and dullness of the hearers would be certain to remain fixed in the memory of such an eyewitness as the Evangelist. Cf. Allo, S. Jean l'Apocalypse, p. cxcviii.; Procksch, Petrus und Johannes, p. 3, " The opposition between Jesus and Judaism, which led finally to the crisis, is worked out in its development far more clearly by John than by the Synoptic writers." But it was not his invention.

complete change of time, place and circumstance may well
account for the writer's aloofness ; while the severity of
his attitude to his fellow-countrymen can be explained by
his devotion to his Master and his whole-hearted champion-
ship of His cause.[1] We conclude, therefore, that there is
nothing in his references to his countrymen to oblige us to
refuse the assignment of the Gospel to one who had been
long ago an Apostle of " the circumcision," but was now
living in a great Greek city, had come into touch with its
modes of thought, and had learned to employ its language
with ease and freedom. There had been an entire change
of perspective. He could now look on the conduct of his
fellow-countrymen with the eye almost of a stranger.

Another striking phenomenon of the Johannine discourses presents itself after we have been reading Synoptic
accounts of the sayings of our Lord. There is a certain
sameness and monotony of tone—a monotony like the
moaning of the incoming tide. It arises partly from the
subject to which the discourses are largely devoted ;
partly from the circumstances connected with the composition of the Gospel itself. The topic seldom strays
away from our Lord's Person and the attitude of men
towards Him. To impress upon those for whom he wrote
its extreme significance is the main object of the Evangelist.
Hence his choice from the store of his Master's sayings
with which his memory was furnished. The Gospel is
avowedly written for a special purpose ; and to that purpose
the author resolutely keeps. He will not be diverted from
the end that he has in view. He has chosen the most vital
subject on which a man can write, and he will let nothing
distract him from it. But it is to be noted that *his choice is
dictated by his experience, it is not his invention.* Can we

---

[1] A similar attitude is discernible even in St. Mark (vii. 3). It is
frequent in St. Luke's descriptions of the relation between St. Paul and
his Jewish opponents. Acts ix. 23, and *passim.* Thus there is abundant
support for the historical character of St. John's references. Cf. H. Delff,
Neue Beiträge zur Kritik des vierten Evang., p. 4, " It is clear that Jesus
was initiated into the manner of thought and speech of the Rabbis : how
else could He attempt to contend with them ? The Synoptists also
confirm this view."

prove this? Only if elsewhere, in other Gospel reports, there are to be found actual sayings of our Lord of the same Self-regarding character; sayings which, while undoubtedly proceeding from His own lips, prove that, as in so many of the Johannine discourses, He considered that a true estimate of His own Person is a vital necessity for discipleship. No passage answers more fully to this requirement than the famous saying from the Logia of St. Matthew, "All things are delivered unto Me of My Father: and no man knoweth the Son, but the Father; neither knoweth any man the Father, save the Son and he to whomsoever the Son will reveal Him."[1] How deeply our Lord was impressed with the value of a true realisation of His Messianic claim and of His unique relation to the Father, appears in the fervour of His recognition of the confession of St. Peter at Cæsarea Philippi.[2] But the most striking instance of all is the revelation that the eternal issues of life and death for man will hang upon the practice or the neglect of kindness and succour to those who need, and why? The Son of Man has made their cause His own.[3] Nothing in the Fourth Gospel exceeds the range and implications of this tremendous claim. The King, Who is the Son of Man, is seated upon His throne; all nations are gathered before Him. The eternal destiny of each individual is to be determined by one practical test —*their attitude to Himself*, as shown by care for His redeemed, or by the lack of it.

To the charge of a monotonous insistence upon His own personal dignity and claims, that seems to stand by itself as reported in the Johannine discourses, we can therefore

---

[1] Mt. xi. 27; Lk. x. 22. With its corollary (in Mt. xi. 28 f. only). For a discussion of this passage, *v. The Person of Our Lord*, p. 163 f. Grill remarks, "Often as the Synoptic Christ emphasises in His speeches the unique authority of His Person, His self-revelation is nevertheless more indirect," *op. cit.*, i., p. 32. But Grill does not quote the passages named above and he goes on: "On the contrary, in the Fourth Gospel throughout, the context of His sayings is essentially Himself, conceived as direct, trustworthy and complete revealer of God." The comparison is defectively stated and therefore valueless.

[2] Mt. xvi. 15 f.

[3] Mt. xxv. 31 f. *V.* H. Holtzmann, *Neutest. Theologie*, i., p. 295 f.

reply that this supposed isolation is not borne out by fact. We have ample grounds for believing that, behind the repeated challenge to thought and consideration in those discourses, lies the certainty that the subject was very near to the mind and heart of Christ; and why? Simply because it is very deeply bound up with the eternal welfare of every soul that He came to save. It is the sublime egotism of the lowliest of men, Who " came not to be ministered unto but to minister," and could best fulfil His task by opening men's eyes to their need of Himself, as their one hope in life and in death. What wonder if the memory of a disciple who stood nearer to Him than any other, played more constantly upon sayings of his Master in which these aspects of His Person were specially prominent, and that, at the cost of iteration, he recorded them in his Gospel !

A more serious charge against the historical character of the Johannine discourses was brought so long ago as in 1820 by Bretschneider.[1] The speeches, whether of our Lord Himself or of John the Baptist, are said to be cast in the same mould ; and even the language of the First Epistle of St. John corresponds in style and manner with the Johannine discourses of Christ. Now, " le style, c'est l'homme." Does not this similarity betray the actual author of the discourses, that is to say, the Evangelist, not the Lord ?

The question is largely a matter of psychology. Had the same phenomenon appeared in one of the Synoptic writers, we should be disposed to say, if the discourse of one of the speakers is accurately reported, that of the other is not. Both would not speak alike. The time between the utterance and its record would be too short to allow the difference between the utterances of speakers, so unlike to one another as the Forerunner and the Messiah, to become obliterated. We should hesitate long before accepting both versions as accurate reports of what was said.

[1] *Probabilia*, p. 169. Recently by W. Heitmüller in *D. Schriften des N.T.*, ii., p. 689. Cf. Keim, *Jesus von Nazara*, i., p. 123 (*E.T.*) ; Inge in *Dict. of Christ and the Gospels*, i., p. 889.

Here the case is different. A much longer time had elapsed before the recollection of what had been said was placed in writing ; and time blunts the edge of a man's memory of variations in so delicate a thing as the style of a speech. St. John had passed from discipleship of the Baptist to that of Christ. The latter was the preponderating influence. He lived over again the life which he had shared with our Lord, and the sayings of the Baptist came back to him through the intervening medium of his recollection of the sayings of the Master and Lord of both. What wonder if the earlier and more fragmentary sayings took something of the tone and style of the later ! if the Baptist's utterances about Christ and his relation to Him (while reported with substantial accuracy) are coloured by the Evangelist's more vivid recollection of sayings which surpassed them in interest and in weight ! The thing is likely and would be freely allowed in any ordinary literary discussion. It is only fair that it should be considered in the present case.

Again, it is alleged that the mind and style of the Evangelist are to be found not only in the speeches of Christ and of the Baptist, but in sayings which he puts into the mouth of various people with whom our Lord was brought in contact. To show this, a saying of the woman of Samaria is compared with a question of the Jews.[1] The similarity is thought to betray the composition of the writer, not the genuine utterances of the respective speakers.[2]

[1] Jo. iv. 12, μὴ σὺ μείζων εἶ τοῦ πατρὸς ἡμῶν Ἰακώβ ; viii. 53, μὴ σὺ μείζων εἶ τοῦ πατρὸς ἡμῶν Ἀβραάμ; Scholten, D. Evang. nach Joh., p. 229, draws attention to this parallel as suspicious. But the question may well have been asked independently on each occasion, the Evangelist unconsciously repeating himself in the actual form of the question—a frequent occurrence in literary composition. Other examples given by Scholten have no significance. The recurrence of a word in incidents separate from one another proves nothing.

[2] Similarity of style between the sayings of Christ and of Nicodemus, and of Christ and the woman of Sychar, has been thought to prove that the dialogues " did not actually occur in the exact words recorded by John." E. A. Abbott in Enc. Bibl., ii., col. 1801, n. 3. But St. John's Greek is a translation from his record, written or memorised, of what was said on those occasions. A translation is apt to show the translator's style in choice of words and in turn of phrase, even when the sayings of

M

The similarity of style and material which exists between the discourses of Christ in the Fourth Gospel and the language of the First Epistle of St. John presents a different problem, and yet one which is patient of a similar solution. Here, again, I believe that the phenomena are due to the fact that the personality and attraction of the Saviour wrought a deep impression upon the mental habits of His disciple. It is evident that St. John was peculiarly susceptible to certain distinctive phases of our Lord's teaching. This susceptibility, while it led him to attach great weight to these phases, helped to determine the bent of his own thought ; with the result that his independent writings constantly reflect the Master's mind, and form the best commentary upon His teaching as recorded in the Fourth Gospel. I should therefore explain the similarity, not by tracing the character and style of the discourses to the creative faculty of the writer of the Epistle,[1] but, on the contrary, by deducing the literary and stylistic peculiarities of the Epistle from the effect of the writer's intercourse with his Master.

This explanation rests upon the fact that the mental atmosphere of the writer was permeated by the recollection of early days.[2] From that time, to him " to live was Christ." He had, what another disciple claimed to possess —" the mind of Christ." [3] When, therefore, recalling and, at the instance of his disciples at Ephesus, putting into writing his reminiscences of the great time in Palestine, or again, when indications of incipient misbelief impelled him to write the Epistle, he could not, if he would, divest himself of the influence of those discourses of his Master which had most powerfully impressed him. As he lives over again the wondrous days—how wondrous to such a mind as his we can scarcely realise—he thinks Christ's thoughts

different speakers are concerned. The presence of a certain similarity reveals the *recorder*. It does not prove that he is the *originator* of what was said.

[1] As Scholten does, *D. Evang. nach Johannes*, pp. 228, 230.

[2] This is apparent from the frequent mention of events trivial in themselves, but bound up in his memory with some word or act of Christ.

[3] I Cor. ii. 16.

and breathes His spirit. It is not surprising if the tide of an inspired recollection surged over its natural boundaries and made itself felt in other regions of his literary activity.

Exception is also taken to the predominance of abstract and metaphysical conceptions over ethical in the teaching attributed to our Lord by the Fourth Evangelist. But, already in the earlier narratives, the great, vital questions of Christian morality had been dealt with. There was no need for another Sermon on the Mount, or of a repetition of the one which we possess. The Fourth Evangelist had other ends in view. His mind played round the mystery of his Master's Person; Who and whence He was; His relation to the Father and its significance and bearing upon the salvation of men, with the call it made upon them. It was these deeper aspects of his subject, suggested by actual words of Christ, that arrested the Evangelist's attention and constitute a marked contrast to the general character of Synoptic reports of His teaching.[1]

[1] If, in the discourses of the Fourth Gospel, Christ speaks in a way that the disciples did not understand, but which later thought and meditation came to enter into, this does not mean, as H. Holtzmann (*Evang. des Johan.*, p. 269) seems to think, that their source was not Christ, but the Christian consciousness. It *was* the Christian consciousness, stirred by reflection and enlightened by the Spirit which, in the person of the Fourth Evangelist, was able to recall and fix in writing what had actually been spoken by our Lord. But not to invent the sayings. Yet Dr. P. Gardner seems to imply this: " Though the Fourth Gospel contains valuable historic material, yet what is its main treasure, the speeches of our Lord contained in it, belongs not to the lifetime of the Founder, but to the early experience of the Church." *The Ephesian Gospel*, p. 335. Against this verdict it may suffice to quote the Cambridge Reader in the Talmud, I. Abrahams. Speaking of recent Jewish criticism of the New Testament, he says, " Most remarkable of all has been the cumulative strength of the arguments adduced by Jewish writers favourable to the authenticity of the discourses in the Fourth Gospel." *Cambr. Biblical Essays*, 1909, p. 181. I cannot agree with Heitmüller, " The prudent investigator will feel bound to employ the discourses and sayings essentially only as sources for the religious and theological view of the author and of the community to which he belongs ": in *D. Schriften des N.T.*, ii., p. 702. Harnack rightly characterises as " misleading " the Canon " to which unfortunately so many adhere nowadays in the criticism of the Gospels, that Gospel material which *can* probably be derived from developments of the Apostolic age and the succeeding time, *must* be derived therefrom ": *Beiträge*, vi., p. 31. V. Lücke, *op. cit.*, i., p. 238: " It was his (St. John's) daily task to preach Christ, to tell of His doings and sayings. Thus his life was an unbroken, and at the same time a ministerial, reminiscence of what He had seen and heard of Christ." Ramsay protests against the frequent suggestion of " the growing

But such a contrast is to be expected according to the natural order of the development of religious thought. Teaching which embodied the concrete and the ethical would be more likely to receive attention and to be recorded before men's minds began to dwell on the metaphysical elements of Christ's discourse. Yet, in the Synoptic reports of our Lord's references to His own Person, few as they are in comparison with what are preserved in the Fourth Gospel, we can trace the workings of a self-consciousness which is in thorough harmony with the self-revelation that we meet with in the later work. The transition is quite natural. Between the two periods of Gospel writing, Christian thought was busying itself with the subject of the Personality of Christ. We can trace its working in the Pauline Epistles and in Hebrews, and the effect of the process appears in the Fourth Gospel.

We therefore decline to allow our confidence in the trustworthiness of the Fourth Gospel to be shaken by a comparison with the Synoptic record of Christ's teaching. With all the differences caused by variety of method and purpose in the Evangelists themselves, and by the action of time and circumstance of composition, the two strains of the narrative are not inharmonious or incompatible with one another. It is the same Jesus Who speaks. It is His voice we hear ; not that of the Church of the second century. The Fourth Gospel, in its report of Christ's words, is not a clumsy anachronism. The criticism of the extreme left makes too great a demand upon our credulity. We can repel its claims by appeal to the assured results of

consciousness of the Church " as an explanation of noteworthy phenomena of the New Testament. *The First Christian Century*, p. 96. Dr. Rashdall incurs this censure when he says, " The speeches of the Fourth Gospel, where they go beyond the Synoptic conception, cannot be regarded as history, valuable as they may be for theology." *Mod. Churchman*, Sept. 1921, p. 278. Gardner and Heitmüller, in attributing the origin of the discourses to the Evangelist or his circle, go beyond Loisy, who speaks of their being written in the style of the Evangelist. *Le Quatr. Evang.*, p. 54. Cf. Delff, *Neue Beiträge*, p. 3, " It is quite unlikely that a learned Jew of the second century composed the sayings of Jesus . . . for the root idea of the sayings lay not only beyond the horizon of Judaism but of this later period. . . . If the root idea is original, so is the form of it historical." *V.* above, p. 22 f.

scientific research.[1]   While the date of its composition has been forced back from the middle to the opening years of the second century, with the possibility of the close of the first, it is, after all, the Gospel itself, its own narrative of the Saviour's sayings, that best bears witness to its truth ; a witness approved by the life-experience of the children of God in every succeeding age, who, as they have listened to St. John, have known by an intuition that needed no outward proof, that " the words of eternal life " that fell upon their ears had been first upon the lips of Jesus.

---

[1] As to the Fourth Gospel generally, Dr. B. Weiss, of Berlin, writing to me in 1908, stated that, with all allowance for its freedom in representation, he is confident of his ability to prove its historical character. Dr. Inge took a very similar view about the same time : " In spite of its free handling of historical detail, it has created a portrait of the divine-human Personality which has sunk deeply into the mind of the Church as the supremely true interpretation of Jesus Christ."   Cambr. Biblical Essays, p. 288.   " In the course of the previous Christian centuries," wrote Delff, " they founded Christianity on the Synoptists and on Paul.   The future belongs to John.   For him history speaks.   His Gospel is a faithful mirror of the time of Jesus."   Neue Beiträge, p. 8.

CHAPTER XI

THE PHILOSOPHY OF ST. JOHN

THERE is no question that the author of the Fourth Gospel was a profound thinker. It could not be otherwise with one whose mind was always dwelling on those problems of the relation between God and the world, of life and death, of eternity and time, which form so unique a feature of his work. Test his theology at any point and you find throughout a consistent strain of thought, which presupposes the conviction that all life is rational and ordered, that " every man " possesses a capacity for receiving light and guidance, if he will but use it.[1]   In this respect St. John stands unique among the writers of the New Testament. Others show signs of this kind of apprehension. But it is subordinate and intermittent. No one else so plainly shows that his theology is disciplined, even in its highest flights of speculation, by a constant reference to the just claims of reason.

Yet withal, it may at once be said that there is no trace in his writings of any attempt to construct a philosophic system.[2] Such a purpose would be foreign to the task he had set himself to carry out. His mind is set, not on the favoured few to whom alone such a work could make appeal, but on the wide world embraced by the love of the Father and the mission of His Son.[3] Hence his thought is everywhere controlled by the end he had in view—the spiritual welfare of his readers, the deepening and confirming of their faith and their power to live the Christian life.[4]

[1] Jo. i. 9.   [2] V. below, p. 192.
[3] Jo. iii. 16.   [4] Jo. xx. 31.

172

The philosophic turn of his mind appears partly in his own direct statements, partly in the choice of our Lord's recorded sayings and his own comments upon them. For the first, we at once turn to the prologue. In the whole range of literature, there is not to be found within so short a compass so great an array of great topics, or so decisive a handling of them. The truths presented are elemental. They lie at the base of all right thinking. They are, therefore, philosophic in the highest sense of the term. But there is no hint that the writer has any metaphysical end in view, when he sits down to write. His purpose is entirely theological, and even then it is a theology of which the one aim is to provide a sure foundation for right living. With all its mysticism, there is no more practical treatise than the Fourth Gospel taken in connection with its inseparable adjunct, the First Epistle.

While, therefore, we decline to see a philosophical purpose in the book, we shall realise, if we judge it rightly, that it is impossible to enter thoughtfully into its teaching without finding ourselves brought up against some of the most vital issues that the mind of man can contemplate.

But, before they are dealt with, it is to be noted that, like the inspired poet of Genesis i., St. John makes no assertion of the existence of God ; still less does he set out to prove it. In each of these two hymns of origin, as they might well be called, the sane man is dealt with as one who has no need of any proof of the fact of God. That fact is his by right of birth and in virtue of his share in the illuminating power of the Λόγος, Who " lighteth every man that cometh into the world." [1] Man, as man, possesses this divine gift of reason. He has that within him which is capable of discerning his Maker. As face answers to face in a glass, man made in the image of God reflects Him ; mind meets mind and understands.[2]

The Evangelist can therefore begin at a high level of

[1] Jo. i. 9. For the theological significance of the Logos doctrine, v. below, p. 254 f.
[2] Belief in a higher power is practically universal and is a proof of this fact.

thought. He starts with God. He has not to work up to Him. He takes His existence as an assured datum of human experience.

Against that fixed, eternal background, he projects a conception which, to a degree unknown in Old Testament writings, modifies and enriches the thought of God. Nowhere else has language said so much in so short a space. The first verse contains one main subject of his Gospel, the theology of the Λόγος as seen from above, *sub specie æternitatis ;* as the last verse of the prologue contains the other subject, the Incarnation of the Λόγος, as seen in time. Thus, in the prologue, he touches the keynote of his book, and outlines his own conception of what a Gospel writing should contain,[1] if it is to correspond with reality.

As seen from above, as though a window were opened in heaven, the Λόγος is perceived to be πρὸς τὸν Θεόν, and this from all eternity, for ἐν ἀρχῇ ἦν. The meaning conveyed is that of the closest fellowship and unity of will and mind with God—such is the force of πρός ; while at the same time there is such a partaking of the Divine essence as to constitute the possession of Godhead, καὶ Θεὸς ἦν ὁ Λόγος,[2] " the Word was God."

Why does the Evangelist preface a writing, which makes so solemn and reiterated an appeal to the historic character of its subject-matter, by the use of so impersonal and abstract a term as Λόγος ? [3] a term, moreover, which he no longer cares to employ in the body of the Gospel, and which he takes no pains *expressly* to identify with the central

---

[1] Few criticisms of the Fourth Gospel are more futile than those which presume to dictate what it should contain and what omit. They show that the critic has failed to see the connection between the rationale of the Gospel as presented in the prologue and its working out in the details chosen by the Evangelist for his purpose.

[2] " John represents the Λόγος as something personal, indeed a person who, though πρὸς τὸν Θεόν, yet operates and appears in a certain distinction from God " : Lücke, *Comment. über d. Joh. Evang.,* i., p. 252. Cf. J. Réville, *Le Quatr. Evangile,* p. 98, " Tourné ou dirigé vers Dieu, *i.e.* qu'il existe comm être Divin distinct de Dieu, et dont toute l'activité est reportée sur Dieu." For the way in which this relation to God comes out in the course of the Gospel, *v.* p. 196.

[3] " Half abstraction, half hypostasis." Grill, *Untersuchungen,* i., p. 170.

Figure of his story. Why does he take it up only to lay it aside ? I believe that the answer lies partly in the source or sources from which the writer deliberately chose his phrase ; partly in the local and temporal conditions under which he set himself to write the Gospel. That so Jewish a thinker as the Evangelist would quarry his thought and phraseology from the thought and language of his own religion is rendered probable by his habit of employing the Old Testament throughout the Gospel. We can hardly fail to see in the Λόγος of the Prologue the *Dabhar* of the Old Testament and possibly the *Mēmra* of Palestinian Aramaic, " the Word (of the Lord)." [1] The ultimate root of his theology is to be found in the religious experience and the Scriptures of his own people, in Palestine rather than in Ephesus. He would be led to his choice by the suitability of the expression for his purpose, as well as by a sense of loyalty to the past. " The Word " not only conveys the idea of a manifestation, a going forth in energy. To a writer of the first Christian century its use in the Old Testament would suggest the idea of a distinction in the Divine Being ; and for the Evangelist's purpose, the double meaning is exactly what he required. There would rise to his mind the thought of those Theophanies which—whatever their precise explanation—were held to visualise the presence of God to those whom He favoured. In each case, the invisible God made Himself felt and known to men, whether by dream or vision, and the effect may be said to have received its explanation in the words of Jacob, " Surely the Lord is in this place." [2] It was an appearance of God in the form of an angel or a man. The most High, " Whom no man hath seen nor can see," [3] so revealed Himself that he who beheld the vision believed that he had seen God ; [4] and in fact did see Him to all intents and purposes.

Another source of the Evangelist's conception is to be

---

[1] מֵימְרָא, דָּבָר. The Mēmra of the Targums belongs to the third and later centuries after Christ, but they contain older elements.
[2] Gen. xxviii. 16.   [3] 1 Tim. vi. 16.   [4] Cf. Jo. xiv. 9.

found in the Scriptures of his own people. It is clear that he wrote with Genesis i. in his mind. Creation is there conceived as due to the utterance of the word of command, "He spake, and it was done." "God said, Let there be light." It was a natural stage of thought to give an almost independent existence and to assign a personal power to the Divine Word ; and we find the Psalmist saying, " By the Word of the Lord were the heavens made." [1] Creation is the result of the *going forth*, the expression of His mind and will ; yet this going forth, while it conveys the idea of a certain separation or distinction from its source, does not imply another centre of being. Rather, it is to be regarded as a personification of the Creator's will, attributing the existence of the phenomenal world to a Divine energy or quality rather than to the direct action of the Supreme Being. Yet, as Lücke has observed, the germ of later doctrine is there, the mould of the future divinity of the Word.[2]

Another root of the Johannine Christology is to be found in the Old Testament conception of Wisdom. As it appears in Job and in Proverbs,[3] it sometimes looks like another form of the personification of the Word. Like the Word, Wisdom is pre-existent to creation—a possession of God, which at the same time seems to have a substantive existence of its own, while it is never to be found out of touch with Him. In the Apocryphal books of Sirach and Wisdom, the language used is very remarkable. In Sirach i. wisdom is eternally with God, yet "from Him." It is His own handiwork and poured out by Him over all His works.[4] In the praise of herself which the writer puts into the mouth of Wisdom, she is almost identified with the Word, " I came out of the mouth of the Most High." [5] As in the prologue of the Gospel, " in the beginning was the

---

[1] Ps. xxxiii. 6 ; cxlvii. 15 ; Is. lv. 11. Cf. Ignat., *ad Magnes.*, viii., τοῦ υἱοῦ αὐτοῦ, ὅς ἐστιν αὐτοῦ λόγος, ἀπὸ σιγῆς προελθών.

[2] *Evang. d. Joh.*, i., p. 257.

[3] Job xxviii. 12 f. ; Prov. viii. ix.

[4] Sir. i. 1, Πᾶσα σοφία παρὰ Κυρίου, καὶ μετ' αὐτοῦ ἐστὶν εἰς τὸν αἰῶνα. v. 9, αὐτὸς ἔκτισεν αὐτήν . . . καὶ ἐξέχεεν αὐτὴν ἐπὶ πάντα τὰ ἔργα.

[5] Sir. xxiv. 3, ἐγὼ ἀπὸ στόματος ὑψίστου ἐξῆλθον.

Word," Wisdom cries, " He created me from the beginning
before the world," and as " the Word was made flesh and
dwelt among us," so with Wisdom, " He that made me
caused my tabernacle to rest and said, Let thy dwelling be
in Jacob and thine inheritance in Israel.[1]

In the somewhat later book of the Wisdom of Solomon,
the writer speaks of Wisdom in terms that we have learnt
to associate with the eternal Word : " She is the brightness
of the everlasting light, the unspotted mirror of the power
of God, and the image of His goodness."   " She is the breath
of the power of God, and a pure stream flowing from the
glory of the Almighty." [2]   It is perhaps true to say that
at this stage of thought, the personification of Wisdom has
attained a more definite degree of substantive being than
in the earlier books ; [3] but she is still an expression for the
power and love of God : there is no independent existence,
unless it is implied in such a passage as " Give me wisdom,
her that sitteth by Thee on Thy throne." [4] Not only is
wisdom described in terms which are elsewhere applied to
the Word, but the function of creation is attributed to her
as fully as to the Word : " O God of the Fathers . . . Who
madest all things by Thy Word and by Thy Wisdom didst
form man." [5]

The importance of the book in the evolution of Christology is plain. Written about the middle of the last
century before the Christian era, it was at the disposal of
Philo, and if it stopped short of his theory of the $\Lambda\acute{o}\gamma o \varsigma$ as
$\acute{o}$ $\delta \epsilon \acute{v} \tau \epsilon \rho o \varsigma$ $\theta \epsilon \acute{o} \varsigma$, it was not far removed from such an
enrichment of the Divine being as is contained in the
theology of the Prologue.[6] In any case it forms a notable

---

[1] Sir. xxiv. 9, πρὸ τοῦ αἰῶνος ἀπ' ἀρχῆς ἔκτισέ με ; xxiv. 8, καὶ ὁ κτίσας με
κατέπαυσε τὴν σκηνήν μου καὶ εἶπεν, Ἐν Ἰακὼβ κατασκήνωσον, καὶ ἐν Ἰσραὴλ
κατακληρονομήθητι. Cf. Jo. i. 1, 14.

[2] Wisd. vii. 26, ἀπαύγασμα γάρ ἐστι φωτὸς ἀϊδίου καὶ ἔσοπτρον ἀκηλίδωτον
τῆς τοῦ Θεοῦ ἐνεργείας, καὶ εἰκὼν τῆς ἀγαθότητος αὐτοῦ. vii. 25, ἀτμὶς γάρ ἐστι
τῆς τοῦ Θεοῦ δυνάμεως, καὶ ἀπόρροια τῆς τοῦ παντοκράτορος δόξης εἰλικρινής.
Cf. Heb. i. 3 ; Col. i. 15.

[3] So Lücke, ib., p. 268.

[4] Wisd. ix. 4, δός μοι τὴν τῶν σῶν θρόνων πάρεδρον σοφίαν.

[5] Ib., ix. 1, 2, Θεὲ πατέρων . . . ὁ ποιήσας τὰ πάντα ἐν λόγῳ σου, καὶ
τῇ σοφίᾳ σου κατεσκεύασας ἄνθρωπον.

[6] V. Lücke, ib. ; Philo, Fragments, ii. 625. Cf. Justin M., Dial., 56.

stage in the long process of thought by which men tried to understand more clearly the true nature of God and His relation to the phenomenal world.

So far, we have briefly reviewed the preparation for Johannine thought which is presented in the Old Testament and the Apocryphal writings which are so closely connected with it. The question arises whether it suffices to account for the phenomena which meet us in the prologue, when taken in conjunction with the personal experience of the writer. We have to bear in mind the contribution to his outlook which was made by his intercourse with the Master in Whom he had learnt to see the fulfilment and realisation of Old Testament prophecy and foreshadowing. Or, on the other hand, has the writer gone farther afield for his material and taken from the thought of the Gentile world something of the form, if not the content, of his philosophy ? The suggestion is not unreasonable. The Wisdom literature of the Old Testament itself bears many a trace of modes of thought which would become familiar to the educated Jew of the Dispersion. If the Gospel of St. John appeared in Ephesus, its author was in a position to know something of the speculative questions which were agitating men's minds at the time. He may have been acquainted with the writings of his early contemporary Philo, and have been emboldened by his example to express himself in terms which recalled the schools of Alexandria rather than those of Palestinian Rabbinism. But, as we shall see, the assumption of a *necessary* indebtedness of St. John to Philo is not required. The traces of similarity in the choice of language are more than outweighed by the contrasts which he presents ; while everything that appears to be reminiscent of Philo can easily be accounted for by the prevailing intellectual atmosphere of such a city as Ephesus. The Stoic and the Platonist Jew abounded there as elsewhere in the large centres of population of the Græco-Roman world. A mind like that which is revealed in the composition of the Fourth Gospel would hardly need the help of Philo in the formulation of his thought. Yet the partiality of Christians for the writings of Philo and the use made of them in the literature of the second century justify us in believing that the Author of the Gospel would not be averse to employ the phraseology and, to some extent, the ideas of a writer so learned both in the Scriptures of his own people and in the thought of the larger world with which Judaism was in contact. We have only to think of Apollos, of his antecedents at Alexandria and his period of speaking and teaching at Ephesus, to be sure that, when the Fourth Gospel came to be written, there would be many Christians in Asia to whom Philonian modes of thought would be familiar. It was likely that the Evangelist would, for his own purposes, take advantage of this familiarity and make it subsidiary to the reception of his teaching.[1]

But he quickly shows that if he employs Philo he is in no wise subservient to his authority. If there is one conception that is wholly alien to the mind of the Alexandrian, one thought that runs counter to the whole spirit of his philosophy, it is the Incarnation of the Logos. Nothing could be further from the view of a man who, while deeply read in the Old Testament Scriptures, was at the same time a Hellenist and a precursor of Gnosticism. It had been Philo's aim to interpret the anthropomorphic representations of God which had contented his countrymen in the past, by a higher and more worthy conception of the Divine nature ; to insist upon the sublimity and seclusion of the Ruler of the Universe and to explain His relation to the world by the theory of intermediaries, who might bridge the gulf between the Infinite and the Finite and so make possible some kind of relation between God and the world.

Against this view St. John sets his doctrine of the Incarnation. He is with Philo in what he taught of the

---

[1] I find that F. Heiler takes a somewhat similar view of the influence of Philo. After observing that " in Philo the prophetic, revealed religion of the Old Testament is united with Platonic mysticism," he says that these two opposite types of piety appear in St. Paul unreconciled with one another. " In the Fourth Gospel, which stands under the influence of Philo and the Hermetic mysticism, their union is already effected ; a tender mystical union with God speaks in all the words of the Johannine Christ." *Das Gebet*, p. 234.

action of the Logos in creation and of His close relation to God, although he would define that relation very differently from the Alexandrian scholar. But he breaks away from him entirely in the great saying, Καὶ ὁ λόγος σὰρξ ἐγένετο. The higher was Philo's sense of the Divine character of the Word, the more he would have shrunk from so complete an identification with humanity as is implied in the Incarnation. Whatever the debt of St. John to Philo—if debt there were—we can trace no connection between that fundamental conception of his Gospel and the mind of the Platonist Jew of Alexandria.

But, if St. John's use of the Logos can be partly accounted for by the force of tradition in the Scriptures and in the experience of his own people, it is also true that his choice of the term with its associations was probably dictated by the end that he had in view in the composition of his Gospel. The Church at Ephesus, for which it was primarily intended, was largely composed of Hellenistic Jews and of Greeks, to whom the term meant much. The term would irresistibly bring to their minds the part which it played in Greek thought from Heracleitus of Ephesus downwards.[1] It would be only natural for the Evangelist to engage their interest in his work by at once showing that in Christ the best thought of their own philosophy was met and fulfilled. As other Evangelists had shown Him to be the answer to the longings of His own people, St. John, writing for a wider Church, Gentile as well as Jewish, will suggest that in Christ, the Incarnate Word, the problems which had occupied their greatest thinkers find their only solution. He is writing for a world predominantly Greek, and he writes accordingly.[2]

---

[1] Cf. von Dobschütz, Studien u. Kritiken, July, 1924, p. 246, "As old Heracleitus of Ephesus had long ago waxed hot over the unreasonableness of men who do not follow the Λόγος, so John of Ephesus sorrowfully meditates upon their lack of reason." i. 5, 11.

[2] There is a tendency in the present day to assign a special significance to terms which do not necessarily require it. In the second part of his Untersuchungen über die Entstehung des Vierten Evangeliums, 1923, J. Grill rightly describes the purpose of the Evangelist in dealing with his material. He will " make the revelation of Christ the Logos and the religion which was to be based upon it as intelligible, sympathetic, and familiar (anheim-

Whatever our view of the actual sources of his terminology,[1] we can hardly avoid the conclusion that its use
was diplomatic. He will at once arrest attention and
arouse interest, before he tells his story. He introduces
the term as though it must be well understood by his
hearers, and yet it is only as we read on that its application
is perceived. Then we see that it must refer to the Son of
God, Jesus the Christ.

Startling and sudden as its introduction is its disuse.
It occurs only in the Prologue, not in the body of the
Gospel. As a term expressive of the Person of Christ it
disappears. Its application to His life as the Jesus of
History would have been unhistorical ; [2] and it is history
that the Evangelist sets out to write.

We are, therefore, presented at once with a problem.
Why is the term employed ? There must have been a
definite object before the writer's mind, an object dictated
by the purpose which he set before himself when he began
his work.

His object is clear. It is the confirmation of the faith
of the Christian Church in the Messiahship and the Divine
Sonship of Jesus.[3] This faith is intended for all who will

elnd) to his Greek and Hellenistic circle of readers as possible." P. 376.
But few will go so far with Grill as to find throughout the Gospel constant
references and allusions to the cult of Dionysus in its many forms, introduced with the intention of recommending his teaching to those who
were adherents of that widely spread devotion. Points of resemblance
are capable of a very different explanation. One of the surest proofs of
the divine origin of the religion of Christ is the way it meets and fulfils
the best thoughts and the highest aspirations of earlier seekers after God.
But many of Grill's parallels are too fanciful to need refutation. The
desire to establish his theory causes him to find intentional allusions in
passages which are clearly descriptive of actual occurrences in the Gospel
story, told because they so happened and with no typological reference.
Cf. pp. 348–355.

[1] Harnack, who reads for δ $\upsilon i \delta s$, δ $\dot{\epsilon} \kappa \lambda \epsilon \kappa \tau \delta s$, in Jo. i. 34, as the more
ancient, observes that it shows how deeply the Fourth Evangelist was
rooted in Jewish Theology ; and he adds : " To find fresh proofs of this
fact . . . is at present a special duty, since an un-Jewish Hellenism, out
of which the most important features of his religious thinking are thought
to be explained, is imputed to him." *Sitzungsberichte der Königln.
Preussn. Akademie der Wissenschn.* for 1915, p. 556. Cf. Burney, *The
Aramaic Origin of the Fourth Gospel*, p. 39.

[2] Not as a matter of fact, but because it would have been premature,
implying the reflection of a later period.

[3] Jo. xx. 31 ; cf. xix. 35 ; xxi. 24.

receive it. But to the non-Jewish world, Messiahship meant little. Thought ran in a different channel. What prophecy had been to Judaism, philosophy was to the Græco-Roman world. The Evangelist recognises this fact, and the tradition of the place where he wrote would turn his mind in the same direction. To many of the converts, both of St. Paul and of himself at Ephesus, the Logos was a familiar conception. It was there that Heracleitus, in the sixth century B.C., taught that there is an eternal and universal principle which is immanent in all things, the Logos, or world-reason, in which all things partake and the following of which is man's bounden duty.[1] Through his pupil Cratylus, the master of Plato, the conception was known to Plato himself and may have contributed to the formulation of his view that the idea of Goodness is to be identified with the Supreme Deity. Nor was Aristotle untouched by the spirit of the Ephesian sage. With the Logos of Heracleitus in mind, he seems to imply that God, as the supreme intelligence or reason, dwelling in thought upon Himself is, in Himself, both subject and object.[2]

The immanent reason of Heracleitus is found again in Stoicism ; but it is at Alexandria and in the schools of Hellenistic Judaism that the conception acquires its chief significance, both for philosophy and for religion. The Logos has become the recognised term for the action of God upon the world. It is true that the authority of the Septuagint version of the Psalms[3] could be cited in this connection. But that version itself was produced when there was close contact between Jewish and Hellenic thought and, if the conception was rooted in Judaism, it had caught something of the wider outlook which prevailed in the Hellenic world.

Shortly before the Christian era, the writer of Wisdom

---

[1] V. Ritter et Preller, Historia Philos., i., § 31 ; Bywater, Heracl. Ephes. Reliquiæ, ii., xci., xcii., xcvi.; Zeller, D. Philos. der Griechen⁶, 1920, Teil i. 2, pp. 793, 922 ; Ueberweg, D. Geschichte der Philos. (E.T.), i. p. 42. V. above, p. 180, n. 1.

[2] Metaphys., xii. 9 ; v. W. D. Ross, Aristotle's Metaphysics, i., p. cxli.

[3] Ps. xxxiii. 3 ; cxlvii. 15 ; cxlviii. 8 ; cxix. 105 ; where νόμος = λόγος, דבר. Cf. Ecclus. xxxiii. 3.

finding, like others before him, a difficulty in the thought of any direct action of God upon the world, regards Wisdom as the intermediary between the Creator and His creation. But, although he does not often employ the term Λόγος,[1] it is clear that he is in touch with the range of thought to which the term belongs. He imputes to Wisdom the close connection and the intimate fellowship in thought and action with God, which is elsewhere ascribed to the Logos. In one passage, the writer addresses God as having " formed all things by His word and made man by His wisdom." Here the terms Λόγος and Σοφία appear as names of the same thing.[2] The idea is that of a living force or activity present with God as one of His attributes, and going forth from Him as an agent or messenger endowed with a personality of its own. But no attempt is made by the writer to distinguish between attribute and person. Now Wisdom speaks as a being separate from God, and now as a quality inherent in the Godhead. At the back of the whole conception lies the thought of the Greek world. It was soon to pass through the minds of the Christian writers of the first century and thereby render the greatest possible service to the Church in its task of commending the Gospel to both Jew and Gentile.

The Book of Wisdom saw the light in Alexandria, and it was an Alexandrian Jew who carried its idea of mediating action between the Creator and His works still farther. Philo was living and writing at Alexandria while Christ was teaching and healing in Palestine.[3] Their paths never crossed. Whether the Jewish writer ever even heard of Christ, we do not know. Nothing in his later writings points to such knowledge, and as he died about A.D. 49 there was hardly time for the effect of the knowledge, if he possessed it, to make itself felt. But his appearance on the stage of religious history was nothing less than epoch-making. He was first and foremost a theologian and was,

[1] But v. xviii. 15 ; xvi. 12.
[2] Ib., ix. 1. Cf. vii. 21 ; viii. 4 ; ix. 9 ; Prov. viii. 27, 30 ; Job xxviii. 12 f.
[3] V. above, p. 178.

perhaps, the earliest writer who could lay claim to the title. He was also a philosopher ; but one whose hold on his religion was unshaken by the speculative knowledge in which he was so deeply versed.

It was this double character of theologian and philosopher that gave him his great importance in the progress of religious thought. Like John the Baptist, he did much to prepare for the Kingdom of God : a kingdom which, like the Baptist, he never entered. What the Forerunner effected in preparing the hearts and the wills of men for Christ, Philo accomplished for their minds. His doctrine of the Logos and the part played by the Logos both in creation and in the communion between God and man, largely influenced Christian thought and helped to bridge the intellectual gulf that, at first, seemed to bar the passage of the Gospel from the Jewish to the Hellenic world.

It is, of course, impossible to prove any direct indebtedness to Philo on the part of New Testament writers. What is tolerably certain is that educated people in Ephesus and its neighbourhood were familiar with his attitude both to Judaism and to Greek philosophy. In both regions of thought the conception of the Logos as the Word or expression of the mind and will of God, and as the Reason which pervades all things, appealed to all that was best in them. Both St. Paul and the writer to the Hebrews show that, if they had not sat at the feet of Philo, they had at least been well acquainted with ideas to which he gave so full an expression ; and it is easy to see that both of those New Testament writers did much to shape the phraseology of the Fourth Evangelist.[1]

When St. John came to write his Gospel, he had at his disposal three main sources from which to draw his material. There was his own experience as an eyewitness of Christ tested and confirmed, as it was, by that of the general body of believers and the testimony of the writers who preceded him. There was the rich inheritance of the Scriptures of his own people with their accompanying Apocalyptic

[1] Cf. Col. i. 15-20 ; Heb. i. 1-4 ; iv. 12, 13, with the Prologue.

literature : and there was also the tone of thought, largely philosophic, with which he was necessarily brought into touch during his residence at Ephesus.

There is no need to ask how far he was directly indebted to Philo. It is evident that thought and language characteristic of the Alexandrian Jew occur frequently in the Prologue.[1] The speculations of so remarkable a thinker could not fail to be known in the cultivated circles of Ephesus well before the Gospel appeared. In his desire, so evidently expressed both in Gospel and First Epistle, to enlist the interest and adhesion of those for whom he writes, the Evangelist would not shrink from any right expedient to gain a hearing. He chooses a term with which his Greek hearers are familiar. With them its associations are of a high order. It is bound up with ideas of the Godhead which had gradually been purified through ages of reverent thought, until something approaching the stern Monotheism of Judaism was the result.[2]

But if the Logos had a long and, recently, a dominating history in the Greek world in which the Evangelist now found himself, it was also deeply rooted in the minds of his own people. Whether as Word or Wisdom, Jewish thought had for a long period conceived of a quality, or perhaps an entity, standing so close to God as to form part of His being, while at times, it seemed to take the appearance of a separate existence. While the principle of Monotheism, which since the Exile had become supreme in Judaism, kept men true to the worship of the One God and Father, the spirit of reverence which it begat, led, strange to say,

---

[1] For proof of this statement, v. Weinel, *Bibl. Theologie des N.T.*, p. 531.

[2] Thus Xenophanes, in the sixth century B.C., spoke of one Spiritual Being who knew and pervaded all things, v. Arist., *Metaphys.*, i. 5. The noble saying of Socrates, as he was about to die, points in the same direction : " It is now time to depart, I to die, you to live ; whose is the better destiny is unknown to all save God." Plat., *Apol. Socr.*, p. 42. So in his *Timæus* (p. 29) Plato speaks of the goodness of the Creator in desiring that all things should be as like Himself as they could be. Aristotle from change and movement argues that there must be one eternal Being Who is Himself unchanging. *Phys.*, viii. 6 ; *Metaphys.*, xii. 7.

to a certain loosening of its hold upon them. How could Jehovah, invisible and inaccessible in His majesty, enter into communion with His creatures? The gulf that lay between Creator and creation seemed too profound for any direct approach. Besides, contact with Persia had introduced dualistic conceptions among Jews of the Dispersion. The evil nature of matter and all material things was a tenet which greatly affected their outlook and appeared to widen the distance that separated God from man.

God seemed to be too high enthroned above the world, too far removed in His purity and majesty, for any kind of direct communion and intercourse with man. Reverence demanded an intermediary. The Logos, as Philo conceived it, seemed to contain within itself the precise qualities which the thought and aspiration of the time demanded. Pre-existent to creation, the Word or Wisdom of God was, as a Son, begotten by Him; and when He willed to create, was by Him as His agent, fully aware of His mind and will and empowered to act for Him.

It was in the midst of a community familiar with these conceptions that the Fourth Gospel was composed. It is not surprising that its author, in his desire to bring the knowledge of Christ into touch with the prevailing mode of thought, used its terminology and showed a certain sympathy with its ruling ideas; all the more because Jewish religious thought had itself been influenced by them. Jewish piety coincided with Greek philosophy in its emphasis on the Divine transcendence. In each case, there was a belief that God is Absolute, Infinite, separated, in virtue of His perfection, from his creatures by a gulf that they could not hope to cross. Each system held that God, supreme as He was, thought and felt for the creatures whom He had brought into being.[1] Plato taught that love was the mediator between God and man;[2] making it possible for the mortal to have communion with the immortal. Jewish religion saw in the Logos the connecting link between

---

[1] But this was not the view of Aristotle; *v.* below, p. 261, n. 2.
[2] *Sympos.*, p. 202 E.

heaven and earth.[1]   These two streams of thought met in Philo.

Now, a comparison of the Prologue of the Gospel with the language of Philo shows a remarkable similarity of form and idea.   But an equally remarkable degree of unlikeness is to be noted.   The Evangelist marches with Philo in the belief in the Divine transcendence, in the sympathy of the Creator with His creatures, in the conviction that all men are capable of enlightenment and that a being, to whom Philo at times attributes personality [2] while St. John is consistent in such attribution, is the medium of enlightenment and the agent of the Father's good will.   So far for the resemblance.

When the Evangelist, after proclaiming in Philonic terms the Divine character of the Logos, goes on to identify Him with a man whom he had seen and with whom he had lived on terms of friendship, he parts company with the Alexandrian writer.[3]   The Incarnation of the Logos was a conception which, if it could ever have occurred to Philo, ran counter to his philosophy.   There was too much evil in matter ;   the dualism that pervaded the universe, according to his thinking, was too pronounced for him to allow that the Son of God could become man.

From the nature of the Word, the Evangelist passes to the sphere of His activity ;   and in so doing emphasises the fact that the Logos is no mere abstraction.   He had said that He was God, but he now proceeds to illustrate this truth by describing His relation to the phenomenal world. And here comes out a remarkable feature of Johannine thought.   He delights in antithesis :   God and Man, God and the World, Light and Darkness, Truth and Error. So strongly does he enforce the contrasts ;   so irreconcilable do they seem to him that, at times we are almost tempted to suspect the influence of Iranian dualism which must have

---

[1] *V.* above, p. 182.
[2] *V.* Zeller, *Philos. der Griech.*, iii. 2, p. 324 f.   So, too, Wisdom is personified, Prov. viii. *passim ;* Sir. xxiv. 3.
[3] *V.* Rendel Harris, *Odes and Psalms of Solomon*, p. xiv.

long ago penetrated as far west as Ephesus.[1] But his own language forbids the thought. He knows of only one source of being. There is no ὕλη of independent origin, evil in its nature and standing over against the source of all good in rivalry and opposition. " All things came to be by Him and apart from Him there was not one thing that came to be." [2] Manichæanism can find no support in St. John. There is no room in his philosophy for a conception of matter as inherently evil and as owing nothing to God's creative power. Nor does he, like Philo,[3] regard it as the necessary condition of God's creative activity, enabling Him to produce new forms, while lacking all responsibility for their essential nature. If there is a dualism in St. John, it is not one of opposition and contrast in the created world, but of inward harmony—that of God and the Word—in the creative power ; a conception already prepared for the Evangelist by the writer to the Hebrews.[4] The process of thought must have been gradual. It needed time and reflection to pass from belief in the One Source and Maker of all things, to belief in the creative function of the Eternal Son, Whom men had known in the flesh as Jesus of Nazareth. *But the transition was effected*, and the special contribution of St. John is the triple

---

[1] " Tout l'Évangile n'est que la lutte et le triomphe du Verbe à qui résiste le monde des ténèbres."   Allo, *S. Jean l'Apocalypse*, p. cxcviii. Cf. Jo. i. 5.

[2] Jo. i. 3. I adopt the punctuation of A.V. and R.V. rejecting the Valentinian gloss (of R.V. margin) which, as Lücke said, " gives no meaning that one can put up with " (keinen erträglichen Sinn), *Comment. über d. Evan. Joh.*, i., p. 305. According to Zahn, it is unjustifiable " sprachlich und sachlich," *Evang. des Joh.*, p. 50. Clemen considers that Zahn has proved the originality of the usual punctuation, *D. Entstehung des Joh. Evang.*, p. 49 ; while Heitmüller agrees with the comment of Lücke, *D. Schriften des N.T.* (J. Weiss), ii. p. 719. Bp. Westcott *ad loc.* tries hard to make the best of the punctuation suggested by the R.V. margin, but admits that " the interpretation of the passage is undoubtedly most difficult." Broadly speaking, a reading in so vital a context, which gives no tolerable sense, may be safely put aside. B. Weiss, *ad loc.* (Meyer's *Comment.*, vi., p. 59), while rejecting the Valentinian punctuation, suggests its early adoption in Versions and Fathers as due to a sense of tautology in the expression ἐγένετο οὐδὲ ἕν, ὃ γέγονεν.

[3] *V.* Drummond in Hastings *D.B. V.* art. "Philo." p. 201. Cf. W. D. Ross, *Aristotle's Metaphysics*, 1924, i., p. cliii.

[4] Heb. i. 2, δι᾽ οὗ καὶ ἐποίησεν τοὺς αἰῶνας ; cf. 1 Cor. viii. 6 ; Col. i. 16.

identification of the Logos, the Eternal Son, and the Man Christ Jesus.

It is doubtful if St. John felt any philosophic need to bridge the antithesis between God and the World, between the Absolute and the Relative, the Infinite and the Finite. It had been experienced from early times in Israel, as anthropomorphic terms and theophanies, as well as the expressions of the Wisdom literature, clearly show. But for one who had accepted the full revelation of God in Christ, such a necessity would have ceased to present itself. In Christ, the gulf was crossed, God and the world had met. The bridge was there in the perfect Manhood. The discord was resolved.

There was still indeed the great contrast which must always exist between the Divine and the human. But it presented no obstacle to union, spiritual and moral. If God could express Himself in terms of humanity, not excluding its material element, it was made possible for man to become a partaker of the Divine nature : " Now are we the Sons of God, and it doth not yet appear what we shall be." [1]

The philosophic standpoint of St. John in regard to his view of God and the world may be summed up in the assertion that all that is not God was made by Him. He alone is Self-existent and is the Author of all that is not Himself. There is, therefore, the strongest possible negation of pantheism. A deep dividing line is drawn between the Creator and the created, between God and what is not God. The antithesis is one of fact, quite apart from the ethical value of the created world. That is only hinted at in the Prologue. In the First Epistle it is a leading feature, and the contrast is raised to the highest degree of mutual exclusiveness. St. John here appears to be frankly pessimistic. He can see no glimmer of hope for " the world " as he conceives it. The term he uses is remarkable, ὁ κόσμος, an ordered, organised whole ; human society

---

[1] 1 Jo. iii. 2. Cf. Chrys. in *Joan. Homil.* on Jo. i. 14, p. 63 c, Ἐγένετο γὰρ υἱὸς ἀνθρώπου, Θεοῦ γνήσιος ὢν υἱός, ἵνα τοὺς τῶν ἀνθρώπων υἱοὺς τέκνα ποιήσῃ Θεοῦ.

consciously and willingly living without reference, if not in
actual hostility, to God. The classical expression of his
mind is " The world as a whole lieth inert within the
influence of the evil one." [1] This does not mean that the
world, in the widest sense, is entirely subject to that evil
influence. The writer has already specified an exception,
ἐκ τοῦ Θεοῦ ἐσμεν. He is speaking of the sphere, rather than
of the success of evil. Satan, ὁ ἐν τῷ κόσμῳ is powerful but
he is not almighty, cunning but not omniscient. And
St. John's recognition of this relieves his pessimistic outlook, as it seems, from the charge of dualism. He is alive
to the tremendous power of evil ; but he is aware of its
limitations. It is the enemy, but never the equal, of God.
His philosophy rests on the sure basis of a personal experience of the power of goodness as he had seen it in Christ,
the Incarnate Word. He was never in doubt of its final
triumph ; but he felt acutely the sharpness of the struggle.
Of this we are assured by his report of our Lord's own
forecast of victory : " The prince of this world is judged."
" I have overcome the world." [2]

Here should be noticed another form of the antithetical
mode of writing in which St. John delights. The contrast
between God and the world is exchanged for one between
κόσμος and κόσμος used in two senses : " He was in the
world and the world was made by Him and the world knew
Him not." [3] The world in the first two clauses is clearly
the world in its larger, comprehensive sense, the world as
the result of the creative power of the Logos and in which
He is immanent.[4] But in the third clause, " the world
knew Him not," the connotation is different. Here it is
the world of rational beings all of whom have by nature—
qua men—the illumination of reason, the gift of " the true

---

[1] 1 Jo. v. 19, ὁ κόσμος ὅλος ἐν τῷ πονηρῷ κεῖται. Κόσμος is, as compared with the Synoptics, chiefly Johannine. They use αἰών generally
with the notion of duration (as always when used by St. John).

[2] Jo. xvi. 11, 33.   Christ could so speak even before the Cross.   Cf.
Lk. x. 18.   The whole question of a pessimistic view of the world, especially
as so frequently seen in persons of saintly life, requires closer investigation
than it has yet received.

[3] Jo. i. 10.   [4] Cf. Col. i. 17.

light " ; but by perverse exercise of the will, " knew Him not," or as St. Paul states the case, " they did not approve of retaining God in their knowledge." [1]   Thus we have the ordered world of creation, good and pure from the hand of its Maker, and within, yet over against it, the world of men, who by wrong use of their will, have declined to recognise their Maker.

Closely connected with this antithesis is that between truth and error, light and darkness : " the light shineth in darkness and the darkness comprehended it not." [2]   There is the same conception, but in a more abstract form.   Light and Truth are almost synonymous in the Prologue.   Darkness is symbolical of error. [3]   The opposition is moral and spiritual.   It is concerned with the will.   There lies the tragedy.   Light is the portion of every man (v. 9).   All in greater or less degree partake of the gift of reason from Him Who is " the true light."   But only here and there is the gift taken and used : for when the true light came into the world and offered Himself to His own people, His own as a body received Him not.   There was found no room for Him, as at Bethlehem He had no place among men, but was among the beasts of the stall.   " The world knew Him not " ; " His own received Him not."   The prologue anticipates, while it is a reflection from, the Saviour's own lament : " Ye will not come unto Me, that ye may have life." [4]   " It is the sad refrain that we shall hear throughout the Gospel." [5]   " Men loved darkness rather than light, because their deeds were evil." [6]

It is in the body of the Gospel and in the First Epistle

---

[1] Rom. i. 28.

[2] Jo. i. 5 ; cf. v. 9, τὸ φῶς τὸ ἀληθινόν. There is the same touch of pessimism in ἡ σκοτία αὐτὸ οὐ κατέλαβεν, " comprehended it not." Both Westcott ad loc. and Zahn ad loc. (p. 62) translate " overcame," " zu unterdrücken." On the other hand, Lücke, Evang. Joh., i., p. 309, H. Holtzmann ad loc., and Heitmüller in D. Schriften des N.T., ad loc., incline to " comprehended " " hat es nicht ergriffen."

[3] Cf. Proper Pref. for Whit-sunday, " Whereby we have been brought out of darkness and error into the clear light and true knowledge of Thee."

[4] Jo. v. 40.

[5] " Das traurige Lied, das wir durch das ganze Evangelium hören werden." Heitmüller, op. cit., ad Jo. i. 26.

[6] Jo. iii. 19.

that the contrast of light and darkness, which is so prominent in the Prologue, takes the form of truth and error, or
unreality.   The antithesis is a keynote of the Johannine
writings.   Truth, in its eternal war with error and half-
truth, is a passion with the Evangelist.   It comes out in
those asseverations which to some minds appear so strange
and so conclusive of the non-Apostolic authorship of the
Gospel ; [1] but to others are seen to be the natural utterance
of one to whom truth is no mere academic interest, but a
vital necessity of all right living.

The question hardly arises whether writings which
bear so clearly the impress of a mind that moved easily in
the region of philosophic thought are to be credited with
the intention of forming a system.   It is true that, as we
have seen, many of the deepest problems that confront the
thinking man come up in the course of his writings ; but
there is no attempt to systematise, or to give logical
connection to, the subjects discussed.   He tells us very
clearly what was his object in writing.   It was spiritual
and moral rather than intellectual ; to kindle in his disciples
and hearers a life-giving faith in Jesus as the Christ and the
Son of God ; not to provide for them a rationale of that
faith.   An answer is given to many of the questions that
lie at the root of the Christian life.   But he takes no pains
to co-ordinate his teaching.   The Gospel with its attendant
Epistle is a message of Salvation.   In its course, it deals
with the deepest mysteries of the Faith.   It opens the
windows of heaven and gives glimpses of what is passing
within.   It touches Reality with a hand all the surer for
its evident freedom from the language or the aims of the
schools.   Its motive is never speculative ; it always has
life in view.   Yet, by its disclosures of historic facts, by
its inspired vision of what lay behind them, it has made it
possible for an open and teachable mind to feel that, without disloyalty to the divine gift of reason, it may hold with
all certainty the truth that in Jesus Christ, Son of God and
Son of Man, the Eternal Godhead has been and is revealed
to men.

[2] Jo. xix. 35 ; cf. xx. 30 ; xxi. 24.

CHAPTER XII

THE THEOLOGY OF ST. JOHN

The Humanity of Christ

THE Gospel, which is commonly thought to place the highest significance upon the Person of Christ, is equally remarkable for its insistence upon His true and complete humanity. This fact is due partly to the lateness of the appearance of the Gospel. So many of the original eye-witnesses of our Lord had passed away that some Christians had begun to doubt whether One, Whose Deity had become a fixed tenet of the Church's faith, was indeed the Jesus of Nazareth Who had lived and suffered here among men. It was only natural that as the truth of His Deity became more and more impressed upon men's minds, there should be a certain weakening of the belief in His perfect humanity. The two great master truths of His Person are not easy to balance. In different ages, there has been an inclination in one direction or the other. Although the two sides of the truth are in no sense contradictory, the firm holding of the one has often led to a certain depreciation of the other. So marked was this tendency at the close of the first century, that some other cause than the lack of balance of mind must be sought to account for the state of things which is disclosed both in the Fourth Gospel and in the First Epistle.

One result of the passing of the new Religion from its cradle in Judaism to the world of Hellenism was contact with Stoic and Platonic modes of thought. The hard line of demarcation between matter and spirit, between man and God, which was drawn in these schools, was bound to have some influence on the convert's reception of the Gospel of the One Who was proclaimed to be both God and man. So strong was this influence in certain quarters that men who had welcomed the message of a Divine Saviour rejected the thought of human nature as involved in His appearance upon earth. They confessed not " that Jesus Christ is come in the flesh." [1] If He were what His disciples and Evangelists said He was, the Son of God, His appearance as man must have been an illusion. Of the two alleged constituents of His Person, one could have had no basis in fact. They accepted Him as the Eternal Son; they rejected the thought that He was true man.

At first sight, it might seem that this attitude of mind was, if erroneous, an error on the right side. To believe and confess that Jesus is Lord might well be the sum and substance of the Gospel message. To the Jew, it was the hardest demand that the Gospel made upon him. To acknowledge the crucified to be both Lord and Christ might suffice. But the Gospel of Christ is a message of Redemption. To give effect to it, it needed the humanising of God. He Who could save must come among us, as one of ourselves, stepping into the arena, where the conflict raged, as one of us, in our own flesh and blood, meeting and conquering the evil which we have to meet and through His victory only can, ourselves, overcome.

Reverent as that Docetic teaching may appear, it was therefore necessary to show that it cuts at the very root of the Christian Faith; and this necessity had to be faced by the leaders of the Church as the first century was closing. If it has left its mark in the most direct form in the Johannine Epistles, where those who deny that Christ came in the flesh are branded as possessing the spirit of Antichrist, it is met indirectly, but no less effectively, by the narrative of the Fourth Gospel. If it is there that Christ is heard to speak more clearly and decisively than elsewhere as the sharer of the Godhead, it is there that appear most unmistakably the lineaments, the manner, the

[1] 1 Jo. iv. 3.

mind of One Who is truly man. The Evangelist, whose choice of his Master's language and whose own reflection on what he has experienced, tends naturally to the highest idealisation of His Person, is surpassed by no other writer in his conviction of His humanity. To St. John, Christ is true man. In each case, the conviction is unhesitating. If in the Epistles its expression is polemical, in the Gospel it appears as a natural and necessary element of the historical recital which he claims to give. At the time he wrote, the need for insistence upon the humanity was even more urgent than the need to insist upon the Godhead. We cannot doubt that it unconsciously affected his choice of incidents and gave force and directness to his report of them.

Indeed, in this respect the Fourth Gospel is closer to the Second than to the other two.[1] This will appear when we call to mind some of those passages in which Christ's human nature is most apparent. It is the two Gospels that most certainly have behind them the eye- and ear-witness of Apostles—St. Peter in the one case and St. John in the other—which in the most downright fashion disclose our Lord's humanity. St. Mark has been charged with crudeness and harshness of language. But St. John is quite as plain-spoken and goes as far as St. Mark in the uncompromising character of his report. Each Gospel tells of such signs of human nature as bodily weakness and weariness. Each reveals the access of strong mental emotion. We even read of states of feeling which, in ordinary persons, very readily become liable to error, and in which the borderline between right and wrong is at times hard to trace. Thus, if St. Mark speaks of the anger of Christ at the hardness of men's hearts, in the Fourth Gospel we read of that peculiarly human trait of favouritism. In " the disciple whom Jesus loved " there is that singling out of an object of attachment, with its result of special con- sideration, which has often been attended with disastrous

---

[1] Cf. J. Weiss, *D. älteste Evang.*, p. 97, " The Christology of Mark stands far nearer to that of John than people usually admit."

consequences. Natural as it is to be drawn to one friend rather than to another, favouritism is, perhaps, of all human emotions, most open to abuse, because it so easily passes into weakness.

It is not only in the sphere of the emotions that the humanity of Christ is disclosed with perfect frankness in the Fourth Gospel. Nowhere else do we find that reiterated disclaimer of independent thought and action, which is so startling and, to some, so perplexing a feature of St. John. Here, it is one of our Lord's chief concerns to guard against the thought that He had come in His own name, or that what He did was in any sense something apart from the mind and will of God. He rejects the idea of any initiative. He subordinates Himself to the will and purpose of the Father, almost to the point of merging His personal identity. He is One with Him in all things. At times He seems to regard Himself as little more than God's messenger, an instrument in the hand of God, a Servant rather than a Son. This feature is absent, not only from St. Matthew and St. Luke, but from St. Mark.[1]

And yet, according to some, such is the idealistic tendency of St. John that in his desire to exalt Christ's Person and to bring out everything that proclaims Him Son of God, he places His humanity in a dim background, making incidents that point to it mere material for his process of idealisation. Thus, Wernle's dictum—" Here (in the Synoptics) the Man : there (in St. John) the God." [2] It would be nearer the mark to state the converse : in St. John, if anywhere in the New Testament, we see the Man of Sorrows.[3] In the other Gospels shines out the glory of the Eternal Son.[4]

If, as we have some reason to think, the incipient Docetism of the close of the first century led the Evangelist to emphasise even more than the Synoptic writers had

[1] V. below, p. 226.
[2] D. Quellen des Lebens Jesu, p. 25, quoted above, p. 149.
[3] Cf. Burkitt, The Gospel History and its Transmission, p. 233, " In no early Christian document is the real humanity of Jesus so emphasised as in the Fourth Gospel."
[4] Cf. Mt. xi. 27 ; xxv. passim ; Lk. x. 22.

done, the true humanity of our Lord,[1] his language, if
occasioned, was not dictated, by the needs of the period
at which he wrote.   It discloses the vivid experience of an
eyewitness, who reports what he has seen.   The style is
that of an impressionist.   The colours are laid on without regard to values.   Thus, the earliest and the latest
of the Gospels that have come down to us, containing, as
they each do, the recollection of an eyewitness, combine
to give the most life-like portrait of the Son of Man.   If
in St. Mark we see Christ through the eyes of St. Peter as
He walked among men, in the Fourth Gospel we see Him
as He appeared, not merely to the faith and piety of the
close of the first century, but to the people among whom
He lived.[2]   Nor does the writer care to correct or explain
when the view taken is wrong and misleading.   He lets the
matter pass, recording what actually occurred, and leaving
it to time and further knowledge to effect a reconciliation.[3]

Now, this is not the procedure of one whose object is to
idealise his subject and who cares for historical incidents
only so far as they can be made to lend themselves to a
spiritual interpretation.[4]   His historical interest is maintained throughout.   It stands side by side with the result
of his meditation on the mystery of our Lord's Person.   It
mingles with his apprehension of His Divine nature, and
that without confusing it.

It is also to be observed that while the humanity of
Christ in the Fourth Gospel is as complete as in St. Mark,

---

[1] V. 1 Jo. iv. 3.   For the reading λύει (in place of μὴ ὁμολογεῖ)
" divides," Vulg. " solvit," v. Harnack, *Sitzungsberichte der Königl".
Preuss". Akademie der Wissen".* for 1915, p. 556; cf. 1 Jo. ii. 22.   " 1 Ep. of
John already combats this rending of Jesus Christ into a Jesus and a
Christ."   Bousset, *Kyrios Christos*, p. 258; v. Westcott, *Epistles of St.
John*, p. 163 f.

[2] Cf. Jo. vi. 42 ; vii. 4 ; viii. 48 ; x. 20, 33.

[3] Cf. Jo. vii. 28, 29, with viii. 14 ; v. vii. 41, 42.

[4] Cf. Loisy, *Le Quatr. Évangile*, pp. 93, 129; Bacon, *The Fourth
Gospel*, p. 349, " We do injustice to this Gospel when we try to force it
to our demand for the ' historical.'   It is not historical but ' spiritual.' "
Why not historical because it is spiritual ?   So, too, E. Meyer, " (The
writer) moves throughout in a mysterious, transcendental world in which
the natural factors of the earthly life pass entirely into the background ;
his narratives are enveloped in a mystic cloud which makes it impossible
to obtain a clear view of what goes on."   *Ursprung u. Anfänge des
Christentums*, iii., p. 321.

it betrays no sign of development.   There is no attempt to qualify, by any kind of explanation, its intense reality.   In the weak, as in the strong, constituents of human nature, Christ is true man.   In view of this fact, which appears when the two Gospels are placed side by side, the attempt of Scholten and others to explain St. John's omissions of the Temptation and the Agony in Gethsemane [1] by the desire to eliminate from his narrative everything that seemed to conflict with his idealising purpose, is quite unjustifiable.   The Evangelist, if we may judge from his procedure elsewhere,[2] is not expressing disapproval of the Synoptic recitals by his omission of them ; rather he confirms them by his silence.   They have been adequately given.   There is no need to repeat them.   Had the Synoptic narratives been to his mind misleading, the importance of the considerations involved in them would, we may be sure, have led him to intervene.

The demand made by a certain section of criticism that the Evangelist should have followed *its own* conception of order and of consistency with the writings that lay before him (for that is what this attitude implies) shows mis-conception of the actual relation of the Gospels to one another.   To be in any true sense of the word historical, the last Evangelist must reproduce what the others have said, and must report nothing that has been omitted by them.   To break this rule is to place himself out of court as a writer of history in the true sense of the term.   Such is, in effect, what is demanded of him.

But, if the omissions of St. John are reckoned against his own asserted claim to write true history, what are we to say of the contention that accuracy of detail is the mark of legendary, apocryphal writing rather than of actual knowledge ? [3]   Can bias appear more plainly ?   Whether

---

[1] But the mental anguish of Gethsemane is at least paralleled, though not so minutely described, by what St. John reports in xii. 27 ; *v.* above, p. 120.

[2] Cf. Jo. iii. 24.

[3] Bacon, *The Fourth Gospel*, p. 337.   In this he may be confronted with Wrede, who considers that this accuracy is a mark of the trust-worthiness of the Gospel : *Character u. Tendenz des Joh. Evang.*, p. 25.

he omits altogether or describes in a manner which agrees with the known situation, according to this view, he is unworthy of credit. Neither procedure can satisfy. A theory has been formed. The contents of the Gospel, if they are to pass muster, must accord with it. There is no question of shaping the theory to the facts. The theory is the criterion of judgment. It is so much the worse for the Gospel narrative if it does not conform to it.

A noteworthy omission of Synoptic material which deals with Christ's humanity is the absence of any clear and direct allusion to the Virgin Birth. Here, again, St. John is in agreement with St. Mark rather than with the other Gospels, although for quite a different reason. St. Mark does not set out to deal with origins. He starts from Christ's public ministry. The silence of St. John is due to another cause. While deeply concerned with the appearance of Christ in the flesh, he appears to show no interest in the way it came about. There is one reference to it in the Prologue ; but unless we abandon the received reading and thereby do violence to the logical connection of the passage, it is rather an indication of the Evangelist's agreement with what had been said in the First and Third Gospels than a pronouncement of his own. The logical trend of thought requires that the relative clause [1] in v. 13 should apply to the subject of v. 12, which is clearly the plural term, " the Sons of God," not a singular,

And Bacon himself elsewhere assigns greater historical value to the Johannine than to the Synoptic duration of the Ministry and the date of the Crucifixion. *Ib.*, pp. 394, 416.

[1] The reading ὅs . . . ἐγεννήθη is found in no good MS., but was known to Justin Martyr, Irenæus and Tertullian. It is, of course, a clear reference to the Virgin Birth of Christ ; but the absence of authority and the logical construction of the whole passage are against it. The verses 11b, 12, 13, *form a parenthesis.* The idea of 11a after this interruption is taken up again in v. 14. Consistency requires that the relative clause should apply to the subject—" those who received Him "—of the passage of which it forms a part. Zahn regards ἐγεννήθη without the singular relative ὅs as the original reading and as referring directly to the Virgin Birth of Christ, whereas the received text refers to it indirectly. *Einleitung in d. N.T.*, ii., pp. 514, 528 ; *D. Evang. des Joh.*, p. 700 f. But, as H. Holtzmann points out, " Manuscript authority is almost entirely wanting, and it remains unexplained how the Plural could have arisen out of the Singular." *Evang. des Johannes, ad loc.*

which would have to be extracted from the expression
" His Name," a mere incident in a clause—" to them that
believe on His Name "—which is epexegetical of the leading
thought of the passage—" to them gave He power, etc."
It is the spiritual generation of the children of God of
which the writer is thinking, although it may be allowed
that the mode of what was the cause of that generation,
the Virgin Birth of the Incarnate Son, is shown, by his use
of terms,[1] to be in his mind.

But passing and incidental as the allusion is seen to be,
the character of the writer's language and the probability
that the Birth stories of St. Matthew and St. Luke were
known to him, suffice to assure us that he was in agreement
with what, by this time, was the received explanation of
our Lord's entrance into the world. Against his adhesion
to that explanation it is as unfair to cite his comparative
silence on the subject as to take the absence of any allusion
in St. Mark as disposing of the narratives of St. Matthew
and St. Luke.

By the time St. John was writing, the belief that Christ's
human nature was prepared for Him by the power of the
Holy Spirit overshadowing the Virgin Mother, had become
an element of the Christian Faith. This " mystery of
godliness " was not at first manifested to the Church at
large. Outside the Holy Family and its nearest kindred,
the birth of Christ had been made known to two distinct
classes—peasants of the surrounding country and a small

---

[1] Οἳ οὐκ ἐξ αἱμάτων, οὐδὲ ἐκ θελήματος σαρκός, οὐδὲ ἐκ θελήματος ἀνδρός, ἀλλ᾽
ἐκ Θεοῦ ἐγεννήθησαν. But H. Holtzmann, ad loc., regards the reference
of this passage to the Incarnation excluding, as it appears to do, all
human participation in the production of life, as contrary to St. John's
own views as to the earthly origin of Christ, and quotes vii. 28. But v.
Westcott on v. 27. Harnack, who discusses the question in Sitzungsberichte der Königl. Preuss. Akademie der Wissenschaften, 1915, p. 542 f.,
reads ὅς . . . ἐγεν[ν]ήθη and considers that " the verse very early, i.e. ' in
the Johannine circle,' must have been written on the margin of the Text
and indeed in reference to the clause καὶ ὁ λόγος σάρξ ἐγένετο, either to
establish conformity with the birth-history of Matthew and Luke, or to
explain so abrupt an expression as σάρξ ἐγένετο, or on both of these
grounds." He remarks that the Virgin Birth is only mentioned in this
passage ; but that it conflicts with not a single verse in the Gospel (p. 550).
Burney, The Aramaic Origin of the Fourth Gospel, p. 34, is inclined to
read ὅς . . . ἐγεννήθη.

group of learned Gentiles. These last had been attracted
to the scene by a visible sign, which accorded with a conviction that at the time was generally entertained throughout the East, that a great deliverer was soon to appear in
the world. But in each case, the experience seems to have
made no lasting impression. " All they that heard wondered
at those things which were told them by the shepherds."
But the nature of the Birth itself was not one of those
things : and the story seems not to have passed beyond
the hills of Bethlehem. The shepherds went back to their
flocks. When their visit was over and their worship and
offerings had been presented, the Magi returned to their
own country by another way. If they took with them a
Gospel of hope for man, we can trace no sign of it. The
unchanging East was still unchanged.

But in one heart, that knew what was hidden from
shepherds and Magi, " all these things " were kept and
pondered.[1] Only after lapse of time, and then with deep
reverence and reserve, the few who knew the sacred mystery
would care, with bated breath, to speak of it. It is reasonable to suppose that, when the primitive community came
to tell up the treasures of Divine wisdom and truth with
which they were entrusted, their minds must have constantly dwelt on every distinguishing factor of their Saviour's
Person and character. Origin and parentage are among
the first questions of interest that occur to a reflecting
mind. And along with the questioning of a reverent
curiosity, there would be the comments of the world outside, which, though it had rejected, was not allowed to
forget Him, if it would. There arose the clash of argument
and controversy. The slander of some of those who
rejected the Gospel message has come down to us ; and
we can understand that the truth that was locked in the
memories of a few—Joseph, if still living, Mary, Elizabeth
—needed to be spoken. Very early it began to pass from
one to another, and a little later to be put down in writing,

[1] Lk. ii. 19, 51.   *V.* W. H. Rigg in *Church Quarterly Review,* Jan. 1925,
pp. 231 f.

or at least to take the settled form of what has been committed to memory. It is these stores of memory or document which, in their singularly primitive form and style, underlie the two first chapters of the First and Third Gospels. If their gift to the Church at large was in itself an act of devotion to the Person of our Lord, it was also a necessary rejoinder to the strictures and comments of those who rejected Him. The purity of the home-life of Nazareth, as well as the sinless character of Him Who shared it, called for this expression.

And it sufficed for the purpose. St. John had no need to tell the story over again. Whatever may prove to be the original reading of the passage we have been considering, there is clear, if indirect, reference to the range of ideas which are involved in the dogma of the Virgin Birth. This being the case, the attempt that has been made to discredit St. John's historical conception of the true humanity of Christ, by claiming that the sole object of His Gospel was to set forth a Christ idealised and exalted,[1] falls to the ground. If it contains an ideal picture of our Lord, the idealism is reflected from His own Person, not from the imagination of the writer. Nor does it obliterate the facts of history and experience which the Gospel contains. The true humanity of Christ was evident to those who were associated with Him. Their report is not contradicted by the intimations of a higher nature of which they were made aware and to which their writings bear solemn witness. The two conceptions of His Person are found side by side. St. John no more than the Evangelists who preceded him made any attempt to effect a synthesis. If he felt the need of a reconciliation, he does not show it. The two aspects

---

[1] Cf. Loisy, Le Quatr. Évang., p. 129. According to Loisy, the idealism of the Fourth Gospel extends even to the persons of people mentioned in it. "The loved disciple is the young Church to which is entrusted the heritage of Judaism and Judaic Christianity. Nothing proves that this disciple ever existed," pp. 128, 129. The Mother of Jesus is symbolical of the Messianic Judaism from which Christianity proceeded, p. 125; cf. p. 75. Cf. Bacon, The Fourth Gospel, p. 317, " The disciple of Jo. xiii. 23–30, is not a disciple of flesh and blood." Cf. p. 319, where he denies the actuality of Jo. xx. 4. In this way, the data of any historical narrative can be explained away. V. B. Weiss, D. Leben Jesu, i., p. 105.

upon all that he had seen and heard while in contact with Christ, he must acknowledge that he had had experience of One Who, for all His claims to a higher nature than that of man, was no less truly one of the same flesh and blood as ourselves. And it is just because the writer is so careful to deal accurately and minutely with details of Christ's human life that he is worthy of confidence when he bids us believe that these human traits did not comprise the whole of His Personality.

It stands to reason that the steps by which this conviction was reached were gradual. The principle of the Incarnation is the revelation of God in and through man. " God was in Christ." The beginning of discipleship consisted in association with one who had all the appearance of being a teacher of quite distinct character and authority ; yet a teacher, doing his work among a people who had been accustomed to pay special respect to the teaching office. " Ye call Me Master and Lord, and ye say well, for so I am " [1] It was through the force and originality of His teaching that Christ made His first appeal to the people for a hearing. It was felt that " He taught them as one having authority, and not as the scribes." [2] But, if we take the Synoptic presentation of His appeal and of the response of His hearers, there is for some time [3] no indication that He regarded Himself as more than man. It is true that in the Birth narratives of the First and Third Gospels things are said of the Holy Child which cannot be applied to one who is bound by the limitations of ordinary human nature. But, as we have seen, these mysterious allusions do not appear to have made any general impression upon other people. There is nothing to show that, as He grew up to man's estate, these signs and hints of future greatness had any effect in determining the character of His career. He adopted, as any other young man of his time would do, the trade of His reputed father. He only quits it at the age of thirty. The reason was probably that which is suggested,

---

[1] Jo. xiii. 13.   [2] Mt. vii. 29.
[3] " For some time," *v.* p. 121.

though not actually stated, by the Evangelist. His kinsman, John the Baptist, had come forth as a new prophet—
when we do not know ; but his appearance by the Jordan
in the wilderness of Judæa is precisely timed.[1] Christ was
thirty years of age, the Baptist six months older. Moved
apparently by an impulse which He could not bring Himself to resist, Jesus leaves His home and His work and
mingles with the motley crowd which gathered round the
Baptist. It was clear to every one that it was the voice of
a prophet that they were listening to : [2] and later on Christ
uttered a remarkable panegyric of His Forerunner, setting
His seal upon the popular verdict.[3]

Now, the question arises : how is Christ distinguished
from the Baptist ? Like St. John, He was popularly
regarded as a Prophet [4] ; and much is being made of the
fact that when, on hearing that John was cast into prison,
He began to teach in Galilee, He repeated the message of
the Baptist : " the kingdom of heaven is at hand." [5] It
was as though He would take the place of the Forerunner,
now that he could no longer fulfil his office, and warn the
world of the coming kingdom. This assumption of the
prophet's rôle in Galilee only took place, as the Fourth
Evangelist assures us, after a considerable period of active
work and teaching which does not appear in the Synoptic
account.[6] If the nearness of the Kingdom was still at that
period the burden of Christ's prophetic teaching, it would
appear that He was still presenting Himself and being
regarded merely as a Teacher and a Prophet. But was
that all that could be said ? Here, again, we are confronted
with a double strain of evidence which reminds us of the

---

[1] Lk. iii. 1–4 ; cf. Mt. iii. 1.
[2] Cf. Mt. xxi. 26.   [3] Mt. xi. 11, 14.
[4] Mt. xxi. 11.   [5] Mk. i. 14, 15.
[6] Jo. iii. 22–25. The οὔπω γὰρ ἦν βεβλημένος εἰς τὴν φυλακὴν ὁ Ἰωάννης,
v. 24, silently corrects the notion which those who had read Mk. i. 14
=Mt. iv. 12 f. might have—that Christ's public ministry only began after
the Baptist's imprisonment. We may conclude that His preaching of
the kingdom, with its prophetic element, formed a feature of that earlier
ministry : v. Zahn ad loc., p. 213 ; Eus., H.E., iii. 24 ; Badham in American
Journal of Theology, 1904, p. 550.

problem presented by the Birth narratives when thought of in relation to the simple ordinary life of Nazareth.[1]

On the one hand, there is the Synoptic insistence on the prophetic ministry of our Lord, giving to some the impression that it was the main factor of His life. Closely connected with it was His work as a Rabbi and the fact that He was generally regarded as one, although of exceptional gifts and authority.

Then, on the other hand, there are incidents which point to a higher order of life and experience. Although the Fourth Gospel has no mention of the Baptism, it concurs with the rest in telling us that there was witnessed a descent of the Holy Spirit upon Christ, and that He it is Who Himself baptizeth with the Holy Ghost.[2] Again, all the Evangelists agree in imputing to Him Sonship to God of a special character. St. John reports the solemn asseveration of the Baptist : " I saw and bare record that this is the Son of God." The Synoptic narrative states that a voice from heaven—the voice of God—was heard saying, " Thou art (This is) My beloved Son in Whom (in Thee) I am well pleased." In each case Divine Sonship is implied.[3]

Now, just as the intimations of a higher nature than that of man which accompanied the Birth of Christ seem to have had little or no effect on the conditions of His life in early manhood, so the signs and portents that attended His Baptism in the Jordan appear to play no part in moulding the character of His early ministry. They do not seem to have been talked about as marking Him out at the very first as One Whose Personality was not that of an ordinary man. In each case—His entrance into the world ; His entrance upon His ministry—the heavens opened and the voice of God or of His angels proclaimed that a great event was occurring. In each case, as silence

[1] V. above, p. 200.
[2] Cf. Jo. i. 32, 33, with Mk. i. 8, 10, and parallels.
[3] Mk. i. 11 and parallels. ὁ υἱός μου ὁ ἀγαπητός. The meaning is " My Son, the only One," according to the use of ἀγαπητός, both classical and in the Septuagint. Cf. Gen. xxii. 2.

fell, at Bethlehem and at the Jordan, the world went on, unheeding. In each case, when " He came to His own, His own received Him not." The lessons which these voices and intimations meant were not learned by their means. Christ entered on His redeeming work as a man among men. It took time and intercourse and discipleship to bring the full truth home.

The comparison that we have drawn between the Synoptic and the Johannine accounts of what happened at the Jordan bears upon the historical character of the latter narrative. If it contains no account of the Baptism, its agreement with the Synoptic narrative of accompanying incidents shows that, as in other instances of Johannine omission, the writer is fully acquainted with what happened. But this omission is sometimes cited as proof of the determined attempt of the Fourth Evangelist to exalt the Person of Christ at all costs. Yet, what do we find on comparing the Synoptic account ? There, as in the Fourth Gospel, and perhaps to a greater extent, the mystery of Jesus stands out in a way that we cannot mistake. If St. John exalts His Person—as his omission of the actual Baptism is thought by some to show—the Synoptic writers do the same. If there is any difference, their emphasis on the character of His Divine Sonship is the more pronounced. " The Son of God," of the Fourth Gospel, is " My Son, the Only One " of the others.[1] Comparison of the idealism of the Synoptic writers with that of St. John in the incidents at the Jordan gives no warrant for the assertion that St. John is too much concerned with exalting Christ's Person to care to narrate what seems to reduce Him to the level of ordinary humanity.

However this may be, the fact remains that what occurred at the Baptism appears to have had little or no influence upon the process of thought by which men came to see in Jesus not a Teacher only, or a Prophet, or the Messiah, but the Eternal Son of God. It was the daily intercourse, the close association, the discipleship with One

[1] Jo. i. 34 ; Mk. i. 11 ; Mt. iii. 17 ; Lk. iii. 22.

Whose character of perfect Holiness and Grace made itself increasingly felt, that led them to the full perception of the truth. The God was revealed in the Man ; true Man, yet exhibiting so much that manhood will not explain, that they came by degrees to understand what He meant when He said, " He that hath seen Me hath seen the Father."

And this consideration helps us to see that there is no contradiction between St. John's narrative of early confession of Christ as Messiah and his insistence on His full and complete humanity. For, if he tells us that the Baptist foretold the redemptive work of Christ ; and if he imputes to Andrew and to Nathanael a perception of Christ's Messiahship which, according to Synoptic accounts, was reached by the disciples generally at a later period, he is not going beyond the stage of faith and understanding which might be expected from the Synoptic disclosure of what happened at the Baptism. Nothing more than Messianic rank is indicated by the sayings of both Andrew and Nathanael. " The Son of God " in the mouth of Nathanael is explained by what immediately follows, " the King of Israel." It is Messianic—not metaphysical— Sonship which is acknowledged ; [1] and the prevailing state of Messianic expectancy to which the Gospels bear witness was quite sufficient to elicit from devout and thoughtful men the utterances which St. John reports.

The testimony of the Baptist is on a different plane. St. John twice affirms the Baptist's belief that Christ, Who in point of time appeared among men after himself, was in fact before him.[2] How are we to interpret this priority ? Is it temporal or qualitative ? The comparison suggested by the use of the terms " after," " before " seems to point

---

[1] Cf. Zahn, *Einleit. in d. N.T.*, ii., p. 544, " It is a long way from the confession of the upright Nathanael to Jesus as the Son of God to the confession of Thomas . . . ' my Lord and my God ' " ; H. Holtzmann, *ad loc.*, p. 68, " The theocratic meaning of υἱὸς τοῦ Θεοῦ comes out clearly from the more definite term βασιλεὺς τοῦ Ἰσραήλ. Each is a heightened expression for Μεσσίας."

[2] Jo. i. 15, 30.

to time, rather than rank or dignity.[1] If so, St. John credits the Baptist with a belief in Christ's pre-existence, which, indeed, is supported by later words of Christ Himself, but seems to conflict with the course of gradual apprehension to which the Gospels as a whole bear witness. But, as we have said,[2] the theory of evolution when applied to human thought and action must not be pressed unduly. It is quite conceivable that in spiritual perception and grasp, a man may be far before his time. One such figure of light and leading, if we accept the Synoptic narrative, was John the Baptist. We have Christ's own authority [3] for regarding him in character and prophetic gifts, though not in privilege or opportunity,[4] as the greatest of men. Such praise sounds exaggerated if there is no outstanding achievement to warrant it. According to the Fourth Gospel, it is to be found in what occurred at the Jordan. Looking upon the man whom he had known as his own kinsman and as the village carpenter of Nazareth, he sees in him, One Who, though younger in the span of human life than himself, was " before " him. This means that by a gift of insight which placed him above all the prophets who preceded him, the Baptist was able to bear witness to the fact that before He was born at Bethlehem, Jesus was living in the heaven from which He came.[5] The Baptist was thus the first to proclaim to the world the pre-existence of Christ. And therein lay his greatness.

How he came to have this intuition, we do not know ; but it is only reasonable to infer that, from his kinship with the Holy Family of Nazareth, he must have heard something of the events that accompanied the Saviour's birth. We have also to remember that from the first the Baptist was a child of promise. Great things were said of him and a high destiny awaited him from the outset : " He shall be

[1] As Zahn points out, if priority in dignity or rank were intended, ἐστι would have been used instead of ἦν, ad loc.

[2] V. above, p. 122.

[3] Mt. xi. 11 ; Lk. vii. 28, from " Q."   [4] Ib.

[5] Cf. Jo. iii. 31, ὁ ἄνωθεν ἐρχόμενος . . . ὁ ἐκ τοῦ οὐρανοῦ ἐρχόμενος. It is probable that v. 31, which, as Zahn says (ad loc., p. 219), shows an unexpressed connection with v. 30, ends the actual words of the Baptist.

great in the sight of the Lord . . . and he shall be filled with the Holy Ghost even from his mother's womb." [1] If we place these early anticipations beside his own early opportunities of knowledge and of intercourse with his kinsman [2] and then think of the place assigned to him by Christ in the long prophetic line, we may well hesitate to charge the Evangelist with lack of historic proportion when he reports the Baptist's declaration of Divine pre-existence. All the information at our command assigns to the Baptist a position of unique significance at the dawn of Gospel history. He must have been, and have done, something to justify this impression. In the Fourth Gospel, the impression is confirmed. In his testimony to Christ as pre-existent, lies the very kernel and heart of the Gospel of the Incarnation.

Nor is this his only service to truth. He takes his place beside the second Isaiah as a prophet of the Atonement. Nothing in Gospel incidents is more dramatic than his sudden unveiling of the Cross, when " looking upon Jesus as He walked, he saith, Behold the Lamb of God," or as he cried, the day before, " Behold the Lamb of God, Which taketh away the sin of the world." [3]

When the Fourth Evangelist is charged with lack of historical perspective in his report of these early confessions of the Person and work of our Lord, as the pre-existent One and as the World's Redeemer, the character and gifts of the Baptist form the ground of an adequate reply. All the Gospels bear witness to his insight and prescience. He stands pre-eminent as a herald and witness of the Lord. As from another Pisgah, he looks upon the kingdom which he may not enter. Only in the person of his disciples does he pass within. He is content to fade, star-like, before the brighter beams of the Light of the World. Like all great preachers of righteousness, he was before his time and

[1] Lk. i. 15.
[2] The reiterated assertion, " I knew Him not," Jo. i. 31, 33, seems to deny that such intercourse had existed. But if the Baptist had been living for years in the desert, it is quite likely that, when Christ appeared at the Jordan, he would not have recognised Him.
[3] Jo. i. 36, 29.

therefore a solitary. No grander figure of a man, nor a more pathetic, appears on the scene of the Old and the New Testament history. And it is here in the Fourth Gospel, rather than in the others, that the explanation of his greatness is to be found. They give Christ's pronouncement of the fact ; St. John gives the ground of it.

The Evangelist's own experience as a disciple of the Baptist may suffice to account for the difference. As he afterwards thought of the two stages of his spiritual experience and of the reason of his passing from the school of the Baptist to that of Christ, memory brought back to him many a significant episode and striking phrase. He speaks in this chapter as one who is living over again every detail of an experience that meant so much to him. No one was so well equipped for the telling of the story. Life and truth shine out in every line of it.

The criticism which rejects the historic value of the Baptist's proclamation of the pre-existence of Him in Whom he foresaw the world's Redeemer is largely *à priori* and based on a theory of development which is applied without heed to special circumstances. It is true that the Synoptic Gospels represent the recognition of the character and Personality of Christ as a gradual process in the case of the Twelve and, in doing so, we feel that they are telling us what was actually the case. But this does not mean that the Fourth Evangelist is unhistorical when he assigns, to a man of gifts so special and unique as the Baptist's, a power of intuitive perception and of spiritual insight, which distinguished him from all who came in touch with Christ, and enabled him to grasp with quickness and with certainty what was laboriously reached by lesser men.

Whether we attribute his utterances to an unique faculty of intuition, or to the inspiration of the Holy Spirit Who had possessed him from his birth, they are the words of a Seer and Prophet, who, on the testimony of our Lord Himself, surpassed in the fulfilment of his office all who went before him.[1]

---

[1] *V. The Person of Our Lord*, p. 274 f.

And it is this acknowledged greatness in the prophetic order, with the singular gifts which it implies, that furnishes a sufficient answer to those who point to the Baptist's declaration of our Lord's pre-existence as an instance of the Evangelist's transference of the theology of the close of the first century to the earliest time.

The Baptist's own language shows that, in his study of Old Testament prophecy during his retirement in the desert, he had obtained a deep insight into what was involved in the coming of the Kingdom and the character of its Messiah. With advantages quickened and strengthened by what St. Luke regarded as a direct and unusual endowment of the Holy Spirit,[1] he could see farther and deeper than other men into the mystery that surrounded the coming One. In the spirit and power of Elijah, and under the influence of the converging beams of light from all the prophets who preceded him, he could say, " He was before me." [2]

To sum up what has been said. The well-attested state of expectancy that prevailed suffices to account for those early confessions of Jesus as Messiah and Son of God which, by running counter to their theory of an orderly development of understanding, are thought by some to lack historical ground. That the combined effect of the Baptist's testimony and the personal power of attraction in Jesus Himself drew men, who had been disciples of the Baptist, to desert him for the new Master, is proof of the existence of a state of mind which very naturally expressed itself in the language which St. John reports. A band of disciples gathers round the new Rabbi ; some of whom, as we learn, have already made up their minds that He is the Christ.

But it should be clearly understood that, apart from the Baptist's declaration of His pre-existence, whatever meaning that conveyed to the people, the confession of Christ had not gone beyond the belief—not yet a certainty —that He was the Messiah of Old Testament and Apoca-

[1] i. 15. [2] Jo. i. 30.

lyptic prophecy, and as such, stood within the limitations of human nature. We can even gather this conclusion from Christ's own words in reply to the generous and enthusiastic confession of Nathanael. Accepting it as a confession of His Messiahship, he speaks of Himself in similar terms, only using the Messianic title of Son of Man, which from its frequent employment He seems to have preferred as His Self-designation.[1]

A further stage of Self-revelation is reached at Cana. Our Lord is now attended by a small band of adherents whom He had attracted to Himself at the Jordan. The miracle is one of those which cannot be accounted for by personal influence, through suggestion or other action of of mind upon mind. It shows Christ's command over nature. As St. John looks back upon it, he sees the presence of more than human power and regards it as a manifestation of (Divine) glory. It had a purpose beyond that of a kind and timely relief of friends from a state of embarrassment through the apparent failure of their hospitality. It was directed towards the forging of the links of trust and reverence that were to bind His disciples to Himself. And it was so far successful. " His disciples believed on Him." [2] In the evolution of their faith, the miracle may be said to mark the first step in that process of apprehension which culminated in St. Paul's declaration of the cosmical office of the Eternal Son : " by Him were all things created . . . by Him all things consist." [3] Such an act of power was natural to Him. The restraint that He put upon its exercise, rather than its use, should excite our wonder.

What was the religious value of the disciples' belief we cannot say : but, as in the early confessions of Christ's Sonship, it may safely be asserted that the belief itself was of a rudimentary character. The conception of Christ's glory as manifested at Cana was formed by the Evangelist when, from the distance of years, he recalled and described the character of the miracle. To him with all his subse-

---

[1] Jo. i. 51.   [2] Jo. ii. 11.   [3] Col. i. 16, 17.

quent knowledge and experience, it was an act of Divine power entirely in keeping with what he knew to be the action of One Who was more than man. He could compare the immature belief of himself and his brother-disciples with the ripeness and depth of spiritual apprehension which he now possessed. Again, therefore, we note that in its account of the faith of the primitive community, the Fourth Gospel is not answerable for that appearance of un-historical precocity which is so frequently imputed to it. The statement of their belief is true. The Manifestation of Divine Glory is the Evangelist's own interpretation of what happened, as he looks back upon it ; not that of the disciples as a body, or at the time. A similar stage of belief is expressed by Nicodemus, not yet a disciple, but a seeker after truth. Impressed by the miracles which Christ had been performing when at Jerusalem for the feast, he con-fessed for himself and others, " Thou art a teacher come from God ; for no man can do these miracles that Thou doest, except God be with him." [1] It is hardly at the same level with the " belief " of the disciples, but is rather a tentative admission. Nicodemus has taken the first step in the acceptance of the Messiahship of Christ. His subsequent history shows that he never went back upon it.[2]

The visit of Nicodemus is notable from its bearing on the theology of our Gospel. This third chapter abounds in problems raised by the writer's method of narration. We cannot say with certainty where either the discourse of Jesus and that of the Baptist end, or where the original words of the speaker pass into the comment and meditation of the Evangelist. We can only draw the dividing line by estimating the probabilities ; our conclusions must remain subjective and uncertain. What is more, the style of the narrative is much the same throughout ; a phenomenon which has given rise to the suspicion that in each case the words attributed to the speaker are the composition of the Evangelist [3]—a crude and superficial theory which takes no account of the psychological aspect of the question and

[1] Jo. iii. 2.   [2] *V.* vii. 50 ; xix. 39.   [3] *V.* p. 166 f.

P

fails to realise how great an effect on thought and style close companionship of the Master must have had in the case of such a disciple as the Evangelist. At the same time, it is to be remembered that the *ipsissima verba* of the speaker would be reproduced by the writer with a certain amount of flexibility due to lapse of time.

With this proviso, we may proceed to distinguish with some confidence between the actual words of Christ and the comment of the writer. The discourse itself ends at the close of *v.* 15 ; *vv.* 16–22 are the language of the Evangelist.[1] From this it follows that the use of the term " Only begotten Son of God " is not an anachronism imputed by the Evangelist to Jesus but a reflection of his own, as he looks back upon the whole incident. We have to distinguish very carefully between the language of Christ and the meditation of the writer, who would otherwise incur unjustly the charge of writing bad history. Here there is no ground for such a suspicion. Christ speaks of Himself, as elsewhere in the Gospel and in the Synoptics, as " Son of Man " ; and in thus reporting Him, the Evangelist shows that he is in close touch with what was said on the occasion itself. When commenting upon it, he naturally uses a term, " the Only begotten Son," which expresses his own stage of conviction at the time of writing. In the discourse itself the Evangelist found a topic which appealed to the bent of his own mind. As in the discourse at Capernaum, he who gives no account of the institution of the Eucharist has furnished us with the very mind of Christ on all which that

---

[1] Heitmüller assigns *v.* 14 f. to the Evangelist. This breaks the connection of thought (" ascension," " lifting up ") which holds between *v.* 13 and *v.* 14. Still more convincing is the fact that elsewhere in the Gospel ὁ υἱὸς τοῦ ἀνθρώπου is only to be found on the lips of Christ Himself, and therefore presumably this is the case here. Zahn, on the other hand, thinks that Christ's discourse only ends at *v.* 21. But that the transition from the speaker to the reporter is made at *v.* 16 is rendered probable by the change from " Son of Man " as Christ's (Self-)description (*v.* 14) to " Only begotten Son " (*vv.* 16, 18). There are also other differences of expression. The absolute ὁ πιστεύων of *v.* 15 passes into ὁ πιστεύων εἰς αὐτόν. " Only begotten Son of God," *vv.* 16, 18, compares with " Only begotten Son " (*al. lect.* " God ") in i. 18, which is language of the Evangelist. That it is the Evangelist (not Christ) who plays with the words τὸ σκότος, τὸ φῶς is likely, because it is he who observes (*v.* 2) that Nicodemus came to Jesus νυκτός.

Sacrament implies ; so in the discourse with Nicodemus, the writer who left it to others to report Christ's command to baptise, himself gives in Christ's own words the reasons for that command. And in so doing, he unconsciously shows that the idea of the coming Kingdom of God was as close to the heart of the Christ of the Fourth Gospel as to the Christ of the Synoptics.

In *v.* 16, which we assign to the Evangelist, it is probable that we have the central and most vital passage of the New Testament. On the one hand, it is in full accord with the Prologue of the Gospel ; but it gives the assurance that Christ is not only the revealer or declarer of the Father, but is Himself a gift bestowed out of the Father's love for a sinful world, that all who accept Him may have Eternal Life. On the other hand, it is in agreement with the conviction of our Lord, which is so frequently [1] expressed in this Gospel, that He is " sent " by the Father—a plenipotentiary in every way representing Him, and responding in accents of complete obedience, " Lo, I come to do Thy will, O God."

The same strain of thought is to be found in the meditation into which the Evangelist passes after recording the speech of the Baptist. He gives us to understand that Christ, as the Son of His love, is fully endowed for His Mission by the Father. He "hath given all things into His hand " ; He " giveth not the Spirit by measure unto Him." [2] Faith in Him, therefore, as in *v.* 16, is the necessary and all-important response on our part ; " He that believeth on the Son hath everlasting life." With all the force of a life-long devotion, an unrivalled experience of the mind and heart of his Master, fused and deepened by the action of the Holy Spirit on thought and memory, the writer makes it plain that to turn from such a gift and such a Giver is to expose the soul to the direct and abiding wrath of God. [3]

---

[1] *V.* Aug., *In Joh. Evang. Tract.*, xiv. 11 D, " Pater mittens Filium, Se alterum misit."

[2] Jo. iii. 35, 34.   [3] Jo. iii. 36.

So far, we have seen that our Lord's Self-disclosure
in this chapter is not out of harmony with that of the
Synoptic narrative at about the same period of His career.
Where there are signs of an advanced stage of conception,
the language is not His own ; it is the musing of the
Evangelist.

In the Discourse with the woman of Samaria, we
encounter a mode of self-disclosure which is certainly
unusual and for a Synoptic parallel to which we have to
look to the end of the ministry To the remark of the
woman, " I know that Messias cometh, which is called
Christ," our Lord replies with a signal outburst of graciousness, " I that speak unto thee am He."   Taken apart from
its context, such a disclosure made so early in His ministry
would seem doubtful. It does not correspond with His
ordinary practice. But the occasion was exceptional. He
was passing through an alien country and people, which
were not included in the scheme of public ministry which
He had marked out for Himself. The whole tone of His
conversation with the woman shows that, as He looked into
the past life which lay open like a book before Him, He was
moved with a deep compassion. Here, in this unlikely
soil, He will sow good seed. He will make Himself known ;
and in what we afterwards learn of the readiness of Samaria
for the Kingdom and of the early progress of the Gospel
there, we find that His grace and pity were not thrown away.
On the woman's testimony, " many of the Samaritans of
that city believed on Him." [1] To the objection that this
disclosure of Messiahship is lacking in probability, so little
does it correspond with His usual attitude of reserve,[2] it
may be replied that the circumstances were different.
He was not in His own country ; and the results of His
interview and Self-disclosure show that the whole incident
moved on the plane of history.

In the sayings and events connected with the healing
of the impotent man, a further stage of our Lord's Self-

---

[1] Jo. iv. 39 ; cf. Acts viii. 5–9 ; cf. p. 145 f.
[2] V. Heitmüller in J. Weiss, D. Schriften des N.T., ad loc.

disclosure is reached. The occasion marks the beginning of the hostility of the Jews. Like St. Mark, the Evangelist traces the struggle, which ended only at the Cross, to the indignation felt at the breaking of the Sabbath.[1] But in the present instance, the broken law was not the only cause of complaint. Our Lord used remarkable language in justifying His action. With tacit reference to the rest of the primæval Sabbath when the work of Creation was finished, He declared that His Father knew no pause in His activity. If He ceased to create, He had still to sustain His work in being : " My Father worketh hitherto." This would be a new thought to His hearers and might, on reflection, have commended itself to the more intelligent of them. But he went on, " and I am working." At this co-ordination of His own work, in the healing of the man, with the perpetual ($ἕως$ $ἄρτι$) working of the Father, the rage of His opponents already excited by His breach of the Sabbath hardens into a plot to destroy Him. The Evangelist explains the reason of the outburst. It was bad enough to violate with so high a hand the immemorial law of the Sabbath. But the crowning offence lay in the claim of an unique and particular Sonship which they detected in the words, " My Father is working up till now, and I am working." This statement, says the writer, they regarded as an act of blasphemy, " making Himself equal with God."

The whole episode forms a critical moment in our Lord's revelation of Himself to the Jewish people. In determining its precise significance, we have to distinguish between the meaning which Christ's words had for His hearers, according to the Evangelist, and their meaning for himself and the Church at the time he was writing. Anything in the nature of a footing of equality with God on the part of a man—even though he were Messiah—was abhorrent to the Jewish mind. There could be no arguing with such a pretension. The very notion was a blasphemy. To the Evangelist himself whatever the words meant to

Mk. iii. 6 ; Jo. v. 16, 18 ; cf. Mt. xii. 14 ; Lk. vi. 11.

him at the time, the interpretation put upon them by the Jews was in agreement with the facts. Thus to speak of God as " His own Father " [1] was, in modern language, to claim the value of God. And as a matter of fact, this was the view to which, at any rate after the Resurrection, the Apostolic Church attained.

In the discourse which follows, at what interval we do not know, our Lord proclaims His Sonship to the Father in words which to the Jews, and to the disciples at the moment, could not have been fully understood. That He did so speak, appears not only from the character of the language itself, but from its close resemblance to other sayings which have the best attestation. After declaring the perfect harmony of will and action existing between the Father and the Son, He continues, in words strongly reminiscent of St. Matthew xi. 27 (Lk. x. 22),[2] " " the Father loveth the Son and showeth Him all things that Himself doeth." [3] It is clear that the two sayings belong to the same circle of ideas. Our Lord in the oldest Synoptic source, as in St. John, asserts that all the Divine Mysteries are open to Him as to the Father. Nothing is hidden from Him. It is the prerogative of His Eternal Sonship. His mind is the mind of God. What comes out clearly enough in the passage from the Logia, is reiterated and emphasised in the Fourth Gospel. There is no doubt that our Lord so spake and that, in so speaking He had a twofold object in view. He would make known in language which could only be understood later under the teaching of the Holy Spirit, His essential unity with the Father and consequently His power as the complete and plenary Revealer of the Father's Will. In this discourse we approach the highest stage of

[1] πατέρα ἴδιον.

[2] From " Q." " This word of ' Q ' is the best and purest expression of the religious certainty which lies over all words of Jesus." Weinel, *Bibl. Theologie des N.T.*, p. 141. Heitmüller tries in vain to evade its full metaphysical meaning. *Jesus*, p. 71.

[3] Other phrases in this discourse are reminiscent of Johannine and other sayings, and are on that account all the more likely to have been employed by our Lord. With Jo. v. 26, " As the Father hath life in Himself, so hath He given to the Son to have life in Himself," cf. Jo. vi. 35, 57 ; x. 10 ; v. 40 ; Rom. viii. 2. With Jo. v. 46, 47 cf. Lk. xvi. 31.

our Lord's disclosure of the true character of His Person
and are still in close touch with the most assured sources
of Synoptic testimony.

At this point we can take into account a remarkable
confession of St. Peter. After the feeding of the 5,000,
followed by the discourse on the Bread of Life in the
Synagogue at Capernaum, came a crisis in the course of
Christ's public ministry. First, " the Jews strove among
themselves saying, How can this Man give us His flesh to
eat ? " But soon the spirit of revolt spread to actual
disciples. Many of them began to say, " This is a hard
saying. Who can hear it ? " There is some indication of
a feeling on Christ's part that He had gone too far in His
estimate of the faith and receptivity of those who followed
Him. " Many of His disciples went back and walked no
more with Him." His teaching had made a greater demand
upon them than they were prepared to admit. Almost
anxiously and pleadingly He turns to the Twelve : " Will
ye also go away ? " Characteristically the reply comes from
the Apostle who appears in the Synoptic record as the
great confessor of the Apostolic band,[1] " Lord, to whom
shall we go ? Thou hast the words of eternal life." He
shows that he has grasped something of the meaning of
Christ's discourse.[2] In the Master's teaching is contained
the secret of eternal life : and then, in a fervent outburst
of faith and devotion, he assures Christ of the trust of himself and his brother-Apostles in language which implies
deep spiritual perception : " We have made an act of faith
and have come to know that Thou art the Holy One of
God." [3] It expresses much the same stage of belief as

[1] Cf. xvi. 16 ; v. Zahn, *Einleitung in d. N.T.*, ii., p. 566.
[2] vi. 68, ῥήματα ζωῆς αἰωνίου ἔχεις, *i.e.* words which impart eternal
life ; cf. v. 63.
[3] There is little doubt of the true reading. The received Text of v. 69
has been brought into correspondence with the confession of Mt. xvi. 16.
The MS. authority points to a wholly different saying and another occasion,
σὺ εἶ ὁ ἅγιος τοῦ Θεοῦ. There is nothing to support the view of Heitmüller
in *D. Schriften des N.T. ad loc.*, that this confession is an echo of that of
St. Mt. xvi. 16. The conception of the Holy or consecrated One of God
may have been suggested to St. Peter by Ps. cvi. 16, where it is applied to
Aaron (cf. 2 Kings iv. 9), and he had been present when, in the same

that to which St. Peter gave utterance at Cæsarea Philippi. The title is Messianic, if nothing more. And a little later, it is justified by the admission of Christ Himself that God had " sanctified " Him.[1] Thus the confession of the disciple is met and confirmed by the Self-revelation of our Lord.

When Christ, as so often in the Fourth Gospel, speaks of Himself as sent into the world by the Father, His language came to be interpreted later on, if not at the time, by the idea of pre-existence. At first, the sending may have meant to the hearers no more than it meant in the case of prophets, like Isaiah, who were taken in their ordinary course of life and charged with a special commission. They were, and believed themselves to be, really sent. But Christ Himself shows that His Mission was conferred in a quite different manner. He was not taken from his ordinary occupation of carpenter, as was Amos from the herd, and given a special work to do. He was " sanctified " and empowered before He entered into human life.[2] This was quickly recognised in the early community. If we naturally turn to this Gospel for the most complete expression of the idea, we also find it held and taught by St. Paul. To him Christ was the pre-existent Lord from heaven, Who " though He was rich (in His former state of glory) yet for your sakes became poor " ; " Who being in the form of God . . . emptied Himself, taking the form of a bondservant." The same idea appears in the sending forth of the Son " when the fulness of the time was come."[3]

---

synagogue at Capernaum, the man with the unclean spirit cried οἶδά σε τίς εἶ, ὁ ἅγιος τοῦ Θεοῦ, Mk. i. 24. That was the cry of the guilty in the presence of One felt to be all-holy. This, the utterance of a loving devotion.

[1] Jo. x. 36, ὃν ὁ πατὴρ ἡγίασε. The title itself is used as an epithet, Acts iii. 14, and occurs in 1 Jo. ii. 20, and Rev. iii. 7.

[2] This is implied in the passage quoted above, Jo. x. 36. " ἡγίασε still more clearly than ἀπέστειλεν presupposes an existence of the One Who is to be consecrated and sent which precedes these operations." Zahn, ad loc., p. 463 ; Einleitung in d. N.T., ii., p. 554. " This fact belongs to the eternal order." Westcott, ad loc. The sanctification of the Son is His consecration for His work on earth. In Jo. xvii. 19, our High Priest in His prayer, on the eve of the Cross, dedicates Himself, ἐγὰ ἁγιάζω ἐμαυτόν.

[3] 2 Cor. viii. 9 ; Phil. ii. 6, 7 ; Gal. iv. 4. The same term ἐξαπέστειλεν is used (v. 6) of the sending forth from God of the Holy Spirit.

Now, St. Paul must have had very clear and definite authority for this belief. It formed part of his Gospel, and we may conclude had been referred, with other essential doctrines, to the Apostles who were in Christ before him, for their agreement and consent. What was the source from which he and they derived it ? Clearly it could have been nothing short of Christ's own words that lived in the minds of His first disciples, some of which were afterwards to be recorded in the Fourth Gospel.

Among these recorded sayings is that which formed the climax of the dispute with the Jews as to their true relation to Abraham. After a manifestation of increasing hostility and perverseness, which the Evangelist, as usual, does not try to hide, they are confronted with the startling assurance, " Your father Abraham rejoiced to see My day : and he saw it and was glad." Whether this mysterious saying is to be understood of the faith of Abraham, who, as a prophet,[1] saw in the unlooked-for birth of Isaac a pledge of the birth in his own line of One in Whom all the families of the earth would be blessed ; or whether it refers to his knowledge in Paradise of what was even then passing in our Lord's life on earth, we cannot say with any certainty. The former is the more probable interpretation, as the past tense (" he saw it and was glad ") seems to show.

When the Jews, reversing the words of Christ, exclaimed " Thou art not yet fifty years old, and hast Thou seen Abraham ? " He suddenly lifts the subject of dispute into the eternal order. He had been speaking of His " day," the Messianic day, which began with His birth at Bethlehem and had been " seen " by the patriarch. Now, when the Jews refuse to admit that there could have been any relation in time between their ancestor and this new Rabbi of early middle age, comes the solemn and august saying, " Verily, verily, I say unto you, before Abraham was, I

[1] " The period of revelation begins (according to the Jews) with the time of the patriarchs. The patriarchs were prophets and spoke through the Holy Spirit." Weber, *System der altsynag. Palestinischen Theologie*, p. 78. *V. E.* König in *Expos.*, Feb. 1921. Cf. 4 Ezra iii. 14, 15 ; Heb. xi. 13 ; Jo. xii. 41.

am." Little as they understood the meaning of His words, they were quick to see that here was a Man standing before them, Who appropriated to Himself a mode or quality of being which, as they knew, was a prerogative of God. They treated Him as one who has committed the offence of blasphemy : " Then took they up stones to cast at Him." [1]

It is only natural that the conception of pre-existence in the Fourth Gospel should assume an importance in the writer's theology greater than we find in St. Paul. What pre-existence means to St. John is determined by the fact that he ascribes it to the Person of the Word Who, as he says, " was with God and was God." St. Paul himself, although the Logos idea is absent from his writings, assigns God-head to the Christ, Whom, as we have seen, he declares to be pre-existent.[2] But, on the whole, it is to the Fourth Gospel that we look for the fully developed idea of the Divine pre-existence of the Son of Man.

At the winter Feast of the Dedication, as He walked in Solomon's Porch, our Lord made a statement of His relation to the Father which has generally been regarded as the foundation stone of the doctrine of His Person : " I and the Father are One." [3] That unity of a high degree is here predicated is shown by the use of the neuter gender, ἔν. That it meant in the mouth of Christ, metaphysical, essen-

[1] Jo. viii. 59. The precise cause of offence was either the appropriation to Himself of a phrase famous in their history when God disclosed His Name to Moses, " I am that I am," Ex. iii. 14 (v. R.V. margin) in which case, if He were no more than they thought Him to be, He was self-convicted of blasphemy : or, they were reminded, by His phrase, of the language employed in 1 Enoch xlvi. 1 ; xlviii. 2, of the Elect Son of Man, the Messiah, and may have thought that He was putting forth a Messianic claim. Existence in heaven before His manifestation on earth was a familiar idea of the Messiah in apocalyptical literature, v. 1 En. lxii. 7. Cf. Baldensperger, D. Selbstbewusstsein Jesu, p. 144 ; Charles, Apoc. & Pseudep. of the O.T., ii., p. 216. " The Parables (of 1 Enoch) assert the actual pre-existence of the Son of Man." Dalman, however, is doubtful if the idea was ever very prevalent in Jewish circles. D. Worte Jesu, p. 107. H. Holtzmann thinks that such passages as Jo. iii. 13 ; vi. 62, are modelled on the Prologue, Neutestam. Theologie, ii., p. 450. Is it not rather the actual sayings of our Lord as to His pre-existence which gave St. John the Vorbild for his Prologue ? On Jo. viii. 58, v. Martensen, Christian Dogmatics, p. 268 ; Lücke, ad loc. ἐγώ εἰμι, " the timeless present " ; Zahn, ad loc., " existence beyond the range of history, (dem übergeschichtlichen Sein)."

[2] 2 Cor. viii. 9.

[3] Jo. x. 30.

tial oneness hardly follows from the passage *taken alone* :
for unity (neuter gender) is contemplated by our Lord for
His disciples, according to the pattern of His own unity
with the Father.[1] And in that case, metaphysical unity
would be out of the question. But it is much more than a
moral unity or agreement of will that is intended here.[2] It
is a fellowship in operation, in the work of Salvation,
" according to which, the Father only works through the
Son and the Son only by the power of the Father." [3] And
when we think of it along with the assertions of pre-
existence and the deductions, which the Evangelist himself
draws, in the Prologue, from our Lord's own Self-revelation,
we can hardly be wrong if we see in this mysterious saying
the consciousness of an unity of Son with Father which is
metaphysical and essential.[4] In any case it conveyed to
the hearers the impression that our Lord was placing Himself in an attitude to God which savoured of blasphemy.
They " took up stones to stone Him " ; " because," as
they said, " that Thou, being a man, makest Thyself God." [5]
Their interpretation of His words was nearer to the truth
than they knew ; and so far was He from withdrawing
anything from His pronouncement, that He went on, " Say
ye of Him, Whom the Father hath sanctified and sent into
the world, Thou blasphemest, because I said, I am the Son
of God ? " Taken in conjunction with the saying, " I and
the Father are One," we here touch the highest point at
which the Johannine Christ arrives in the disclosure of
His Deity.[6]

[1] Jo. xvii. 22, ἵνα ὦσιν ἕν, καθὼς ἡμεῖς ἕν ἐσμεν: Cf. *vv.* 11, 21, Eph.
iii. 28.

[2] *V.* Schmiedel in *Encycl. Bibl.*, ii., col. 2533.

[3] B. Weiss, *ad loc.* (Meyer). Weiss, like Lücke, *ad loc.*, ii., p. 435,
does not regard this passage as a direct proof of the ὁμοουσία doctrine.
But Lücke sees in it a unity which is peculiar to the Son as ὁ μονογενής.
Zahn thinks that the ἕν implies unity in operation and in suffering, *ad
loc.*, p. 460.

[4] " It seems clear that the unity here spoken of cannot fall short of
unity of essence." Westcott, *ad loc.*

[5] Jo. x. 31, 32.

[6] Jo. x. 36. " While Jesus neither could nor would disavow this
testimony, He brings forward a proof which goes beyond it, that He
could call Himself God, without speaking blasphemy." Zahn, *ad loc.*,
p. 463.

Indirectly, His saying to Martha, " I am the Resurrection and the Life, he that believeth in Me, though he
were dead, yet shall he live," is almost on the same level of
Self-assertion. It unfolds a relation of mankind to Himself
which implies that He is more than man.[1] At the same
time, the fidelity of the Evangelist to truth is shown by the
way in which he makes our Lord's power to perform the
most stupendous of His miracles to depend on His communion with the Father in prayer.[2] In all His Self-
disclosures, the Johannine Christ, either directly, or by
implication, remains in touch with the Father. It is as
the Son, or as the Messenger of the Father, that He makes
His appeal to men and claims their allegiance. It is a
remarkable feature of the Gospel, which is thought to
exceed the others in the height of its Christology, that it is
far more careful than they are to safeguard His entire
concurrence with the Father in every part of His redeeming
work.[3] He will give no occasion to His hearers to suspect
Him of posing as a " Second God." Coming forward, as
He did, in the true line of the prophets as a preacher of
righteousness, He stands on their firm monotheistic ground.
He is less careful to assert His own essential Deity than to
guard, in a world which was chiefly polytheistic, the truth
that the Lord is One God, that beside Him there is none
else. Moreover, His appeal to the Jewish people, which was
primary in His purpose, could have gained no hearing if it
appeared to sanction a rivalry to the God of Israel. No
Evangelist brings out this fact so fully as St. John. Its

---

[1] Jo. xi. 25. It is to be compared with the relation which is implied
in the great parable of judgment, Mt. xxv. 31 f. ; and in the invitation,
Mt. xi. 28 f.

[2] Cf. v. 19, 30. " Inseparabilis operatio est Patri et Filio, sed a Patre
est Filio." Aug., de Trin., ii. 3. V. Inge, Dict. of Christ and the Gospels,
i., p. 894, " By co-ordinating His own activity with that of the Father
Jesus claims Himself to be Divine."

[3] V. Jo. v. passim ; viii. 28, 50 ; ix. 4 ; xi. 41 f. Cf. Ignat., ad
Magnes., 7, ὥσπερ οὖν ὁ Κύριος ἄνευ τοῦ Πατρὸς οὐδὲν ἐποίησεν. On
Jo. v. 19, οὐ δύναται ὁ υἱὸς ποιεῖν ἀφ' ἑαυτοῦ οὐδέν, v. Aug., In Joh. Evang.
Tract., xx. § 4, " Quia non est Filius a se, ideo non potest a se." The
impossibility is rooted in the eternal relation of the Father and the Son,
v. Chrys., In Joan. Homil, ad loc. Cf. Van Oosterzee, Christian Dogmatics,
p. 514, § 6 ; v. above, p. 196.

reiteration all through the Gospel is one of its most conspicuous features and, taken in connection with its lofty Christology, amounts almost to paradox. May it not have been the writer's experience of life in Asia with its varied forms of polytheism that led him to recall and fix in his narrative sayings of our Lord that bore specially upon this subject? This practice of his makes all the more telling his assurance that it was the glory of the Eternal Son Who was to become Man that Isaiah saw in his vision in the Temple.[1]

Once more, our Lord speaks of His unity with the Father in terms which almost imply identity: " He that seeth Me seeth Him that sent Me." [2] Christ is thus the complete revelation of the Father in all that concerns the salvation of man. His love is the Father's love. His will is the Father's will. Even the Sacrifice of the Cross is shared, so far as sympathy and purpose are concerned, by the Father. The failure to learn by the experience of years of discipleship and by the recollection of this saying brought upon Philip the reproach, " Have I been so long time with you, and yet hast thou not known Me, Philip? he that hath seen Me hath seen the Father; and how sayest thou then, Show us the Father? " [3] It must have been on such sayings as these that the Evangelist founded his comment upon the witness of the Baptist, " God only begotten which is in the bosom of the Father, He hath declared Him." [4]

So far, we have considered the Self-revelation of the Christ of St. John and the effect which it produced upon the thought of the Evangelist. We have still to form an estimate of the final conclusion which he reached. It is to be found in the first and the last chapters : " In the beginning was the Word, and the Word was with God, and the Word was God." " And Thomas answered and said unto

---

[1] Jo. xii. 41 ; Is. vi. 1 f.   [2] Jo. xii. 45.   [3] Jo. xiv. 9.
[4] Jo. i. 18, reading μονογενὴς Θεός. " The whole course of thought of the Prologue still more than the good MS. evidence speaks for the reading." Grill, *Untersuchungen*, i., p. 104, n. 2. So also Hort, *Two Dissertations* ; Zahn, *Einleitung in d. N.T.*, ii., p. 554 ; Ottley in *Hastings D.B.* s.v. " Incarnation ;" B. Weiss (Meyer), *ad loc.*

Him, My Lord and my God." [1] In these two passages, the
one expressing the mind of the Evangelist and embodying
the experience of a lifetime, the other the mind of his fellow-
disciple at the sight of his risen Master, framing the Gospel,
as they do, in terms of the most exalted faith, Christian
doctrine reaches its climax. The highest point has been
attained and there is no going back from it. It has been
given to man to recognise here on earth in the Person of
Christ " God's Presence and His very Self, and Essence all-
divine." The process of attainment was slow and gradual.
It could not have been otherwise. To live with one whose
family and occupation were known to all, to eat and drink
and move about with him, to watch his actions and listen
to his conversation, might in certain cases lead to a feeling
of respect and affection on the part of his intimates. And
for a time it was so in the present instance. But, as the
days passed, a conviction grew upon the disciples' minds
that He, Who stood before them as man in the truest sense
of the word, was none other than the Son of God.

Like the Synoptic writers, the Fourth Evangelist makes
no attempt to reduce his belief to a system. He records
his experience and the experience of his fellow-disciples, and,
in doing so, he gives the best possible proof that he is aided
and guided in his task by the Holy Spirit. [2] In spite of
the title ὁ Θεολόγος conferred upon him from the third
century onwards, [3] it is the material rather than the ordered
system of a theology for which we have to thank him. [4]
Besides, the title of " The Divine " is largely due to the way
in which he " theologises Christ," speaking of Him as God, [5]
as well as to the impression that while he is as much concerned with details of fact as are the Evangelists who
preceded him, he is still more largely occupied with truth of
doctrine.

---

[1] Jo. i. 1 ; xx. 28, the last chapter exclusive of the Appendix.
[2] Jo. xiv. 26.   [3] V. Zahn, D. Evang. des Joh., p. 6, n. 9.
[4] " The theologian among the Apostles, if we consider early training
(Vorbildung), mode of thought, and language, is not John but Paul."
Zahn, op. cit., p. 7. This is no doubt true, as regards technical training
in Rabbinical learning (cf. Acts iv. 13) ; but any deficiency in this respect
must, in the case of the Evangelist, have been more than made up for by
the advantage of his close intimacy with his Master.
[5] Jo. i. 1, 18.

CHAPTER XIV

THE TRANSITION TO CATHOLICITY

ALL periods of history are transitional. This is especially true of the history of religion. Where there is life there is movement; the current is always flowing, although here and there, we can note backwaters marked only by stagnation.

The life of St. John fell in a time characterised as none other by the flow of incident and thought. Born a Jew in the early years of the first century A.D., reared under the Law which had ruled his people for many centuries, he lived to see it annulled through its complete fulfilment by the work of Christ and the passing of the old Theocracy, with its restrictions to a covenanted people, into the universal kingdom of the Son of God. He was concerned in every stage of this extraordinary development. At times, it hung fire. The force of inherited custom threatened more than once to stifle the free action of the new sources of life that had entered into the world. The Church narrowly escaped the fate of settling down as a sect of Judaism—a condition of things which would have tied it permanently to a career that was solely Eastern and Semitic, and that could never gain a footing among the progressive peoples of the West. If St. John knew the Church as " a sect everywhere spoken against," he left it a world-wide kingdom, himself contributing at every step to this astonishing result.

Little of this process is to be detected in his life as it comes before us in Scripture and in tradition. Indeed, so far as his own action is concerned, he seems to stand rather on the side of a prudent, if not reactionary, conservatism, than of progress and movement. He is a stickler for authority and cannot bear opposition to the cause that he favours. His method of procedure is based on historic precedent, and incurs the stern rebuke of his Master.[1] Quite consistent with this early ebullition is the incident of his meeting with the heretic Cerinthus in the public baths, which Irenæus relates on the authority of Polycarp.[2] Nor do we forget how he manifests the same spirit in his own Second Epistle.[3]

And yet, in spite of this firm and unbending attitude, St. John became, next to St. Paul, the chief actor in the work of extricating the new faith from the constraining environment in which it had its rise, and of placing it on the high road of breadth and liberty along which it was to march to its greatest triumphs. In this, he was only carrying out a principle which was necessarily involved in the redeeming work of Christ. Our Lord could aim at nothing less than the universal acceptance of His claim and the world-wide victory of His Faith. Himself, the world's creator, He could not be content that any part of it should remain a captive to the dominion of sin and evil. The story of the Cross is bound up with the universal supremacy of its Divine Victim: " I, if I be lifted up, will draw all men unto Me." Thus does He foresee and foretell the necessity of a Church limited by no bounds of space or time. Catholicity is of the very essence of Christ's Religion. No narrower conception is compatible with the character of His claim on our allegiance.

The passing of the Gospel from the Jewish to the Gentile world was the first step in the transition to Catholicity. It was an epoch-making phase in the life of Christendom. It meant the conquest of hereditary prejudice, and required fresh and more thorough study of the Old Testament Scriptures, especially of the second Isaiah. As a matter of fact, the universal scope of Messiah's kingdom was a necessary consequence of Monotheistic belief. It could not be otherwise, if He were God's anointed.

The admission of Gentiles to the Christian Church was

---

[1] Mk. ix. 38–41; Lk. ix. 54.   [2] Iren. iii. 3, 4.   [3] 2 Jo. 10.

in strict accordance with Jewish custom and practice. But it was not regarded with favour by legalists. The wider outlook of the prophets was shared by few. Proof of this disposition is seen in the episode of the conversion of Cornelius and in the controversy between the leaders of the Church of Jerusalem and St. Paul. Equality of privilege of Jew and Gentile was not to be gained without a struggle. It was St. Paul's recital of Christ's command during his vision in the Temple, " Depart ; for I will send thee far hence unto the Gentiles," that was the direct cause of his first imprisonment in Rome.[1] The Jews heard him patiently until he made this avowal. Pride of race and privilege could not brook it. If this was the state of popular feeling in wholly Jewish circles, it is not to be wondered at if we find it in the Jewish Christian Church, and if even men of Apostolic rank were touched by it.

It is therefore important for our purpose to take note of the effect of this feeling of prejudice in the widening of the field of the Church's enterprise. Humanly speaking, it almost succeeded in making the nascent religion of Jesus the bondservant of a Judaism which had had its day and admitted no loosening of ancient ties. But prejudice was not to prevail. Our Lord's prescience was to be justified. World-wide was to be the range of the attraction of the Cross. Only if it were universal, could the religion of the Crucified be final. Nothing less could satisfy the love of God, or the need of man. St. John saw this, when he wrote, " The Father loveth the Son, and hath given all things into His hand." [2] The Son Himself confessed it, as He was about to return to Him Who sent Him, " All power is given unto Me in heaven and earth." [3] If His Religion is true, it must be of universal scope and obligation.

Here we are dealing with the first halting steps towards the recognition of this fact. The primitive community was comprised of men of Jewish blood. The place of its origin was to be its home for a time, only to be finally left when events should make the future course clear beyond

---

[1] Acts xxii. 21.   [2] Jo. iii. 35.   [3] Mt. xxviii. 18.

Q

all doubt.   The fall of Jerusalem was " the opening of the
prison " to a Church that was " bound " by iron fetters of
custom and privilege.   But long before the city fell, the
breath of liberty was felt in her streets.   Things were
happening.   Men were thinking.

History abounds in paradox.   It is the unlooked for
that happens.   None of his fellow-disciples would have
thought that the first step in the widening of the Gospel
field would be taken by St. Peter, a man of intense, but
narrow, outlook ; headstrong in his emotions, but often
wayward in his action.   Yet he it was who should hold
the keys and unlock for the Gentile the gates of the Kingdom.
No sooner had his austere reserve been broken down and,
by the baptism of Cornelius and his household, the first
Christian family life had been inaugurated outside the pale
of Judaism, than St. Peter had to defend his action before
the Church.   It is clear that he was not without misgivings
as to the rightness of the step he had taken.   He speaks as
one who acted rather under constraint than from full
agreement with the course adopted : " What was I that I
could withstand God ? " [1]   It went against the grain with
him to admit Gentiles to full communion on equal terms
with God's ancient people.   If he was able to justify the
freedom of his action before the Church, he was arguing
against his own preferences, if not his convictions.   How
strong was the grip of custom and prejudice appears from
the indignant protest of St. Paul against his " dissimulation "
at Antioch.   Even the Hellenistic Barnabas was " carried
away " under the influence of the Apostolic primate,[2] who
had, already,[3] chosen for himself and his friends, the two
sons of Zebedee, " the circumcision " as their special sphere
of work.

At this point it is to be observed that St. John was still
subject to the stronger will of the older man.   As in the
Gospels, he is content to act with St. Peter and to let him
speak for him.   It is the older disciple who takes the lead.
St. John has to pass through the school of Ephesus, with

[1] Acts xi. 17.   [2] Gal. ii. 11 f.   [3] Gal. ii. 9.

its traditions of St. Paul and of Apollos, before he emerges as the John of Asia, warm-hearted and impulsive as ever, but with a mind deepened and enlarged by life and experience. This should be borne in mind when we face the problem which confronts those who regard him as the author of the Gospel. We part with him in New Testament narrative as an Apostle of the Circumcision, in close connection with St. Peter ; we meet him again—this time, in historical tradition—as an Apostle of the Gentiles, in the line of St. Paul rather than of St. Peter.

The change is great ; but we have to think of the disillusionment which this Jew of Palestine must have undergone. The martyrdom of his brother (with the approval of " the Jews "),[1] the cruel death of St. James, the Lord's brother, at the hands of a Jewish mob,[2] the unmistakable signs of God's anger with Jerusalem, as seen in its capture and fall, the previous separation of the Church from contact with the doomed city : all these momentous events tended to show that the future was in the hands of men of other race. They were all consequences of that supreme act of rejection which made itself heard in the cry, " His blood be upon us and upon our children." They accentuated the spirit of detachment which characterises St. John's allusions to his fellow-countrymen when, in his Gospel, he recalls their dealings with his Lord. There is no psychological inconsistency in the identification of the former Apostle of the Circumcision with the aged John of Ephesus, as he comes before us in tradition. There are points of likeness which are evident ; while the differences are to be accounted for, not only by knowledge of the past, but by lapse of time and change of circumstance. The logic of facts had been too hard for early predilections to resist. St. Paul affords a parallel for comparison. Who so inflexible in religious and racial zeal as that " Hebrew of the Hebrews " ? Yet, who so great a champion of " the liberty with which Christ has made us free," after he had seen, in the Vision at Damascus, the glory of the Lord ? If in so short a time,

---

[1] Acts xii. 2, 3. [2] *V*. p. 15.

Saul of Tarsus could become Paul, "an Apostle of Jesus Christ," on what ground can we be precluded from seeing the son of Zebedee in the John of Ephesus, apart from direct evidence to the contrary? At any rate, we are not to be deterred from taking this view by psychological considerations. If, when they are appealed to, the march of events is taken into account, the verdict is very likely to coincide with that of tradition.

But to return to our subject. If his association with St. Peter suggests that the tone of St. John's mind was conservative, we get the same impression from what is told us of the early successes of the Gospel among the people of Jerusalem. At no period of the Church's life has the prospect looked brighter than in that covered by the first chapters of the Book of Acts. From the day of Pentecost onwards, the Apostles marched from victory to victory. If, as Christians, the disciples formed a close corporation knit together by the ties of a common faith and a common fellowship; as Jews, they still kept in touch with their own people and their old religion. For a time they rode on the crest of a wave of popularity. They struck a chord which vibrated in the hearts of the more religiously minded, but got no response from the Sadducean hierarchy. The tension that existed between these opposing sections was all in favour of the disciples. And we have to think of those who, after watching the Cross from afar, "smote their breasts and returned" with the conviction that they had witnessed a tragedy in which they themselves were directly concerned. And now they hear that the Crucified had risen again; and His friends who say so are moving among the people not only with a Gospel of hope and pardon on their lips, but bearing about them a power of healing and beneficence, which none could resist.[1] Conscience is awakened, and many who had "waited for the consolation of Israel," sustained by the Apocalyptic hopes that had bridged the gap left by the cessation of prophecy, came to see in Jesus of Nazareth their true Messiah.

[1] Acts iv. 14, 16.

The cumulative effect of all these converging forces must have been at first a state of bewilderment. But the power and calmness of the Apostolic preaching soon steadied their resolves. The facts could not be resisted. " God hath made that same Jesus Whom ye have crucified both Lord and Christ." They are " pricked in their heart." Like Saul, not long afterwards, they ask, " What shall we do " ? [1] The will is won. They have nothing to unlearn. They come to see that in receiving Jesus as their Lord and Messiah, they are taking God at His word. They acknowledge the fulfilment of " the promise which was made unto the fathers." [2] They have not to abandon their Judaism in order to accept Christ. On the contrary, they have only to act in accordance with its true spirit. All that is wanted is a contrite heart, an open mind, a ready obedience. And these they gave, as in ever-growing numbers they flocked into the Messianic Church.

It is a fact full of significance for the understanding of the situation that neither the disciples themselves, nor their converts, saw any need to forsake either the worship or the customs of their own people. The call of the Temple still made itself heard at the hours of prayer. Children were circumcised on their eighth day. The Sabbath still breathed its balm of hallowed rest. When " a great company of the priests became obedient to the faith," they were not thereby withdrawn from their regular ministry ; only the offices of the sanctuary were filled with a new meaning. It did not at first dawn upon them that sacrifice and offering had been superseded by the " One Sacrifice for sins for ever." Into this Jewish Christian Church, it was only Jews that first found entrance ; Jews and—what, from the legal point of view, amounted to the same thing— proselytes. [3] They used the same Scriptures as their fathers, and they showed a higher appreciation of the Apocalyptic writings than was felt by those who remained outside the

---

[1] Acts ii. 37.   [2] Acts xiii. 32.
[3] Such was perhaps Cornelius ; one of the " Seven," Nicolas, is expressly stated to be " a proselyte of Antioch." Acts vi. 5.

Church. There were no other sacred books in their possession.

But while the infant Church still looked back " to the rock whence it was hewn," the new faith, which it had received, that Jesus is " both Lord and Christ," opened before it a new prospect. Although Christ expressly declared that He " came not to destroy the Law but to fulfil it," in His perfect fulfilling of it, the Law was merged and, therefore, done with. All that was transitory fell away like the husk. All that was vital and essential remained, but in a new form and enforced by other sanctions. " Christ is the end of the Law to every one that believeth." Henceforth only he who lives " in Christ " can " keep the Law."

Very soon this new aspect of their religion began to be seen by Jewish Christians. Questions of consistency arose and tension was caused. The disciples were leading a double life. The practice of the old faith with its unbending legal observances found itself confronted with the free and enthusiastic devotions of the Gospel. A new world had opened before the Church. " The breaking of the bread " " at home," " the prayers," which were reaching out with new forms of expression and meaning, the preaching of Christ even in the precincts of the Temple [1]—how could these observances be always reconciled with the claims of the old ?

While the Church consisted of people who were Jews by birth or by adoption, the pressure of contrasted elements of the Faith was not serious. The strain began when Gentiles sought admission directly, without passing through the stage of the proselyte. The rigorists required them to be circumcised ; to be Christians, they must also be Jews. It required not only the vision at Joppa, but the clear evidence of their possession of the Holy Spirit, to convince St. Peter that Cornelius and his household might receive baptism. Others, who had not had his experience of what was taking place, could not master their old prejudices so

[1] Acts iii. 11 f.

far as to admit Gentiles into the Church on equal terms.
But a decisive step was soon to be taken.

The progressive Church of the Syrian Antioch, from
which St. Paul and St. Barnabas had received their Apostolic
Commission,[1] had awakened the suspicions of the extreme
Judaising element at Jerusalem.   In the winter of A.D. 48–
49, certain emissaries from St. James, who was now the
head of the Mother Church, came to Antioch in order to
restrain those who were showing a liberal spirit towards
Gentiles.[2] St. Paul had won over many Greeks during his
visit to Iconium and, when he returned with St. Barnabas
to Antioch, " they rehearsed all that God had done with
them, and how He had opened the door of faith unto the
Gentiles." [3] It seemed to the men who came down from
Jerusalem that a wholly new departure was being made.
Gentiles were to be received, no doubt ; but only in obedience to the Law : " Except ye be circumcised after the
manner of Moses, ye cannot be saved." [4]

After much discussion, it was felt that the question was
beyond the competence of the Church of Antioch to solve.
It must be referred to Jerusalem.   St. Paul and St.
Barnabas, with others, were sent to bring the whole question
before the Apostles and elders.   A Council was called.
Believers, who were Pharisees, pleaded for the full observance of the Law in all cases.   It seemed as though they
would prevail and that the Church would remain what the
outside world still thought it, a mere sect of Judaism, fast
bound by restrictions and requirements of a past that had
been done away by Christ.

But it was not to be so.   St. Peter rises in the Council
and throws all the weight of his influence into the scale of
liberty and toleration.   He reminds the Church that it is
" a good while ago " [5] since he was chosen by God to bring
the Gospel to the Gentiles, and that to them, as to the Jews,
was given the witness of the Holy Spirit.   Clearly, the case
of Cornelius had made no lasting impression upon the

---

[1] Acts xiii. 1–5.   [2] Acts xv. 1 ; Gal. ii. 12.
[3] Acts xiv. 1, 27.   [4] Acts xv. 1.   [5] Acts xv. 7.

Jewish Church, although it had long been known to every one.

St. Paul and St. Barnabas again [1] speak of their experience among the Gentiles and of the miracles which had accompanied their ministry, regarding them as signs of God's approval.

At this point, after the opposing sections had stated their case, James, the Lord's brother, bids them come to a decision. Referring to St. Peter's action in the case of Cornelius, he shows its complete agreement with the spirit of prophecy,[2] and proposes that a letter should be addressed to the Church of Antioch, assuring the Gentiles of liberty as regards the observance of the ceremonial law. Only let them refrain, as Christian men of whatever race must refrain, from idolatry, from murder and impurity [3]— offences against the moral law. Henceforth, to become a Christian, a Gentile needs not to become a Jew.

The speech of St. James made an epoch in the life of the Church. It was one of the greatest services ever rendered to the cause of true religion. Coming from a near kinsman of Christ, and delivered in what was at once the centre of the old faith and worship and the Mother Church of Christendom, it laid broad and deep the moral foundation on which the Church could always stand, when new races and peoples were pressing into it. And when the gist of the speech was embodied in a formal letter to be carried to the contending factions of Antioch by the returning Apostles and other " chief men among the brethren," the document became for all time the charter of true religious freedom.

The force of habit and custom is strong. It was not easy for born Jews, who had become followers of a Christ Who Himself had been " circumcised and obedient to the

---

[1] Acts xv. ; cf. *vv.* 4 and 12.   [2] Amos ix. 11, 12.

[3] Acts xv. 20, 28. πνικτοῦ, πνικτῶν, in these passages respectively, while absent from *Cod. Bezæ*, are not found in Irenæus or Tertullian. If this ceremonial requirement (*i.e.* that, unlike the pagan process of strangulation of a sacrificed animal, its throat should be cut) is omitted, Gentiles are bound henceforth by the moral law of God which holds good universally ; not by the rules of a code already superseded by its fulfilment in the perfect righteousness of Christ.

Law for man," to shake themselves free from the ceremonial requirements of their race, to which the Founder of the new Faith had submitted in His own person. St. Paul's earlier Epistles show the state of tension that arose.

What was the position of St. John at this critical epoch ? There is little positive evidence. That he concurred in the formulated judgment of the Church of Jerusalem is certain. With " James and Cephas " he " perceived the grace that was given unto " Paul, and gave to him and Barnabas " the right hand of fellowship." [1] His usual attitude at this period is one of acquiescence in the action of others rather than of direct personal initiative. If the widening of his sympathies was, in the first instance, effected by the friendship and influence of St. Peter, it was undoubtedly carried on by the example and teaching of St. Paul. But of this stage of his development we have no evidence apart from what is suggested by comparison of the writings of the two men. To so devoted a follower of Christ as the Fourth Evangelist, the Epistles of St. Paul, together with the recollection of his life and character, would appear deeply impressive. For they evince a zeal for Christ as burning as his own ; an intellectual force to which he could not fail to render homage ; a dialectical subtlety to which his own narratives of controversy between Christ and the Jews present a certain similarity. It is probable that he owed much in the attainment of his Christian position to the greatest of the Apostles. But what he gained in power of insight and expression, in grasp of truth and perception, never came to stand between himself and his Lord and Master. If St. Paul helped St. John to formulate and arrange the experiences of his early discipleship, he never, by his influence, obliterated the sharpness of their outline, nor diverted the gaze of the Evangelist from its Divine object. It is probable that the chief effect of Pauline influence on St. John lay in the help that it gave the Evangelist to recognise and bring out of the storehouse of his memory those incidents and sayings of his Master which

[1] Gal. ii. 9.

were most necessary to meet the exigencies of the growing Church.

But there is another point of view which is generally lost sight of. Much is said about the debt of St. John to St. Paul. What of the debt of St. Paul to St. John ? How eagerly would the Apostle " born out of due time " listen to the " disciple whom Jesus loved "! When he submitted his own gospel to the approval of those who were in Christ before him, would he not try to elicit from one who had been so near to Christ something of the impressions which he had received ? I believe that much of the confidence in the formulation of his doctrine of the Person of Christ, which is shown by St. Paul, is due to his intercourse with St. Peter and St. John ; and especially with the latter. The fact that St. John wrote long after St. Paul is no proof that, if there was borrowing, it was he alone who was the debtor. It is probable that St. Paul received as much as he gave. Facts and personal impressions imparted by the loved disciple would be of untold value to an Apostle who had not seen Christ in the flesh ; and when they had passed through his strong, analytical mind and came to form part of the staple of his own Epistles, they would react upon the thought of that disciple as he wrote his Gospel. There was mutual influence at work. Each Apostle had some share in forming the mind of the other. We can admit this and still be alive to the help which the Fourth Evangelist must have received from his study of the writings of St. Paul.[1]

Here, it is to be remarked that, from St. Paul's own account of his intercourse with St. John, we get a sidelight upon the Evangelist's standpoint at that time. He appears to be unaffected by the reactionary spirit which St. Paul imputes directly to St. Peter and, by implication, to St. James.[2] There is no sign of the highly strained relations which arose between St. Peter and St. Paul. We cannot

---

[1] I find that E. B. Allo takes a similar view of St. John's influence on St. Paul. *St. Jean, l'Apocalypse*, p. cxcii. v. Feine, *Neue Kirchl. Zeitschr.* 1925, p. 299 f.

[2] Cf. Gal. ii. 12. Emissaries of James led Peter to Judaise.

explain the difference by appealing to the impulsive and wayward disposition of St. Peter. All that we know of St. John betrays an equal vehemence of temper. The reason is probably to be found in the fact that St. John was already in possession of the wider hope, and that, in his reflection upon the Person and the claims of his Master, he had come to see that the access of the nations to their Redeemer and Lord could not be barred by the ceremonial restrictions of a Judaism which its own action had rendered obsolete. In this matter, he stood where St. Paul stood— " in the liberty wherewith Christ hath made us free "; [1] and not a little of the anti-Judaic attitude of his Gospel is due to the decisions which were strengthened if not actually formed during his intercourse with St. Paul at this time.

When, years later, he left Jerusalem and, going north through Antioch, reached Ephesus, St. John came again in contact with the influence radiated by St. Paul. For two years that Apostle had preached and taught there, " so that," in the rhetorical language of St. Luke, " all they that dwelt in Asia heard the word of the Lord Jesus, both Jews and Greeks." St. Paul was the Evangelist of Asia, and Ephesus was the centre of his activity. In what St. John could see of the result of that free proclamation of the Gospel, and of its welcome at the hands of Greeks, as well as Jews, his own liberal tendencies were strengthened and justified. At the same time, it was not without significance that the course of action pursued by St. Paul received the approval of the " pillar " Apostle.

After this sketch of the Apostle's career we are in a position to consider his influence on the transition of the Church to Catholicity. When he began to write, he was able to draw upon an experience that extended from the earliest days of his discipleship to the pre-eminent position in which we find him as head of the Church in Asia. The more fully we recognise the unique advantages which he possessed for writing what might serve as the final, authori-

[1] Gal. v. 1.

tative volume of inspired Scripture, the less difficulty do we find in attributing to him the authorship of the Gospel.

If the conception of an universal religion owes much to the faith and the genius of St. Paul, it was to St. John that was due the choice of a single phrase which for ever lifted Christianity out of the confinement of a Messianic cult and set it free to win the allegiance of the world. By his identification of Christ with the Logos, Who at the beginning of all things was already " with God and was God," he made it possible for men, who looked askance at the hopes of Jewish patriotism and took little interest in the latest phase of a religion which had in the past been so much bound up with political considerations, to become whole-hearted followers of Jesus of Nazareth. By a stroke of his pen he brought Christianity into line with the best elements of Greek philosophic thought—while he maintained its connection with the teaching of the prophets of the Old Testament. The Logos was at once the creative expression of the mind of the All-Father, which coming into the world He had formed became the Light of reason and understanding to all His creatures ; and was at the same time the fulfilment of the highest hopes of that people which had been specially trained and prepared to give birth to Him.

It is true that in the body of his Gospel the Evangelist makes no further use of his great phrase, and that there is no reason to think that it had ever been applied by Christ to Himself : yet it is not too much to say that the Gospel narrative as a whole and the conception of our Lord enshrined in it is in strict agreement with the Logos doctrine of the Prologue. If we could not trace this correspondence, the Prologue, instead of being an illuminating summary of the contents of the Gospel, would have the effect of confusing and blurring the picture of Christ which we get from the Synoptics and the Pauline Epistles. It would take us into heights of mystic speculation unrelated to fact and reality. We should be transported from the sure ground of history and experience into a region of vague and uncertain theory.

But so far from this being the case, St. John has carried

out and applied the theology of his Prologue in the rest of his Gospel. He insists on the two constituent elements of Christ's Person which give Him that universal significance which the Church, since St. John's day, has always claimed for Him.

The Logos of the Prologue is revealed in the Gospel throughout as the only-begotten Son of God, pre-existent, of one essence with the Father, sending forth from the Father by His authority the Holy Spirit, acknowledged to be both God and Lord. Such a Person could claim nothing less than the worship and allegiance of all men.

The other fact of Christ's Person shadowed forth in the Prologue and proclaimed from end to end of the Gospel is His identification with Jesus of Nazareth, Who is the Word made flesh and is thereby brought into direct touch with humanity as a whole.

It is these two truths—the Divine Sonship of Jesus and His Incarnation—that constitute the universality of the Christian Religion and form the foundation stone of the Catholic Church. And it is to St. John that we owe their clearest and most authoritative expression.[1]

What, then, are the chief contributions of St. John towards the universalising of the Christian Faith ? St. Paul had treated the subject dialectically. In his argument on justification, he maintains the priority of faith, and its superiority over the later provision of the ceremonial law. The efficacy of faith is absolute. The law was a temporary expedient ; useful so far as it aided men to prepare for Christ ; of no value when He had come. From this it followed that access to Christ was open to all, of whatever race or nation, who would receive and trust Him. But St. Paul was withdrawn from the conflict before the battle was won. Reaction and conservative prejudice were still strong. The Temple was still standing. Many a convert from Judaism found it hard to part with the old restrictions and observances.

And, a few years later, when the seat of the old worship

---

[1] *V.* above, p. 228 ; below, p. 259.

had been destroyed, and it seemed that in its downfall the authority and sanctions of the religion which centred there had become obsolete, there were still many who, if they saw in Christ the end and goal of the law, were hardly prepared to separate themselves from all the observances and associations which had clustered round it.

To men in such a condition of mind, receiving Jesus as the Christ, yet with a backward look of yearning for the old religion, the appearance of the Fourth Gospel came as a voice from heaven. Henceforth, for Gentile as for Jew, the gates of God's kingdom stood open to all who would enter in the Faith of Christ. The universalism of the Gospel is apparent throughout. " Every man " is capable of receiving the " true light " shed abroad by the Logos.[1] " As many as received Him," irrespective of race or custom, " to them gave He power to become the Sons of God." The Prologue is the charter of the universal range of God's grace, which is wide as the love that moved Him to create. The universalism of the Fourth Gospel is bound up with its revelation of the Person of Christ. There can be no " favoured nation," no race pre-eminence among the subjects of His kingdom ; for it is the dominion of Him Who, now manifested in the flesh, " was in the beginning with God and was God." This is the basis on which rests the Catholicity of Christ's Church, and it is the merit of this Gospel that the truth has been placed beyond all doubt.[2] Without it, Christianity might have lingered on precariously in the guise of a Jewish sect, still trammelled with the swaddling clothes that were well enough at its birth, but could only stifle and impede its course through the Western world. Through the Fourth Gospel, the Church attained its manhood. Christian civilisation, Christian ethics, social and individual, are the gradual working out of the principles which it enshrines.

---

[1] Jo. i. 9.
[2] With Jo. xi. 52, recording the prophecy of Caiaphas, cf. *Odes of Solomon*, x. 5, " And the nations were gathered together as one that were scattered abroad."

CHAPTER XV

THE CONTRIBUTION OF ST. JOHN TO RELIGIOUS THOUGHT

No estimate of the contribution made by the author of the Fourth Gospel to the sum of Christian thought can be determined without careful discrimination between the historical data of the writings and the conclusions which the writer draws from them. The space of time that elapsed between the events and their record is a factor which is far less prominent in the case of the Synoptic Gospels. There has been opportunity to test the facts and their bearing upon personal experience. Two generations of life and thought have intervened. The claims of Christ have been put to the proof and have been found to hold good. The proof constitutes a theology, and yet the presence of theological statement and doctrine is never allowed to affect the calm and dispassionate presentation of the facts on which the writings rest. As we have seen,[1] the narrative itself is in keeping with the period and the conditions with which it deals. It bears every mark of being the record of deep and ineffaceable impressions made upon a mind at once receptive and retentive. We see things just as they happened. We hear words as they were actually spoken, save for their transference to another language.

It is true that St. John had a distinct purpose in view when he gave to the Church the closing century the account of his experiences as a disciple in the far-off days in Galilee and in Jerusalem. But the higher his purpose, the more scrupulous was his care to give an accurate account of the facts and events through which he had lived. His

[1] Cf. p. 22, 169, n.

history and his theology are never at variance. Truth of statement is never sacrificed to the interests of edification. No Gospel writer shows so great a concern to state actual fact ; for he clearly feels that it is on fact that the whole edifice of the Gospel and the Faith of the Church depend. For him, the reality of the Incarnation, the facts of the Cross and the Resurrection, are as certain as his own existence. If any one purpose can be said to run through his writings, it is to make others share the certainty which was the joy and strength of his own life.

If this passion for truth and actuality possesses him, we have at once a clue to the interpretation of his thought which should keep it on right lines. Here, if anywhere, we are justified in applying the old canon which lays down that the literal meaning of a passage, if it will bear it, is the right one. Of the use of fact for symbol there is indeed no lack in our Gospel. But the symbolism is never allowed to obscure the underlying reality. To the present writer no criticism appears to be farther from the mark than that which denies to our Evangelist any real concern for the facts of history to which he makes allusion.[1] According to this view, his purpose is wholly didactic. One would think that his own statements to the contrary might be allowed to have some weight, apart from the fact that he gives more than one proof of an anxiety to correct statements in the earlier Gospels that seemed to give a wrong impression of the true state of the case.[2]

This concern for fact finds expression and illustration in his attitude to truth. In the Prologue he speaks of truth as an element of the glory of the Incarnate Word. In so doing he has the sanction of that great saying of Christ, which he alone records : " I am the Way, the Truth, and the Life." Truth is a necessary constituent of Christ's Being ; and His life on earth was an unceasing expression of it. No New Testament writer is so possessed with the conviction that Truth is a primary requisite of the spiritual life. His Gospel is a standing protest against the shallow

[1] *V.* p. 28.   [2] Jo. iii. 24 refers to Mk. i. 14.

and misleading feeling so often expressed : It matters not what a man believes, if he acts aright. Indifference to the claims of truth upon the conscience, he regards as a sign of a wrong condition of life: " Men loved darkness rather than light, because their deeds were evil." The tendency of truth to come out into the open, to be recognised and acknowledged, is a necessary ingredient of the truth itself. It finds its justification in the Incarnation. " In Him was life, and the life was the light of men." It was to manifest the truth about God and man that Christ came into the world. He Who is " the Truth " declares Himself to be " the Light of the World." [1] Human nature is so con- stituted as to be capable of seeing and welcoming the light. " Every man," in a degree possesses this capacity. What- ever the stages of his evolution, he only became man, when this capacity was attained. As Christ, wherever He is seen and acknowledged, radiates Truth from His Person, as the Sun of Righteousness, the regenerate, by a law of their new nature, become capable of transmitting light and truth to others : " Ye are the light of the world. A city that is set on a hill cannot be hid." [2]

Truth and its showing forth being thus united, it is no wonder that St. John carries their obligation into the region of the practical life. In an Epistle, he lays down the rule that no friendly relations are to be maintained with those who " abide not in the doctrine of Christ." [3] As he knew by experience, right thought and right action are bound up inextricably together. False teaching was prevalent in the Churches of Asia. St. John had known and suffered too much in the course of a long life to allow him- self to hold lightly any departure from the truth. He had too vivid a recollection of the Truth, as it shone out in the life and teaching of Christ, to suffer any wilful perversion of it. Moreover, he makes it an unfailing test of the practice of truth in thought and life, that there is a desire

[1] Jo. viii. 12 ; ix. 5.
[2] Mt. v. 14.
[3] 2 Jo. 10. The words sound harsh ; but the dangers of incipient heresy were imminent and justified severity.

to submit conduct to general scrutiny. Such is the implication of his assurance when meditating on the discourse with Nicodemus : " He that doeth truth cometh to the light, that his deeds may be made manifest that they are wrought in God." [1] The open expression of truth by the regenerate is regarded as natural and inevitable. It is a necessary result of the sonship of those who have received Christ as the Incarnate Word, Whose object in coming into the world was to make manifest to all men the mind and will of God.[2] In the view of St. John, nothing in the relations of God and man is more vital than truth of thought and action.

Closely connected with truth as a paramount element of the Christian life is his insistence on the need of certainty. It may be regarded as the subjective side of truth, as an inward conviction that on the matter in question, whatsoever it may be, we are in possession of the truth. Owing to its subjective character, it is too personal and individual to be able to command the assent of others beside the subject himself. So many different factors contribute to, or detract from, the possession of certainty. It is probable that St. John never tried to investigate the psychology of the question. He deals with it in terms of knowledge. As he treats it we get the impression that the fact or truth to which he is referring, stands before him as a reality which admits of no question. He has been in contact with " The Truth " Himself, and his whole soul has been irradiated. He could no more doubt his possession of it than he could be uncertain if his eyes beheld the sun. Certainty is thus the response to what has been revealed ; the natural reaction of an unbiassed mind to what is presented to it.

Nowhere but in the Johannine writings has the importance of truth, with its correlative, certainty, been so strongly emphasised. What the writer himself experienced, he made it his business to impart to his converts, that, by

---

[1] Jo. iii. 21.

[2] Jo. i. 9, 12, 18. St. Paul seems to be feeling his way towards the position taken up by St. John ; but characteristically, his thought moves in the region of faith implicit and explicit. Rom. x. 10 ; cf. James iii. 17.

faith, they might enter upon the same possession. They are to see through his eyes. His inheritance is to be theirs. Thus, of the piercing of the Saviour's side he writes, " He that saw it bare record and his record is true, and he knoweth that he saith true, that ye might believe." [1] But, as we should expect, it is chiefly in the First Epistle, when dealing with the application of the life and work of Christ to human needs, that his high estimate of the value of certainty comes out : " These things have I written unto you that believe on the Name of the Son of God ; that ye may know that ye have eternal life, and that ye may believe on the Name of the Son of God." [2]

There is the same insistence upon certainty in the attestation of the elders of the Church of Ephesus which was affixed to the appendix of the Gospel. " This is the disciple which testifieth of these things and wrote these things ; and we know that his testimony is true." [3] To some, this formal expression of approval appears to render it quite improbable that the writer of the Gospel was an Apostle. It must have been a disciple of lower rank whom they could venture so to commend. The objection is plausible ; but, it should be noticed that the character and style of the approval is quite in the manner of St. John himself, and the elders, who thus declare themselves, show that they have learnt from him the vital need of religious certainty.[4]

The question arises, To what cause are we to assign this extreme concern for the possession of truth and certainty ? The answer is not an easy one. It is to be found, we think, partly in the religious character of the writer himself ; partly in the circumstances of the time when he was writing. His character had been formed by personal intercourse with

---

[1] Jo. xix. 35, " . . . he knoweth that he saith true," ἐκεῖνος according to Westcott, *op. cit.* p. 25, is the writer, but many understand it of another, Holtzmann, *ad loc.;* Moffatt, *Introduction,* p. 568. E. A. Abbott, Zahn, *ad loc.,* Spitta, *Das Joh. Evang.,* p. 386, apply it to Christ, Who is thus referred to several times in 1 John.

[2] 1 Jo. v. 13.

[3] Jo. xxi. 24. *V.* above, p. 32.

[4] For instance, 3 Jo. 12, " and ye know that our record is true."

our Lord. His teaching, His Passion, and Death, followed by His Resurrection and the coming of the Spirit, had convinced the Evangelist that he had been face to face with the Incarnate Son of God, the fountain of all truth. In His light, he had seen light. Whatever the course of his future life, this impression could never fade. He could testify as no one else then living, that " the Son of God is come, and hath given us an understanding that we may know Him that is true." [1] Henceforth, what he said and what he wrote demanded and deserved the whole-hearted acceptance of his converts. To depart from it was to forsake the way of life.

And there was another reason for his attitude. Himself, perhaps the only remaining link between the primitive witnesses of Christ and the Church of the closing century, he viewed with profound apprehension the first signs of a freedom of thought and belief which seemed to threaten the very existence of the Faith, as he and his brother Apostles had received it. Men were saying that the human nature of Christ was only in appearance. They denied that He had come in the flesh. For the purpose of His passion and death, He had borne the semblance of a man. Others, like Cerinthus, were affirming that it was the man, Jesus of Nazareth, Who suffered and died upon the Cross, not the Son of God, Who indeed had descended upon Jesus at His Baptism, but had left Him before His humiliation and death.

To one with the past of St. John, each of these modes of thought was fatal to any sure hold upon the Gospel of the Incarnation. It seemed the very spirit of Antichrist. By his denial of a true humanity, the Docetist lost that vital and essential union with the Son of God from which alone his own sonship could take its rise. By his denial to the suffering Son of Man of personal identity with the Eternal Son of God, the Cerinthian parted with the infinite efficacy which, in virtue of His Godhead, belonged to the Redeemer of mankind. If all that could be said of the

[1] 1 Jo. v. 20.

Saviour is that He was Jesus of Nazareth, the son of Mary, we should be still under the dominion of sin, " without hope, without God in the world."

Against these opposing, but equally destructive, theories, the Apostle threw the whole force of his knowledge and experience.[1] If, as we think, his mind, if not his hand, is to be found in Gospel, Epistle, and Apocalypse, we have to acknowledge that Christ is presented to us as the Eternal, pre-existent Son of God, " with " Him, sharing His throne, the Creator, the Judge ; yet Son of Man, with all the experiences of human nature at its weakest, sin only excepted. This estimate of the being and personality of his Master is set forth in the Johannine writings as the only possible one, in view of the facts which came to the writer's knowledge. In such a matter he felt the claim of truth to be imperative. He lived to hand it on to others that they too, possessing it, might have the peace of certainty. Out of his own deepest experience he can affirm, " This is life eternal, that they might know Thee, the only true God, and Jesus Christ Whom Thou hast sent." [2]

But, to be efficacious, truth needs to be apprehended, to be acted upon. Its presentation makes a demand not only upon the intellect, like a proposition of mathematics. Its appeal is ethical, to will and character. The heart can close against it and, where there is this spirit of opposition, the truth remains outside the life. However fully acknowledged as a matter of intelligence, it remains inoperative. It requires conscious, willing acceptance. Nowhere is this requirement shown more clearly and decisively than in the Prologue : " The light shineth in darkness and the darkness comprehended it not " : or in a more personal, concrete form : " He came unto His own and His own received Him not."

What, then, is needed that the Truth may enter in and have effect ? What is it, on our part, which can reach out and appropriate what is offered ? To St. Paul the first requisite was faith—not a bare, intellectual assent—but a

---

[1] *V*. Iren. iii. 11, 1 ; E. Meyer, *op. cit.*, iii. p. 642.   [2] Jo. xvii. 3.

movement which enlisted the affections : " with the heart
man believeth unto righteousness." Interest is aroused.
There is a movement of the whole being towards its object,
with the result that the object itself becomes a present
possession : " I live, yet not I, but Christ liveth in me."
Faith had established such a relation between himself and
his Saviour, it had so appropriated Him, that the life which
he still felt was his own and for which he was responsible
was, so to speak, an incarnation of Christ.   Christ dominated
him.   He had " the mind of Christ."   His own life was
" hid with Christ in God."   And this was no mere vision
of an unrealised future.   It was a present condition.

This view of the action of faith appears with even
greater clearness in the striking definition given by the
writer to the Hebrews : " Faith is the substance of things
hoped for, the evidence of things not seen." [1]   The believer
is said to possess already what he is hoping for : the object
of his faith is its own evidence : his faith brings about its
own fulfilment.   If this definition was known to St. John,
it supplies a link between himself and St. Paul.   Although
St. John never uses in the Gospel, and only once in his
Epistles [1] the term " faith," $\pi i\sigma\tau\iota\varsigma$, as a substantive conception—perhaps, as has been suggested, in order to avoid
mention of what had been put to a wrong use [2]—his language
is full of references to it.   He employs the verbal forms of
the word freely.   But what is specially to be noted is the
way in which, like the writer to the Hebrews, he regards
the object of Christian faith as already in the believer's
possession.   His use of the present tense is remarkable,
" He that hath the Son hath life." [3]   Faith, as it passed
from the thought of St. Paul through the writer to the
Hebrews to the thought of St. John, has become something
more than itself.   Its action is proleptic.   The believer
can say " I know."   The object of his faith stands before
him.   It is a reality.   " The substance " is there.   He

[1] Heb. xi. 1.
[2] 1 Jo. v. 4.   Cf. his avoidance of the substantive $\gamma\nu\hat{\omega}\sigma\iota\varsigma$, probably
or the same reason.   V. 1 Tim. vi. 20.
[3] 1 Jo. v. 12.

has passed from time into eternity. He is already in heaven, though not yet gifted with capacity for its full enjoyment. He is still in the body, and " it doth not yet appear what he shall be." In any case there will be an organ of receptiveness and of expression corresponding to the earthly body, but as far transcending it as the life of heaven transcends the present life.

If we ask how St. John reached this stage of mystical experience, there appears to be only one satisfactory answer. It was through long meditation on the life and teaching of his Master, as both were recalled to him by the Holy Spirit. The religious experience of St. Paul had been founded on the appearance of the crucified and risen Christ as, full of zeal for what he thought to be the will of God, he drew near Damascus. It was a crisis which changed the whole character of his life. It was otherwise with St. John. So far as we know, there had been no such decisive turning point in his career as that which marked the conversion of St. Paul. He had passed from the influence of the Baptist to that of Christ by what seemed a natural and regular process. Henceforth he had an ever-deepening conviction that, as day by day he walked with Jesus, heard His words and saw His works, he was with One Who belonged to a higher order of being. We, from our position as inheritors of nineteen centuries of thought and experience, find it difficult to enter into the mind of men who were feeling their way towards a true conception of the facts. We can only apprehend and record the separate and distinct impressions made upon the Evangelist's mind by his intercourse with Christ. On the one hand, there is vivid realisation of the fact that Christ had " come in the flesh," that He stood in the direct line of the Prophets as one " sent " from God, that He made no claim to any distinct authority, but always referred His action to the initiative of the Father.[1] On the other hand, we see that the impression made upon the Evangelist by Christ's Personality is not to be explained by anything that comes

[1] *V.* p. 226.

entirely within the category of human nature. If this feature is most apparent and definite in the Prologue, it is evident throughout the course of the Gospel. Indeed, we are inclined to think that, like many a modern writer, the Evangelist wrote his preface after the main substance of the book embodying in it the results arrived at in the course of his narrative. In that narrative, we can trace the effect upon his mind of the acts and words of Christ, at the time they were spoken or done. In the Prologue, we have the reasoned conclusions on the two great parallel facts—the Humanity and the Deity of Christ—to which his immediate knowledge of the circumstances had led him. But, still there is no attempt to reconcile the two contrasted elements, or to bridge over what would seem at first sight to lie poles apart. We have to guard against the temptation to read into his mind the theology of the fourth century. To the Church of all time, St. John has bequeathed his conviction that, while he was always conscious of discipleship with One Who was truly man, he had an overwhelming certainty that He, Who had stood face to face with him, was to be identified, he knew not how, with God.

It is this twofold witness of St. John which constitutes his chief contribution to religious thought. He has set the Divinity of our Lord in a position which it has never lost ; partly by his choice of Christ's own sayings ; partly by his own interpretation of them. He looked with a steadier eye than any one else into the mystery of the Godhead, and without losing himself in metaphysical abstractions, he saw that the Man Christ Jesus, with Whom he had lived and for Whom he had suffered, could only be adequately interpreted as God in human form : " In the beginning was the Word, and the Word was with God, and the Word was God . . . and the Word was made flesh and dwelt among us."

If, as we have seen,[1] the choice of the Logos conception was due to familiarity with Greek circles at Ephesus which had been influenced by the long succession of thinkers

---

[1] *V.* above, p. 178 f.

from Heracleitus to Philo, it was to his own people and
their Scriptures that the Evangelist turned for the thought
that " the Word became flesh and dwelt among us."

The language of the whole passage is reminiscent of Old
Testament ideas and promises in which God's visible
presence on earth is foreshadowed.[1] In the Tabernacle
and later in the first Temple, over the Ark of the Covenant
and between the Cherubim, the Shekinah is said to have
appeared.   The term itself is allied to the word σκηνοῦν, to
pitch a tent,[2] and under the form of shining light symbolised
the fact that God was actually with His people, though
invisible to the eye.   It was His glory that was seen ; not
Jehovah Himself.[3]   But the glory had—to use a modern
expression—" the value " of God.   In that sense, it came
near to being a personification of qualities subsisting in the
Godhead, yet going forth from Him so far as to be recognised by man—a certain intensification of His presence,
revealing His nature and assuring men of His goodwill.[4]

It was not in itself a manifestation of God so separate
as to be spoken of as a Person, in our acceptation of the
term : [5] but we may rightly regard it as a foreshadowing of
what God had in mind in the Incarnation of His Son.   The
correspondence of the language employed with that of
St. John in the passage before us is too striking to allow us
to miss its significance.   What the glory of the Divine
Presence symbolised in God's dealing with Israel became

[1] Ex. xxv. 8, 21 ; xxix. 45 ; Lev. xxvi 11, καὶ θήσω τὴν σκηνήν μου
ἐν ὑμῖν. Hag. ii. 7. Cf. 2 Chron. vi. 18, 41. V. above, p. 175 f.

[2] שכן to dwell, abide ; cf. the root letters of σκηνοῦν, the verb used
in Jo. i. 14, καὶ ὁ λόγος . . . ἐσκήνωσεν ἐν ἡμῖν.

[3] V. Ex. xxxiii. 18 f., " (Moses) said, I beseech Thee, show me Thy
glory. And He said, I will make all my goodness pass before thee . . .
but My face shall not be seen."

[4] Cf. G. F. Moore, Harvard Theol. Review, 1922, p. 59, " Like Memra,
Shekinah acquires what semblance of personality it has solely by being
a circumlocution for God, in contexts where personal states or actions
are attributed to Him." This statement is no doubt true in certain
cases of the use of such terms. But it is difficult to resist the impression
that there was something approaching personality implied in other
instances—a more or less unconscious striving to find a plural element in
the unity of the Godhead to meet the requirements of philosophic thought.
The problem that presented itself to reflecting minds was to explain the
action of an all-holy God upon a sinful world.

[5] Cf. C. C. J. Webb, God and Personality, 1918, p. 61 f.

an actual fact in the Incarnation of His Son, according to the witness of the Evangelist : " We beheld His glory, the glory as of the Only begotten of the Father,[1] full of grace and truth." [2]

The value of the writer's contribution to religious thought on this greatest of all subjects can hardly be over-estimated. He is about to record, in his Gospel, his memories of our Lord as he knew and loved Him in the days of His flesh. He wishes to awaken interest in his narrative. Himself a Jew, not unmindful of his race though living and working in a Gentile city, he shows by his allusions to great historic moments in his people's past that they have a share in the Gospel which he is about to proclaim. In the course of his Gospel, hard things are said of his fellow-countrymen ; but his message, if they will receive it, is for them as for the Gentiles. To that larger world in which he found himself in his old age, the Scriptures, whose phraseology he employed, had not the same signifi-cance. He will do what he can to meet its needs. With one bold stroke, he chooses a term rooted, as in the thought of his own people, so also in the philosophic past of that wider world from which the greater number of his converts were taken : " The Word became flesh and dwelt among us."

But, it is by his identification of the Logos with the

---

[1] The object of the seeing of the Apostle was the glory of Christ, His δόξα, " the LXX equivalent of כָּבוֹד, the splendour which serves as the garment, symbol and instrument of the God Who in Himself is invisible." H. Holtzmann, *Evang. des Joh.*, p. 44. This glory was seen by the three Apostles who attended Christ at His transfiguration. Lk. ix. 32, εἶδον τὴν δόξαν αὐτοῦ. The Fourth Evangelist recalls his own experience, cf. 2 Pet. i. 18. That the sight of the glory of the Word was actual, bodily, a matter of the senses, not a mental vision, is proved not only by the definite purpose of the Evangelist throughout the Gospel, viz. to assure men of the true humanity of Christ. It is proved by the terms of the parallel passage in 1 Jo. i. 1–4. ἐθεασάμεθα " must be understood according to 1 Jo. i. 1 f., as the equivalent of ὁρᾶν. H. Holtzmann, *ib.* Cf. Bacon, *The Fourth Gospel*, p. 456, " (The writer of 1 John) emphasises the visibility and *tangibility* of the incarnation of the Logos as in Jo. i. 13-16 . . . against the doctrine of Cerinthus." The context also requires this meaning, cf. *vv.* 11, 12.

[2] With this ascription of " grace and truth " (πλήρης χάριτος καὶ ἀληθείας) cf. Ex. xxxiv. 6, Κύριος ὁ Θεὸς οἰκτίρμων καὶ ἐλεήμων, μακρόθυμος καὶ πολυέλεος καὶ ἀληθινός.

historical Jesus, which St. John effects in this passage, that he makes his chief contribution to religious knowledge.

From this identification, it follows that Christ is the meeting point of the highest attainments in the thought of both the Jewish and the Gentile world that preceded His birth. Secondly, it follows that what the ancients dimly groped for—a personal Mediator between the Absolute Reality and the world to which He gave being—is made manifest in the life of Jesus of Nazareth. Thirdly, it follows that the weight of the dualistic pessimism, which had oppressed the mind of the old world, is relieved by the fact of which the writer and his fellow-disciples had been witnesses, that Christ appeared in human flesh and yet remained holy and pure, revealing to men in His own Person " the glory as of the only begotten of the Father." In matter itself—the flesh and blood of the Son of God—there is no inherent evil. He has come into contact with it. He has taken it to Himself. By so doing He has for ever bridged the gulf that both for Jew and Gentile seemed to yawn between the all-Holy and His creatures. Fourthly, it follows that He Who became flesh, the man Christ Jesus— by being identified with the Word, Who was pre-existent to all creation [1] and the only-begotten of the Father—is declared to be God Himself with all the implications, metaphysical and ethical, which are bound up with that great statement.

The question arises : How far was the Evangelist breaking new ground, when he identified Jesus Christ with the pre-existent Word Whom he declared to be God ?

It cannot be affirmed that in the identification itself, he is wholly original. If he were the first to find God in the Person of Christ we should have to attribute to him a departure from the teaching of the Synoptics and of St. Paul which would be nothing less than a breach with the primi- tive Gospel. It would be " another Gospel," a corruption of the original. But the earliest Apostolic preaching, as well as the Epistles of St. Paul, combines with the Synoptic

[1] Jo. i. 1.

narrative in speaking of our Lord in terms of Deity. What is new in the language of St. John is his decisiveness. He carries out to their logical consequences the implications of the earlier writers. It is probable that they did not realise all that their confession meant. They saw the Divine in Christ. They could not withhold their worship. St. Paul, at any rate, held His pre-existence and speaks of Him as God.[1] The Synoptic Evangelists record without comment language of our Lord which would be blasphemous in the mouth of one who was less than Divine.[2]

It is St. John who, while portraying an intensely human life and while insisting, in his report of Christ's teaching, on His derived authority and on His eternal subordination to the Father, roundly asserts His Godhead, not only in the Prologue, but throughout the Gospel. Like the writers who preceded him, he is either unconscious of the difficulties presented by the concurrence of the Divine and the human natures in a single person, or he is too firmly persuaded of the facts themselves to allow the difficulties which they suggest to weaken his hold upon them. His testimony is based on personal experience of a life which, while it fulfilled all the conditions of true and complete humanity, revealed capacities and powers, gifts and endowments, to which the life of an ordinary man could make no claim. When this personal experience was met by the Resurrection and by the new experiences of Pentecost, and all the past was seen in the light of those events, surmise became certainty. Hence the constant assurance that forms so striking a feature of the Gospel and Epistle : " We know." It is as though faith, that adventure of the soul into the unseen, which had been the characteristic and necessary attitude of the disciple in the early days of Christian experience, had now passed into a higher stage of development. The future was already present. " The things hoped for " were now substantially in hand. With St. John faith has become

---

[1] *V.* Rom. ix. 5, with Sanday and Headlam's note; Godet *in loc.*; cf. 2 Cor. viii. 9.

[2] *V.* above, p. 165.

knowledge : time is swallowed up in eternity. " We know that the Son of God is come and hath given us an understanding that we may know Him that is true . . . this is the true God and eternal life." [1]

It is not that faith is no longer required. There is always a place for it in the life of the Christian. When new aspects of truth are presented and untried courses of action are suggested, faith must light the way, and both the Gospel and Epistle show that the writer was alive to this. But he had taken his stand upon the bed rock of religious experience. He could speak from knowledge. He had the conviction that he had been with One Whom to see was to look upon God, Whom to know as Christ and Lord was to possess eternal life, here and now. Thus St. John is the Master of the Mystics. He has done more by his own testimony to strengthen and confirm men in their hold upon Christ as the Revelation of the Father, than any other New Testament writer. Looking back upon his daily intercourse with our Lord, recalling by the help of the Holy Spirit sayings which fell unheeded upon the ears of other disciples, he came to see that he had been living with God. He could understand what Christ meant when He said, " He that hath seen Me hath seen the Father." [2] And it is in the Prologue that he gives, in a few bold strokes, the whole result of his experience and the fruit of his long meditation. Jesus Christ is the Incarnate Word, the only begotten Son of God, the Maker of all things, the one Light and Life of all mankind.

If we owe to St. John the most complete and satisfying conception of the Person of Christ, it is to him that we are indebted for the most profound conception of the nature and being of God. It is presented in the form of definitions

[1] 1 Jo. v. 20. "The process of his thought rests throughout on mystical intuition ; it is an attempt to grasp the incomprehensible and to clothe it in language." E. Meyer, *Ursprung und Anfänge des Christentums*, iii., p. 317. Cf. F. von Hügel in *Encycl. Brit. Gospel of St. John*, p. 454.

[2] Jo. xiv. 9. It is probable that St. John had read in Acts xx. the vivid account of St. Paul's farewell address at Miletus to the Elders of Ephesus, or had heard of it from one of them. The phrase " the Church of God which He hath purchased with His own blood " (Acts xx. 28) would tend to mould his thought. The Crucified was God.

—one, that of our Lord's own framing, in the Gospel ; [1] the other, an inspired venture of the writer of the First Epistle : [2] " God is Spirit " ; " God is Love."

That God is Spirit is clearly a revelation. It could only have been imparted by adequate authority, which we have not far to seek. " No man hath seen God at any time ; God only begotten, which is in the bosom of the Father, He hath declared Him." [3] And it was significant of the unearthly character of the revelation that it was given not to priest or Apostle but to a Samaritan woman, " a stranger from the covenant of promise." [4] Our Evangelist was but the recorder of it.

It shed a new light on the being of God. Old Testament writers abound in references to the " Spirit of God " from Genesis onwards ; but there is no intimation that Spirit is the εἶδος, the " form " of the Absolute Himself. It is the pronouncement of the Eternal Son, for " neither knoweth any man the Father, save the Son and he to whomsoever the Son will reveal Him." [5]

And, as all fresh revelation of Eternal truth must do, it has lifted the whole relation of man to his Maker to a higher level. Our Lord Himself draws the consequences. Worship, the approach of man to God, must accord with what is now known of His nature : " They that worship Him must worship Him in spirit and in truth." Time and place have no significance here. His activity, like His nature, is universal, unlimited ; the true worshipper can find Him always, everywhere. His sanctuary is the universe.

It is to St. John himself that we owe the truth that God and Love are in a sense synonymous terms. If love is personified, we must name it God. No lesser title will suffice. In the Old Testament, love is a characteristic attitude of God towards His creatures, an attribute, one among many that are assigned to Him. The book of

---

[1] Jo. iv. 24, Πνεῦμα ὁ Θεός.
[2] 1 Jo. iv. 8, 16, ὁ Θεὸς ἀγάπη ἐστίν.
[3] Jo. i. 18 ; cf. 1 Jo. iv. 12, 20.
[4] V. above, p. 145 f.
[5] Mt. xi. 27.

Deuteronomy is full of the love of God. No more beautiful description of His tenderness can be found in all Scripture than that of the eagle fluttering over her young.[1] But, in his First Epistle, St. John, in a singular flight of imagination, soaring eagle-like to the very throne of God, identifies His nature with Love itself. Love is His very being so far as it can be expressed in language, or made the object of thought. We can only guess at the process by which the writer came to this conclusion. Once arrived at, it is found to be satisfying. It is its own verification, while in its practical consequences it is confirmed by all who have come " to know the love of Christ which passeth knowledge." Out of his own experience of that love St. John could look up to the Father and, from the depths of an understanding that was being moved by the Holy Spirit, was able to give to men the final and supreme revelation of the true being of God.[2]

And is it not fitting that he who, when he came long afterwards to give forth his Gospel, chose to speak of himself as " the disciple whom Jesus loved," should, of all the first preachers of the Truth, be the one to proclaim the divine character of Love, and to draw from it the mystic, yet practical, inference that " he that dwelleth in love dwelleth in God and God in him " ? [3] And this congruity of circumstance is illustrated by what tradition has handed

[1] Deut. xxxii. 11.

[2] 1 Jo. iv. 8, a passage, not only of deep spiritual intuition, but of great philosophic importance. " He that loveth not, knoweth not God, for God is love," *i.e.* only the loving can come to know Him Who is love ; like can only be known by like, a principle familiar to Aristotle, *Eth.*, vi. 1, who, speaking of parts of the mind, adds, " if it be true that they acquire their knowledge through a certain resemblance and affinity to the object of their knowledge."

But, whereas Aristotle, from his theory of God as transcendent, unmoved, and indifferent to all but Himself, regards Him as the *object* of men's desire, yet without love for His creatures, St. John carries out his doctrine of God as Love by assigning to Him the first impulse in the mutual love of God and Man ; *v.* 19, " We love Him because He first loved us." His love is creative. Cf. *Odes of Solomon*, i. 3, " I should not have known how to love the Lord if He had not loved me " ; Jo. iii. 16 ; " All turning to God in the deepest sense must be effected by God Himself," J. Arndt quoted by Heiler, *Das Gebet*, p. 225 ; " Truth finds out the disciple of Christ and not he It," J. B. Mozley, *Essays*, ii., p. 146.

[3] 1 Jo. iv. 16.

down of his old age. His life was one long exemplification
of the spirit of tenderness and consideration for others.
Clement of Alexandria has told of his patient search for a
young disciple who had gone astray, a search rewarded by
his restoration.[1] To St. Jerome we owe the last glimpse of
the Apostle as his strength was failing.[2] Borne into the
assembly of the Ephesian Church, he could only say, " Little
children, love one another." But it meant much. He had
stood beneath the Cross of Christ.

[1] Clem. Alex., *Quis dives Salvetur*, xlii., " a tale which is not a tale
but a true account, handed down about John the Apostle."
[2] *Comment. in Ep. ad Gal.*, vi. 10. *V.* Aug. *In Joh. Evang. Tract.*
cxxiv. 2.

INDEX OF NAMES AND SUBJECTS

THE END

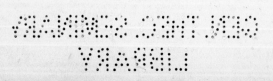